"BUSY TIMES"

*Human Documents of the
Age of the Forsytes*

"BUSY TIMES"

Human Documents of the
Age of the Forsytes

E. ROYSTON PIKE

PRAEGER PUBLISHERS
New York · Washington

BOOKS THAT MATTER

Published in the United States of America in 1970
by Praeger Publishers, Inc., 111 Fourth Avenue,
New York, N.Y. 10003

© 1969 by George Allen & Unwin Ltd., London, England

All rights reserved

Library of Congress Catalog Card Number: 79-99598

Printed in Great Britain

INTRODUCTION
JOHN GALSWORTHY AND HIS FORSYTES

For the purposes of this book 'The Age of the Forsytes' may be taken as being the 'eighties and 'nineties of the last century with an overlap of a year or two into the 1900s.

No other title seems anything like so good. The governing class of the period was 'upper middle'—and it is generally agreed that in John Galsworthy's *The Man of Property* and *In Chancery*, the first of the novels that developed into *The Forsyte Saga*, the upper-middle class of that time is described with wonderful insight and accuracy. Galsworthy's own term was 'embalming', and its use is thoroughly justified.

Furthermore, to countless numbers of readers of the Forsyte chronicles—to an even greater number, perhaps, who have listened to the radio versions, and to a number certainly greater still, to be counted in millions in fact, who have watched, week by week, the extraordinarily vivid and true-to-life representations on B.B.C. Television—the Forsytes have a reality that laughs at the objection that they are nothing more than a set of characters in a work of fiction.

John Galsworthy never made that mistake. He did not invent the Forsytes. He had met them, lived amongst them, known them intimately. Some of them he took straight from life. And of course, he was a Forsyte of Forsytes himself.

Born in 1867, in a house on Kingston Hill on the southern edge of London, within a few yards of the site of 'Robin Hill', he was the son of a successful builder and estate developer, solicitor and company director, who became the original of 'Old Jolyon'. He went to Harrow for five years, and thence, in 1886, the year in which the *Saga* opens, to New College, Oxford. On coming down from Oxford in 1890 he read for the Bar and was 'called' the year following. There followed a trip round the world, and then in 1904 he took chambers in The Temple and set up as a barrister. He had only one brief, and that was given him by the firm of solicitors in which his father was a partner.

The Law did not interest him, nor indeed did any other career that might suggest itself. He never had to work for his living, but was always assured of a comfortable private income. He was never able to understand how any man who was hard up could possibly be happy. He made fun of the sense of property in others, but he could never imagine himself without a good deal of property of his own. And while he was by nature a man of the most sincere and deeply felt human sympathies, he

7

was a poor mixer, and his friends were almost all drawn from his own rather narrow social class.

With the poor he had no real acquaintance. As a young man he was occasionally employed by his father to collect rents from the rather seedy properties in Fulham and Kensington that made a substantial contribution to the family income, and he was apt to be shocked by the conditions of poverty and squalor that he found there. Sometimes of an evening he would walk round the corner from his flat in Victoria Street and explore the adjacent haunts of poverty and vice and crime, but however closely he might observe the drabs and layabouts and worse who congregated there he felt not the smallest urge to make their personal acquaintance. And it has been argued, with much justice, that the working men and women whom he introduces into his plays and novels are little more than caricatures.

In the early 1890s, then, we see John Galsworthy, now in his middle twenties, a briefless barrister, living on the allowance of £350 a year made him by his father. Dissatisfaction was the keynote of his existence, but he felt no strong urge to change it. He took not the least interest in politics. Socialistic ideas made no appeal to him. He drifted, easily and comfortably, on the tide of Forsytean prosperity. And his life might have remained barren and ineffectual if he had not fallen in love with the wife of his cousin Major Arthur Galsworthy. Her name was Ada—Ada Cooper to begin with, daughter of a doctor in Norwich of some standing in his profession—and she was destined to become the original of Irene Forsyte.

Ada was the same age as John Galsworthy, and her husband was six years their senior. The marriage was in 1891, and very soon it was turning sour, just as Irene Forsyte's did. Why did Ada Cooper marry Arthur Galsworthy? Why did Irene Heron marry Soames Forsyte? The one question has been asked as often, perhaps, as the other, and as likely as not the answer in both cases should be the same. The marriage suited the family convenience, and the bride was willing enough to obtain financial security, an excellent establishment, elegant surroundings, and a bank account that was never likely to run dry.

When John Galsworthy returned from his round-the-world travels he learnt, on 'Galsworthy change', that the marriage of his cousin Arthur and Ada was running into trouble. He encountered Ada at family gatherings, and very soon an affectionate relationship developed between them. Then at Easter, 1895, he met her and her mother when holidaying at Monte Carlo: *she* was beautiful and desperately unhappy, *he* was young and eager and full of sympathy. They returned to England, and in the following September became lovers. Henceforth for a number of years they lived together whenever they could, in London, and on holiday trips to Devon and Cornwall and to the Continent. The affair was kept as secret as possible, and conditions must have been much easier after Major Galsworthy had gone off to the war in South Africa.

But for Ada, Galsworthy might never have become a writer. She may have been the first to suggest such a thing; beyond any doubt she encouraged him to persevere in his amateur efforts, suggested subjects, looked over his manuscripts, typed and retyped his drafts, and almost held the pen for him. The first of his long list of writings was a volume of short stories that was published in 1897, and this was followed by several novels. Then at the end of 1904 Galsworthy's father died, leaving an estate of £110,000. Galsworthy's share was sufficient to bring him in an income of £700 a year—a very comfortable competence in those days. Furthermore, there was no longer any need for concealment of his relationship with Ada; and in the next month divorce proceedings were begun by Major Galsworthy, with John Galsworthy as co-respondent. Immediately they had received the papers, Galsworthy and Ada slipped away to Italy together, and in his bag was the greater part of the novel on which he had been engaged for two or three years past. It was *The Man of Property*.

Of course, the theme had been suggested by Ada, and its treatment reflects the attitude of a woman who felt herself to have been deeply injured. But it is only right to say that those who knew Major Galsworthy best—and not least the woman whom he married as his second wife some years later—were at one in maintaining that Major Galsworthy was not at all the kind of man to 'assert his rights' over his wife in the manner that Soames Forsyte is said to have done.

The concluding chapters of *The Man of Property* were written in an hotel room at Levanto, on the west coast of Italy, when the divorce proceedings were taking their course in London. The suit was undefended, the decree nisi was pronounced in April, and in September 1905, on the very first day on which they were legally entitled to marry, John Galsworthy (like 'Young Jolyon') married the woman who had been his cousin's wife. In March, 1906, *The Man of Property* was published by William Heinemann.

The book was well reviewed, and the sales were satisfactory if not spectacular. Galsworthy was encouraged, and in the next few years he achieved well-deserved distinction and popularity as a playwright and novelist. But it was not until towards the end of the Great War that he returned to the Forsytes, and then it was because, as he put it, 'people wanted to hear some more about them'—and what better reason could there be ? The theme was resumed with *The Indian Summer of a Forsyte* (1918), which formed the connecting link with the next full-length novel, *In Chancery* (1920). Another 'interlude'—*The Awakening*—led on to the third volume in the trilogy, *To Let* (1921). Then in the year following all five titles were combined and published under the name that Galsworthy had originally had in mind for *The Man of Property* by itself, *The Forsyte Saga*.

Still this was not the end of the Forsytes. The chronicles were continued in *The White Monkey* (1924), *The Silver Spoon* (1926), and *Swan Song* (1928), in which the third generation of the Forsyte family are described in the vastly different England of the 1920s. But the whole series, from first to last, is held together by 'that more or less fixed quantity, Soames'. This second trilogy of novels was published in one-volume form in 1929 under the title of *A Modern Comedy*. Last of all appeared *On Forsyte Change* (1930), something in the nature of a rag-bag of Forsyte tales.

The first part of the *Saga*—the only part with which we are directly concerned in this book—ends with the birth of Fleur, Soames's daughter (and he had so set his heart on a son!), on November 20, 1901; the second with Soames's death in September 1926 while saving his daughter from the flames that were devouring his pictures. And it was then at last that Galsworthy did something like justice to his superlatively realized character. 'There's no better death', Sir Lawrence Mont tells his son, 'than dying to save the one you're fondest of. . . .'

The completion of the *Forsyte Saga* set the crown on John Galsworthy's life work. Honorary doctorates were showered upon him, in 1929 he was awarded the Order of Merit, and three years later came the Nobel Prize for Literature. He died in 1933, from a brain tumour, and the ashes of his cremation were scattered on the grassy slope of Bury Hill, just above his Sussex home.

* * *

For generations to come, students of social history who want to know how the comfortable classes lived in the latter part of the Victorian Age will turn to Galsworthy's pages, in which, with such clarity, such perceptive accuracy, such warmth of sympathetic understanding, he has described the fortunes of the Forsyte family. They will not be disappointed. But it must be understood that *The Forsyte Saga* gives nothing like a *complete* picture of the period in which its action is set. The upper middle class Forsytes are there in 'full plumage', as he puts it—'pickled' to use another of his expressions—but (not to mention the aristocracy) all the classes below them in the social scale are represented hardly at all.

The thirty-shillings-a-week clerk, the factory girl in her flimsy finery, the London policeman and Tommy Atkins in barracks, the hospital nurse and the Fleet Street journalist, the sweated tailor in the East End, shop assistants who must always *seem* to be busy, the ballet dancer and the Board School teacher, the artful dodgers of the lodging-house and the dreary relics whose only bed is a seat on the Embankment—all these, and many, many more, have a place in the Late Victorian scene. And yet Galsworthy doesn't mention them, or at most gives them only a passing glance. Which is why they must be found a place here.

All the same, it is only right and fitting that we should start off with some account of the class to which the Forsytes belonged. The chapter, 'At Home with the Forsytes', is a very necessary one, the kind of chapter that becomes increasingly necessary the farther we are removed from the days of gas-light and hansom-cabs, of pea-souper fogs (such as Philip Bosinney met his death in), and roads that were channels of mire and horse-dung; of women compressed in corsets and weighed down by layers of underclothes and with dresses trailing; a world without telephones or cinemas, a world in which dockers dreamed of a tanner an hour and processions of unemployed stumbled along the streets, collecting pennies in tin-cans; a world in which children might be ragamuffins, and the old men and women had nothing better to look forward to than the workhouse. These things were part and parcel of the facts of life for those who got *The Man of Property* out of Mudie's Library on its publication in 1906, but they can hardly be imagined by readers who live in this present, ever so different time. Hence this chapter on the houses such as the Forsytes lived in, their rooms and furnishing, the social functions with which they filled their hours of leisure, their servants, the dresses they wore on a variety of occasions, the daring significance of a cigarette between a lady's lips and a dab of powder on her cheeks.

From 'those green pastures where Forsytes flourish' we move on into those vastly larger parts of the metropolis where live the people whose toil makes Forsytean existence possible. There is no better place to meet them than in the pages of Charles Booth's account of 'London Life and Labour'. All the 'documents' in Chapter 2 are taken from this incomparable survey. First, a summary account of the social classes and economic circumstances of the inhabitants of the East End; next, a number of sketches from the investigators' note-books; next again, descriptions of members of the professional groups and the principal classes of tradesmen; and then, finally, short accounts of those who serve the public, ranging from men wearing the Queen's uniform to officers of local government.

Chapter 3 is concerned with a social survey which ranks second only to the one just dissected: 'Rowntree' supplements 'Booth', and it will be noticed how the conclusions of one are ratified by those of the other.

Next comes a chapter illustrating the '£. s. d. of Living', in which the statistics are not allowed to swamp the human material. Reading the personal stories—true stories, be it noted, taken straight from life—contained under 'Family Budgets', reading how a man and his wife might 'make do' on incomes varying from 30s. a week to £10,000 a year —we are enabled to visualize everyday existence in Town houses and houses in the country, flats and tenements and semi-detached villas.

After this come chapters composed of 'documents' drawn from official sources, the reports of the Royal Commission on the Housing of the Working Classes and the Select Committee of the House of Lords on the Sweating System. A later chapter gives a selection of similar documents dealing with departmental inquiries into Dangerous Trades.

The remaining chapters may be described as lively specimens of Victorian journalism inspired by social propaganda. Need that formidable lady, Mrs Sidney Webb, have sniffed quite so loudly when in after years she referred to her 'one and only literary success' that is largely reproduced in Chapter 7? With what cheerful audacity that ebullient red-head, Mrs Annie Besant, championed the London matchgirls when they went on strike! And how W. T. Stead thrust all caution aside in his highly coloured exposure of the crude and cruel manifestations of Victorian vice. And then the curtain comes down on General Booth's grim picture of a land a tenth of whose population is 'submerged' below the level of any society calling itself civilized.

In conclusion, I would make it clear that (as in my previous volumes, *Human Documents of the Industrial Revolution in Britain* and *Human Documents of the Victorian Golden Age*) all the 'documents' in this collection are *original* documents, prepared and written and printed when the 'Age of the Forsytes' was running its course. In my selection from an almost overwhelming mass of likely material I have constantly had an eye for what is essentially 'human'. While in most cases I have shortened the documents, have added headings, and here and there have inserted side-headings and explanatory matter—this in square brackets—I have been careful not to alter them. Full details of source are given at the foot of each extract. All the illustrations, taken from contemporary publications, have been selected for an evidential value that makes them 'documents' in their own right.

CONTENTS

13

ILLUSTRATIONS

PLATES

DRAWINGS IN TEXT

ACKNOWLEDGMENTS

Grateful acknowledgment is made of the assistance rendered by the Publishers of the various works drawn upon in this volume, in particular: Messrs Heinemann Publishers Ltd (John Galsworthy's *The Forsyte Saga* and *The Modern Comedy*), Messrs Macmillan & Co. Ltd. (C. Booth's *Life & Labour of the People in London*), Messrs Thomas Nelson & Sons Ltd. (S. Rowntree's *Poverty: A Study of Town Life*), Messrs John Murray Ltd. (*Cornhill Magazine* articles), London School of Economics and Political Science (Mrs Sidney Webb's *Pages from a Workgirl's Diary*), etc.

In the matter of illustrations: the Librarians of the London Library; the Corporation of the City of London; and the London Borough of Tower Hamlets; also the Editors of the *Illustrated London News* and *Punch*.

CHAPTER I

AT HOME WITH THE FORSYTES

Round the park—Hyde Park, in London's west end—the Forsytes had their high-class residences. Old Jolyon's was in Stanhope Gate, at the lower end of Park Lane, and James's was just round the corner in Park Lane itself. Swithin, being a bachelor, lived in the 'lonely glory' of chambers in Hyde Park Mansions, and Nicholas had his abode in Ladbroke Grove which, though spacious, was probably not a bit too big for a man with a wife and six children. Roger and *his* brood lived on the other side of the park, in Princes Gardens, within a stone's-throw of the Albert Hall. Susan had a husband and a house high up on Campden Hill—a house so tall that it gave you a crick in the neck to look at it. And Timothy had a commodious red-brick residence on the Bayswater Road, overlooking the park, where also there dwelt under his protection his three sisters, the 'old aunts', who on Sunday afternoons were 'at home' to any of the Forsytes who fancied a cup of tea in an atmosphere of family gossip.

So much for the elder generation, the ten children of 'Superior Dosset Forsyte', who in the early years of the century had pushed his way up from a stonemason in Dorset to being a prosperous master builder in London. Of the next generation, Soames Forsyte, the 'man of property', and his wife Irene, had a daintily fastidious 'nest' in Montpellier Square, quite near the Park, between Knightsbridge and the Brompton Road; and his sister Winifred Dartie was nearer still, in Green Street, Mayfair.

Good addresses, all of them; but there was another in the family directory that was nothing like so good. The eldest of this second generation, Young Jolyon, had slipped out of Forsytean morality and ways of living and had a house in St John's Wood—and a pokey little place it was, too, in his father's eyes: why, the rent couldn't be a hundred a year!

For some of these dwellings Galsworthy has handed us a key. We may stumble into Timothy's dark little hall, so dark that Aunt Hester had once mistaken Philip Bosinney's soft grey hat for a cat and tried to 'shoo' it off the chair. We may, if we like, peer into Old Jolyon's vast and dreary apartments, catch a whiff of his cigar-smoke from his gloomy little study, so full of green velvet and heavily carved mahogany and with windows of stained glass to exclude the depressing view. We may give a rat-tat on the copper knocker of Soames's olive green front door, and follow the maid through rooms furnished in First Empire style and with wallpapers of William Morris design, into the little court tiled with jade-green tiles where there are pink hydrangeas in peacock-blue tubs. These are but glimpses, however, brief and tantalizing, serving only to remind us of whole heaps of things that we would very much like to know. Hence this chapter. . . .

To begin with, we are 'shown over' what may be taken as a typical middle-class house of the period. Through the front door into the hall, up the stairs to the main rooms on the first floor, and up again to the principal bedrooms, and higher still to the servants' attics. On the way we may cast a glance at the bath-room, provided with the most up-to-date fittings, and a much more hurried one at the dark little box of a W.C. Then down again to the kitchen, where our attention may well be called to the gas-cooker and the washing-machine.

In the main our guide on this domestic itinerary will be Robert (later Sir Robert) Edis, an architect with something of a reputation as an interior decorator. His book, *Decoration and Furniture of Town Houses*, based on lectures he had given under the distinguished auspices of the Royal Society of Arts, must surely have found a place on the shelf above Philip Bosinney's drawing-board; and by no great stretch of the imagination we may suppose that some of his ideas were given expression in the house at Robin Hill.

Next we are taken behind the scenes to learn something of the arrangements that were necessary to put on a 'dinner at Swithin's' or a 'dance at Roger's' or such a comparatively small affair as an 'at home' at Timothy's. We may observe the Forsytes and their guests 'eating' their soup and steadily making their way through the *entrees* and *rôts*, the *relevés* and *entremets*, with the butler hovering round to fill up the glasses with champagne (at seven or eight shillings the bottle). We are told the correct way to ask a young lady to dance, and how a chaperon makes herself useful, and the dreadful consequences that might be expected to follow when a lady smokes. (Irene Forsyte smoked Egyptians?)

What next? Well, surely the servants deserve a bit of recognition. In the Forsyte class servants were cheap, and they were treated accordingly, if we may judge from some of the remarks made about them. Old Jolyon had half a dozen 'eating their heads off'. Soames had several, and *his* attitude may be gathered from his insistence as a young married man that they must dish up a hot dinner on Sundays, since they had nothing else to do but 'play the concertina'. And how astonished Soames was when his father's butler, whom he had known for years, told him that he had a son in the Inniskillings, who might be sent out to fight in the war in South Africa at any time now. 'Why, Warmson, I didn't know you were married.'

Then in the last section we may learn what the Forsytes wore, in the home and at business, at weddings and funerals, at dinner-parties and dances, on the lawn-tennis court and at the seaside. We may visualize mischief-making Mrs MacAnder on her bicycle, no doubt one of the recently introduced low-built 'safeties'—no lady might ride one of the old 'penny-farthings' for fear of showing too much leg in mounting and getting off—on that September afternoon when she spotted Irene Forsyte and Philip Bosinney emerging together from a grove of bracken; and also that pioneering motorist, young Eustace Forsyte, and his girl-friend, swathing themselves in coats and wraps, veils and goggles, for a run in his car (Panhard or Daimler?) that shook him up so horribly that he broke one of his eye-teeth.

Turn the page, and with no great stretch of the imagination we may take a peep through the door of Irene's boudoir and see her brushing that amber-coloured hair of hers—applying perhaps just a touch of powder to her pale cheeks—struggling with her corset—tying her garters (*above* the knee of course); or, even more intriguing, ready for bed in her frilly, lace-trimmed 'night chemise'.

I

Old Jolyon's at Stanhope Gate?

I can conceive nothing more terrible than to be doomed to spend one's life in a house furnished after the fashion of twenty years ago. Dull monotonous walls on which garish flock papers of the vulgarest possible design stare one blankly in the face, with patches here and there of accumulated dirt and dust, or the even worse monstrosities of imitation *moiré* silk, with bunches of gilt flowers tied up in gilt ribbons, and running in symmetrical lines like soldiers on parade.

Of course, if the flock paper be red, we had red curtains hung on to a gigantic pole, like the mast of a ship, blossoming out at the ends into bunches of flowers, or turned finials, like enormous hyacinth bulbs in water. The curtains trailed some feet on the floor, and, when not taken possession of by the pet dog or cat, became the receptacle for dust and dirt, or the hiding-place of the remains of some pet's dinner.

The chairs were covered with red stuff of some kind; the table had a red cloth, printed all over with elegant designs of flowers in black, in impossible positions; the carpet was probably of some gaudy colour and pattern, covering the whole room with a sprawling pattern of gigantic flowers; the furniture of the stiffest possible kind, rows of chairs seemingly propped up against the wall in straight lines so as not to over-task the bandy-curved legs which bore them, the so-called 'shaped' backs cut cross-grain of the wood so as to snap sharp off with any extra weight; an enormous glass over the miserably ugly mantelpiece, in a still more enormous gold frame, with bits of plaster ornament, also gilt, stuck on like bats and rats on a barn door, and, like them, showing signs of decay and decomposition; a so-called sideboard, with a drawer in the

24

middle, a cupboard on each side, and another enormous glass overhead.

In the drawing-room we had the same kind of monotony, only perhaps in a different colour; a green carpet, with peaceful lilies intertwining with each other; a hearthrug, with a Bengal tiger ill at ease, his back to the fire and his face in the lilies; and a footstool, covered with Berlin wool, representing the pet dog of the period, very much astonished at his proximity to the aforesaid tiger; green curtains, with a Greek fret or honeysuckle border in yellow or gold; a gigantic valance with deep fringe worked into knots over turned wood beads; furniture covered with work of crude colours, marriage offerings to our fathers and mothers; chairs so lightly constructed that you could never be safe upon them; couches that you could not lie comfortably upon; tables with legs twisted and turned into impossible shapes; occasional chairs, which were well named in that they would never stand for the purposes they were intended, except very occasionally indeed; and the whole arrangements of the room stiff, formal, and uninviting. . . .

If there was a bit of colour on the walls, nine times out of ten it was of the tea-tray character, a brilliant illumination of Vesuvius, as it would probably appear in a pantomime, and not in reality; a few family portraits, whose particular merits were spoilt by the painting, and everything miserable and unartistic. . . . This is no exaggeration; there are still hundreds of rooms in which this utter want of taste prevails. . . .

ROBERT W. EDIS, FRIBA, *Decoration and Furniture of Town Houses* (1881), pp. 17-20.

2

Bright Ideas for 'Robin Hill'?

The general arrangement of a Town House consists, as a rule, of a narrow entrance hall, widened out to make room for the staircase which stares you in the face as you enter, and two or more rooms on a floor lighted from back to front. The rooms are without bays or recesses, with flat ceilings, cornices of stereotyped form, mantels and grates of no particular design. The doors are four panel, with weedy-looking mouldings; the windows filled with plate glass, and the general lines and details of the rooms suggestive of anything but harmonious decoration.

But if you will, you may substitute artistic for commonplace decoration; paper your walls and paint your doors and other woodwork, at little or no greater cost than that of the flock or imitation *moiré* silk papers and imitation graining so much affected in later years; and replace the bad and ugly with what shall be in good taste and pleasant to look upon.

Hall and staircase

Let us suppose that the street door—which should be painted in some warm, serviceable colour, either chocolate or brown, and varnished for protection against the weather and to render it easily cleaned—is opened and we are in the hall, the ante-chamber of the house.

Here the walls should be painted with some good colour—not too light to show finger-marks—to two-thirds of their height, with some simple pattern stencilled over the surface and the whole carefully varnished. The upper portion should be divided by a plain wood moulding which can be formed into a narrow shelf on which to place light pieces of majolica or *grès de Flandres* or other ware. Drawings or anything hung on the walls are generally in the way, and are liable to blow about and damage the paint and decoration. The space under the cornice might be distempered; for where gas is used this portion of the wall is likely to get dirty or discoloured in a year.

As a rule, the floors of halls of most town houses are of stone, and these form very good borders for bright Persian or Indian rugs. The door-mat should be sunk flush with the floor, and of large size, so that little or no dirt may be carried on to the rug.

In the ordinary hall there is not much room for furniture, but there is still space for one or two high-backed chairs of plain oak, or a long deal settle, and for a small stand for wet umbrellas. If possible there should be a cupboard with shelves arranged for coats and a sliding rack for hats.

The staircase is usually a cold and dreary approach to the living rooms—often a long vault, walled in with blocks of imitation marble, with cast-iron balustrading of the worst possible design, thin, poor, and unsafe. Of course, all this must remain . . . but we can make them more cheerful and less cold and dull.

As a rule the lower flights are fairly well-lighted, and the walls can therefore be hung with drawings. If possible, put here and there a piece of china, or a good figure on brackets. A carefully-designed lantern light, filled with leaded and jewelled glass . . . a bright drugget . . . here and there, on the landings and open spaces, Persian or Indian rugs or prayer-carpets. If the landing be large, put a comfortably low couch with some bright covering, and a stand for flowers or china.

Dining Room

In the dining room everything in furniture should be as comfortable and convenient as possible, and designed for use, not show. The chairs should be broad-seated and backed and strong, not narrow, high-backed and spindle-legged with knobs and irregularities to torture the back. The seats and backs stuffed and covered with strong, serviceable leather or morocco in preference to velvet, which is liable to hold dust and to drag the laces of ladies' dresses.

The table should be made so that those who are placed at the angles are not made to suffer torture and misery during the long hours of dinner, by projecting legs which are always in the wrong place. I can conceive nothing more suitable for an ordinary room than a round table 4 feet 8 inches to 5 feet in diameter, the top made expanding into almost any length so as to form, when open, an elongated oval.

Instead of the ordinary sideboard, with its grotesque spider-like legs and carved pedestals and utterly useless mass of looking-glass back, with hideous carved scroll frame and top, I would suggest a plain but solidly handsome buffet, arranged for the reception of plate and glass, or for good pieces of china, the lower portion fitted up with a cellaret and liquor tray within a panelled cupboard on one side and a useful cupboard on the other, a few drawers for plate and other necessaries for a dinner-table; and between the cluster of shelves above, a small splayed mirror might be fixed.

Perhaps, for convenience of serving, the central portion might be made into a sliding hatch communicating with the small back parlour or breakfast-room, or a light lift from the basement might easily be made to run up in the lower portion; on either side might be repoussé copper or brass sconces for candles.

As regards the floor, the practice of covering the whole with carpets answers no purpose but to increase the upholsterer's bill and to keep up a dust trap which is not got rid of until the times of the annual spring or autumn cleaning. Paint or stain and varnish the floor two or three feet all round in some good, hard-wearing colour, and put the money thus saved into some good Persian or Indian carpet, which, while warm and comfortable to the feet, is grateful and pleasant to the eye.

Drawing Rooms

The drawing-rooms should be the rooms of all others in which good taste, both in decoration and furniture, should be everywhere apparent. The rooms wherein we practically live, talk, play, and receive our guests are essentially the ladies' rooms of the house, and should be decorated in a pleasant, cheerful manner, without stiffness or formality.

The walls should be pleasant objects to look upon, not cold and dreary blanks of mere one-tinted paper, varied, perhaps, with birds, or bunches of flowers in gold, scattered here and there in monotonous array.

The furniture should essentially be comfortable, couches and chairs pleasant to lounge and really rest upon, not so-called artistic monstrosities on which it is impossible to do the one or the other. The rooms should, above all, look and be home-like in all their arrangements, with ornaments, books, and flowers, not arranged merely for show but for pleasant study or recreation.

But I must protest against fluffy wool mats scattered about the tables, antimacassars of lace, worsted, or other work hung loosely over the backs of the chairs and sofas, velvet-covered brackets, with useless fringe fixed on with brass-headed nails, on which too often are placed trumpery bits of Dresden or other china, in the shape of dogs, cats, or birds. By all means have coverings to protect the chair-backs, but let them be of some good embroidered stuff or well-designed crewel work, fixed securely to the chair or sofa-backs, so as not to be liable to be carried off as pendants to the fringe of a lady's dress or the buttons of a gentleman's coat.

In the illustration 'A Drawing-room Corner', I give a sketch of my own drawing-room, showing what can be done in the drawing-room of an ordinary London house.

The general tone of the woodwork is black, the panels of the doors and shutters being covered with gold leaf as a ground for painted decoration of flowers or birds. The general wall surface is covered with Morris's pomegranate pattern paper of bluish grey ground, with exceedingly good decorative effect in colour of fruit and flowers. The wall space is divided about three feet below the cornice with a plain flat gilt moulding, under which is a simple $\frac{1}{2}$-inch gas pipe, also gilt, as a picture rod. Above this the wall space or frieze has been lined all round with canvas pasted on to the plaster, and on this Mr Marks has painted a decorative frieze, consisting of figures, birds, and foliage.

The cabinet shown is of mahogany ebonized, free from all mouldings and carving, and designed specially for china and books, with drawers for photographs and prints, and the panels filled in with painted heads representing the four seasons. The floor surface is painted dark brown, and the centre space covered with an Indian carpet. The ceiling is slightly toned in colour.

Bedrooms

A bedroom should be clear of everything that can collect or hold dust in any form; should be bright and cheerful, and pleasantly furnished with light and cheerful furniture of good and simple design.

If a room be carefully decorated, curtains are much better away, on the grounds of health as well as of decoration. If you insist on having your room quite dark at night, have double blinds or shutters.

I would have the whole floor stained and varnished, or painted, and strips of carpet, matting, or rugs thrown down only when required; these can be taken up and shaken every day without trouble, the floors washed, and the evil of fixed carpets thus avoided.

Even as it is undesirable to cover the whole of the floor with carpet, equally undesirable is it to cover the whole walls with paper. As a matter of health, it is better to have as little material as possible that will absorb and retain the often impure air of a bedroom; as a matter of light, it is desirable to have a portion of the wall in some light tone, even if the lower portion be papered in a somewhat dark shade.

Any pattern or design which shows prominently any set pattern, or spots which suggest a sum of multiplication, or which, in the half-light of night or early morning, might be likely to fix themselves upon the tired brain, suggesting all kinds of weird forms, are especially to be avoided. The woodwork of the doors, windows, and skirting should be painted in some plain colour to harmonize or contrast with the wall decoration.

The old four-post bed is now almost a thing of the past. We have learnt that to shut ourselves up in the limited space of such monstrosities, by closed tops and coverings, means not only excluding light which may be desirable, but air, which is of the highest importance. Nothing can be better or more cleanly than the painted iron or brass bedsteads, with perhaps some light hangings, cheerful, yet subdued in colour.

Although the wardrobes of the present day combine many conveniences, they are lumbering and unwieldy and occupy far too much space. I would suggest that the recesses formed by the chimney breast should, in part at least, be filled with good hanging closets. These can be made to go up to the ceiling, by which arrangement no spaces would be left to harbour dust and dirt. The top portion may be arranged with shelves, whereon may be stowed away articles of dress not immediately required. The middle space should be fitted with hooks and rails on which to hang dresses and other articles of a lady's belongings; the lower portion being fitted with sliding shelves and drawers, for caps and bonnets.

Naturally chests of drawers are required, but these should stand up well from the floor, so as to allow the space underneath to be thoroughly cleaned and dusted. The dressing-table should have nests of convenient drawers on either side, while cupboards may be arranged on either side of the swinging glass for gloves or jewellery. Now that good painted tiles can be obtained at small expense, they may be used for washing-stands with good effect, or the wall above may be lined entirely with them to a height of 3 or 4 feet. In the window, plain deal boxes, fitted as ottomans, with luxuriously stuffed seats and backs, would themselves suggest rest and quiet.

Children's Nurseries

In the dreariness of town houses, nothing has struck me as so utterly cruel as the additional dreariness which generally pervades the rooms especially devoted to children—the nurseries of the house, the rooms in which our little ones spend so large a portion of their early lives—and yet I know of no rooms which should be made more cheerful and beautiful in their general appearance than these.

While the furniture should be strong and useful, it need not be prison-like; the walls need not be covered with some monotonous imitation tile paper just because it wears better than another.

In the windows of the day nursery there should be boxes of flowers, in which buttercups and daisies, primroses and daffodils might be cultivated, to teach the little ones of the country, and of the nursery rhymes and fairy tales they love so well.

Let the walls be papered with some pleasant paper, in which the colours shall be bright and cheerful; distemper the upper portion of the room for health's sake, and varnish the paper if you please. But nowadays, when really good illustrations are to be found in so many of our weekly and monthly publications, why not cut them out, or, better still, let the little ones do so, and paper them over the the whole of the lower portion of the walls ? A band of colour might be made by buying some of the Christmas books, which Mr H. S. Marks, R.A., Miss Kate Greenaway, and Mr Walter Crane have so charmingly and artistically illustrated, and by pasting the scenes in regular order and procession, as a kind of frieze under the upper band of distemper, varnished over to protect from dirt.

R. W. E D I S, F R I B A, *Decoration and Furniture of Town Houses* (1881), pp. 148-238.

3

Garrets for Servant Girls

The ceilings of all servants' rooms should be whitewashed once a year and the walls colour-washed, unless they are papered with washable sanitary paper. The floor should simply have dhurries [Indian cotton fringed squares] laid down by each bed and by the washing-stands, etc.

Each servant should have a separate bed if possible, and that bed should be as comfortable as can be, without being unduly luxurious.

I should like myself to give each maid a really pretty room, but at present they are a little hopeless on the subject. No sooner is the room put nice than something happens to destroy the beauty, and I really believe servants are only happy if their rooms are allowed in some measure to resemble the home of their youth, and to be merely places where they lie down to sleep as heavily as they can.

The simpler, therefore, a servant's room is furnished the better. A cupboard of some kind should be provided where they can hang up their dresses. But if this is impossible, a few hooks must supplement the chest of drawers, washing-stand, bedchair, and toilet-table with glass, which is all that is required in the room of a maid-servant.

The sheets should be changed once in three weeks, also the pillow-cases, while three towels to each maid a week are none too much to allow them to use, if you wish them to be clean.

MRS J. E. PANTON, *From Kitchen to Garret* (7th edit., 1890); pp. 151–2.

4

A Kitchen out of 'Mrs Beeton'

In a kitchen, of all rooms, it is most desirable that the walls should be divided into two parts, the dado, and what may be called the superdado, by a horizontal chair rail placed at their height. Below the chair rail, the walls that constitute the dado should be panelled or matchboarded; the superdado may be papered according to taste, but with a washing paper which should be varnished.

It cannot be too strongly insisted on that everything found in the kitchen, whether fittings, fixtures, or furniture, should present a varnished exterior. Varnished work may be a little more costly than ordinary painting, but its durability and cleanly appearance after being wiped over with a damp cloth, render it cheaper in the long run. The floor should be stained and varnished.

The kitchen table should be massive, firm and strongly made. Perhaps it will be better without drawers, for kitchen-table drawers but too often become receptacles and lurking-places of a heterogeneous mass of rubbish and odds and ends, most of which would find a fitter resting-place in the dust-bin or ash-pit.

No kitchen can be regarded as completely furnished without a clock. The best kind is an 8-day dial, which requires winding up only once a week. A good English 8-day dial may be obtained from Messrs Benson & Co., Ludgate Hill, London, E.C., measuring 12 inches across the dial, for 35s.

The kitchen dresser is usually a tripartite arrangement, consisting of a range of drawers, usually three in number, with a 'potboard' below and four to five tiers of shelves above. Broad and deep cupboards are an absolute necessity in a kitchen, and the recess formed by the piers that flank the range and the chimney breast above are usually appropriated to this purpose. The board on which the bells of the house are hung, according to the old-fashioned mode of bell-hanging, or the indicator that is used with electric bells, is usually placed above the kitchen door.

By far the most important fixture is the apparatus that is used for cooking, heating water, etc., usually known as the range or kitchener.

Kitchen ranges may be distinguished as close and open. In the open range the fire-grate is uncovered at the top; in the close range the fire-chamber is closed in front by an iron door, and covered in at the top by an iron plate. Close ranges are now chiefly used. Economy of fuel and cleanliness are the chief features of close ranges of all kinds, combined with efficiency of action, provided that the flues themselves, through which the smoke and soot pass off into the chimney, leaving considerable deposits in the passage, are kept perfectly clean. As types of the best ranges yet contrived, we may select Crabtree's Close Fire Range (cost £7 15s. to £11 5s. according to size) and Crabtree's Patent Kitchener (£15 to £21).

Gas stoves. From the consideration of ranges in which cooking is performed by the combustion of solid fuel, it is necessary to turn to those in which gas is the fuel employed, the gas companies in various localities lending all the aid in their power to further it, by supplying their customers with gas stoves, or ranges, at a low annual rental.

There are many features to recommend cooking by gas, chief among which are the cleanliness and the readiness by which the fire can be lighted and extinguished. Again, during the greater part of the day in the summer, no fire is needed even in the kitchen, and it is a genuine comfort to be able to dispense with it. Against this, however, must be placed the fact that a gas range does not present the comfortable appearance that an ordinary range or kitchener has, with solid fuel burning in its box or grate. Moreover, when a gas fire is constantly maintained, it is open to question whether it is not more costly than a fire of coals.

Mr Thomas Fletcher, Warrington, Lancashire, is the leading authority in the country in the use to which gas may be put, and takes rank as the first gas engineer and maker of appliances for the use of gas in the

United Kingdom. Fletcher's No. 4 Gas Cooking Range appears to be the most suitable for family use, being of sufficient capacity to cook for ten persons, the price, complete, being £7.

For bedrooms, and occasional uses, a gas fire is always economical as compared with coal; in fact, the expense and great trouble of coal fires for bedrooms renders their use practically prohibitory, whereas a good hot gas fire can be obtained for half an hour, night and morning, at a cost of 6d. per week or less.

Washing machines. The use of machines for washing, wringing and mangling has now become general. They can be suitable for the smallest as well as the largest family. According to the machines, so do the instructions vary. It may, however, be roughly stated that stains should be rubbed out of clothes before they are put into the machines, and that care be taken in wringing the articles so that the buttons are not dragged off. An ordinary family washing machine when opened out occupies a space of about 4 or 5 feet square, but when not in use it can be greatly reduced.

Mrs Beeton's Household Management (1888 edition), ch. 3.

5

Bath-room, Lavatory, and W.C.

It is now generally acknowledged that a dwelling cannot be considered as complete without a bath-room, and that its adoption should not be limited to the superior mansions of the wealthy, but that all classes of our population should have it within their power to benefit by the comfort, cleanliness, and healthfulness afforded by both hot and cold baths.

In large mansions there should be one or more bath-rooms on every floor, while in all average-sized dwellings one placed in a central position will be found to be all that may be positively necessary.

For superior dwellings, copper baths should be used in preference to enamelled metal of any kind, for enamel after a time flies off and breaks; this objection also applies to japanned zinc and iron. The most useful length for a bath is $5\frac{1}{2}$ feet at the top and $4\frac{1}{2}$ feet at the bottom, with a depth of 2 feet 3 inches.

In numerous instances lavatory apparatus, embracing a hot and cold water supply, may be readily adopted throughout the bedrooms and dressing rooms of the upper floors in the place of the jug and basin system which is now so universal, and by its adoption not only may time and trouble be saved to the occupants but a large amount of unnecessary labour to the servants.

Water-closets. With few exceptions the excremental refuse of superior dwellings in this country is discharged through the medium of water-closets, the only exceptions being those comparatively rare cases where earth-closets have taken their place, and those in which neither earth nor water-closets exist *within* the dwelling, and the inmates therefore follow the old but waning custom of using *external* closets of some kind or another.

Two important objects should be aimed at wherever water-closets are used. (1) They should be so placed that no objectionable smell shall find its way into the other parts of the dwelling. (2) Their machinery should be so arranged that no gases from either sewer, soil pipe, or trap shall escape inwards.

Housemaids' closets. Next in importance to the water-closets in the upper floors of a dwelling the housemaids' closet deserves consideration, as the sink it contains serves for the discharge of all upstairs slops. By their adoption not only is much manual labour saved to servants, but the water-closet apparatus, which most frequently does duty as a sink in the absence of special arrangements, is protected from derangement. Housemaids' closets should never be placed in conspicuous places, as they are generally subject to a disagreeable though slight odour.

EARDLEY F. BAILEY-DENTON, *Hand Book of House Sanitation* (1882), pp. 57-8, 87-9.

(b) SOCIAL OCCASIONS

I

Leaving Cards

Leaving cards is the first step towards forming, or enlarging, a circle of acquaintances. A lady's visiting card should be printed in small, clear, copper-plate type, and free from any kind of embellishment. It should be a thin card, $3\frac{1}{2}$ inches in depth or even smaller. The name of the lady should be printed in the centre, and her address in the left-hand corner. It is now considered old-fashioned for husbands and wives to have their names printed on the same card: they should have separate cards of their own.

Leaving cards principally devolves upon the mistress of a house; a wife should leave cards for her husband as well as for herself. The master of a house has little or no card-leaving to do, beyond leaving cards upon his bachelor friends.

Mostly cards should be delivered in person, and not sent by post. A lady should desire her man-servant to inquire if the mistress of the house at which she is calling is 'at home'. If 'not at home', she should hand him *three* cards: one of her own and two of her husband's; her card is left for the mistress of the house, and her husband's for both master and mistress. If the answer is in the affirmative, she should, after making the call, leave *two* of her husband's cards on the hall-table, and neither put them in the card-basket nor leave them on the drawing-room table, nor offer them to her hostess, all of which would be very incorrect.

When the mistress of the house has a grown-up daughter or daughers, the lady leaving cards should turn down one corner of her visiting card —the right-hand corner generally—to include the daughter or daughters

35

in the call. Maiden ladies of a certain age should have visiting cards of their own.

Manners and Rules of Good Society (1888), pp. 18-21.

2

Afternoon At-Homes

When the answer [to the inquiry, 'Is Mrs A. at home ?'] is in the affirmative, the lady should enter the house without further remark and follow the servant to the drawing-room. On opening the drawing-room door the servant should stand inside the doorway, facing the mistress of the house, and say, 'Mrs . . .'.

The mistress of the house should rise, come forward, and shake hands with her visitor. She should not ask her to be seated, or to 'take a seat', or where would she like to sit, or which seat would she prefer ? etc., but should at once sit down and expect her visitor to do the same, as near herself as possible.

A hostess betrays that she is not much accustomed to society when she attempts to amuse her visitor by the production of albums of photographs, books, illustrated newspapers, portfolios of drawings, and artistic efforts of members of the family, and the like. She should rely solely upon her own powers of conversation to make the short quarter of an hour—which is the limit of a ceremonious call—pass pleasantly to the visitor. She should not offer her visitor any refreshments, wine and cake for instance. But if tea is brought in while the visitor is in the drawing-room, or if the visitor calls while the hostess is having tea, she should naturally offer her visitor tea.

When a second visitor arrives, ten or fifteen minutes after the first, the first visitor should take her leave as soon as she conveniently can. When the hostess has shaken hands, and before crossing the room with her, she should ring the bell, that a servant might be in readiness in the hall to open the door and to call up her carriage.

Manners and Rules of Good Society, pp. 29-40

3

When a Gentleman Calls

A gentleman when calling, should take his hat and stick (or small umbrella if it answers the purpose of a stick) with him into the drawing-room, and hold them until he has seen the mistress of the house and shaken hands with her. He should [then] either place them on a chair or table near at hand or hold them in his hand, according as to whether he feels at ease or the reverse, until he takes his leave. He should not put his hat on until in the hall, as, in the house, a gentleman should never put on his hat in the presence of its mistress.

To leave his hat in the hall would be considered a liberty and in very bad taste; only the members of a family residing in the same house leave their hats in the hall, or enter the drawing-room without their hats in their hands. The fact of hanging up the hat in the hall proves that the owner of the hat is at home there.

Manners and Rules of Good Society, pp. 31-2.

4

Music in the Afternoon

In town, during the season when large and fashionable afternoon at homes are given, it is usual to engage one or two celebrities in the musical world, whose talents lie either in the comic or operatic direction. The fees for such services range from 5 to 25 guineas.

On the other hand, ladies to whom the expenses of an entertainment are a matter of some moment, and who can only afford a small fee, content themselves with engaging talent of a different order, the fees for these services range from 2 to 5 guineas, including pianists and vocalists.

Professors of music and singing—men of undoubted ability, but who have their way to make in the world—are sometimes glad to give their services gratis at the houses of ladies possessing a large and fashionable circle of acquaintances, on the consideration of being presented to the most influential ladies present or those ladies who are likely to require professional services at their own parties, or professional instruction for their daughters. Such an arrangement gives the *artiste* an opportunity of exhibiting his or her talents which might otherwise not be afforded; while the guests have the enjoyment of professional talent, and the hostess the *éclat* that professional talent always confers upon an entertainment.

Party-Giving on Every Scale, by a Member of the Aristocracy (1882), ch. 5.

5

Good Manners at the Dinner-Table

When a lady has taken her seat at the dinner table she should at once remove her gloves, although occasionally long elbow gloves are not removed during dinner, but this is conspicuous and inconvenient. She should unfold her serviette and place it in her lap.

*

Soup should be eaten with a table spoon, and not with a dessert. (In these days no one 'drinks' soup: it is 'eaten'.) Fish should be eaten with a silver fish-knife and fork. All made dishes, such as *rissoles*, patties, etc. should be eaten with a fork only. In eating asparagus a knife and fork should be used. Salad should be eaten with a knife and fork. Peas should be eaten with a fork. Jellies, blancmanges, iced puddings, etc. should be eaten with a fork, as should be all sweets sufficiently substantial to admit of it.

When eating cheese, small morsels of the cheese should be placed with a knife on small morsels of bread, and the two conveyed to the mouth with the thumb and finger, the piece of bread being the morsel to hold as cheese should not be taken up in the fingers, and should not be eaten off the point of the knife.

As a matter of course, young ladies do not eat cheese at dinner-parties.

*

Saying grace, both before and after dinner, is a matter of feeling rather than of etiquette. It used to be very much the custom to say 'grace', but of late years it is oftener omitted than not, especially at large dinner-parties in town.

Manners and Rules of Good Society, page III.

6

Dinner Parties

Advice on dinner giving is rarely offered by one friend to another. People are very thin-skinned and rather touchy on the subject, and a guest would prefer to eat of a dozen bad dinners at his friend's table than to offer the faintest suggestion as to how those dinners might be improved.

Forty years ago people were perhaps more blunt, and a story is told of a *bon vivant* who, when asked to give his opinion by his host of a dinner given in his honour, replied, 'My dear fellow, sell your plate and get a cook'.

The principal points to be considered in dinner giving are, first, the arrangement of the menu, bearing in mind that each course should supplement the other, and that there should be no repetition but constant variety. The time that should be occupied by the dinner is another important point, the best of dinners should not be prolonged beyond an hour and a quarter.

Two descriptions of soup are always given at large dinner parties, one *consommé* and one *purée*. Clear turtle is very much given at both large and small dinners by those who are inclined to pay the price for it, namely, one guinea per quart.

At large dinner parties two kinds of fish are always given, and even at small parties of from eight to ten it is rather the custom to give two kinds; it is needless to add that they would be dressed in different ways, boiled and fried or broiled, and that a large and a smaller kind of fish would be chosen, such as salmon and smelts, turbot and whiting, etc. Oysters when given do not form part of the fish course, but precede the soup; half a dozen would be the proportion to provide for each guest. The cost averages 3s. per dozen.

It is no longer the fashion to give four *entrées*; the number has been reduced to three at large dinner-parties, and to two at small. Formerly the *entrées* were of the most substantial character, and invariably comprised cutlets, patties, and *filet de boeuf;* now the idea is to give *entrées* of the highest possible character to tempt the appetite rather than to satisfy it. Partridge-cutlets are a very popular *entrée*. Sweetbreads appear to have taken their stand as an ubiquitous *entrée*, and few menus are arranged without including them.

At small dinner parties one *relevé*, or remove, would be given, which would consist of a joint. At larger parties, two *relevés* would be given, one of meat and one of poultry. When beef is given, *filet de boeuf* is chosen in preference to a sirloin. Lamb is much given in the summer months. Hot ham with broad beans is considered rather a dainty dish to provide, especially at men's dinners.

The second service is commenced with *rôts*. At large dinner parties two *rôts* are given; at small, but one. *Rôts* considered the most choice in their various seasons are:—ducklings, green goslings, guinea-fowls, capons, spring chickens, golden plovers, wild ducks, partridges, pheasants, grouse, pigeons, snipes, and ortolan.

The vegetables given form quite a feature in themselves. Potatoes are not eaten in the fish course, save when new potatoes are served with salmon, or when dressed fish is served with mashed potatoes; neither are vegetables handed with the entrées. Two plain vegetables and salad are always given with the *relevés* or removes in the first course, and one or two dressed vegetables are given with the *rôts* in the second course. *Pommes de terre frites* generally accompany the *rôts*, with or without a second dressed vegetable.

The roast is followed by *entremets*, savory *entremets* and sweet *entremets*. For a party of eighteen it is usual to give two savories and three sweets; for a smaller number, one savory and a dressed vegetable.

In providing ices it is usual to give one water ice and one cream ice; the proportion would be one pint to every eight guests. The desert is with many an expensive feature. For a party of eighteen, eight dishes of fruit would be the proportion.

The quantity of wine drunk at dinner parties varies so considerably that it is difficult to lay down any hard and fast rule. Thus with regard to champagne, one man would drink from three-quarters of a bottle to a bottle, another would drink say two glasses, while a third would confine himself to claret. Half a bottle of champagne to each man and a third of a bottle to each lady would be a fair proportion; 84s. per dozen is a fair price to give. Sherry is but little drunk at dinner-parties; 72s. per dozen is a price seldom exceeded. When claret is preferred to champagne, a sound dinner claret at 74s. per dozen is provided. Port wine and Madeira are but seldom given, unless they are very choice of their kind, and have been in the cellars some thirty or forty years.

The cost of floral decorations for a dinner table greatly depends upon the season of the year. Those flowers possessing very powerful odours should be avoided, such as hyacinths, cape jasmine, syringa, etc., and the preference given to those which have a refreshing rather than a faint, heavy perfume, as in a dining-room of small dimensions guests often feel a sense of oppression from this cause, by which the appetite suffers and the relish for the good dinner is destroyed.

Party-Giving on Every Scale, ch. 11.

7

Balls and Dances

In town the drawing room is the room usually converted into a ball-room. There are several preparations recommended for preparing floors for dancing, but there is none so thoroughly satisfactory as wax polishing.

Dancing on a polished floor, however, whether it be a fashionable dance or the most modest little piano dance, means the displacing of all the moveable furniture and taking up carpets and consequent inconvenience to the family in general. Thus when the number of invited guests is under one hundred, a dancing-cloth is placed over the carpet.

If the room is a very spacious one, it is usual to place settees or rout-seats around the walls and in the recesses of the windows and in other available spots. The hire of rout-seats with velvet cushions is from 4d. to 6d. per foot. In allowing for seating of guests, seats for one-third of the number invited would be sufficient, as two-thirds of the company at a ball or dance are either dancing or going to and fro to the tea or supper room.

The prevailing idea with most people is that a ball-room cannot be too brilliantly lighted; those who can afford it indulge in a positive blaze of light, and in addition to the usual centre chandelier or gaselier of a drawing-room, half circles, containing from nine to twelve wax lights, are suspended from the walls at the most convenient points, interspersed with girandoles with from three to twelve lights.

Others again consider that this blaze of light should be judiciously toned down, being softer to the eyes and more becoming to the ladies. Thus the wax lights are shaded with coloured shades, and the globes of the chandeliers with tinted glass or coloured muslin.

Balconies, conservatories, and out of door corridors and gardens are often lighted with Chinese lanterns and coloured lamps.

The extent of the floral decorations is entirely a matter of inclination, the cost of which may range from £1 to £100. People who cannot afford to do things well in this department often prefer dispensing with floral decorations altogether to making a meagre display; others confine their outlay to clustering evergreens and foliage plants and a few fragrant cut-flowers, ignoring the use of flowering plants in pots altogether.

The seats for the band or the orchestra, as they are termed, are placed at the upper end of the front drawing-room, or, failing this, in the back drawing-room. The strength of the band depends upon the size of the room, or the expense to which the host is inclined to go. If a string band, the number of performers range from nine to twenty-four, and the charge is from 17s. to £1 per man. A piano band is usually engaged for a small carpet-dance, and consists of two performers only—a pianoforte player and a cornet player; the charge varies from £1 10s. to 3 guineas, according to the standing of the musician. For after-dinner dances, when only one performer is engaged, viz, a pinaoforte player, the charge is a guinea.

A convenient cloak-room is required for the use of the ladies, and a ground-floor room is most suitable for this purpose, however small it may be. A general cloak-room of which both ladies and gentlemen have admission does not offer sufficient privacy and comfort for the ladies as does a small room set apart exclusively for their use, where torn dresses can be re-arranged, and curls and caps readjusted. A cloak-room is also always provided for the gentlemen, with toilette mirror, etc. Gibus hats are always taken by the gentlemen into the ball-room, and are not given up with the coats.

Refreshments are served in the tea-room until the hour of supper. Supper is invariably served in a ground-floor room. From four to ten small round tables are usually provided, in addition to one long supper-table.

Cold roast chicken is a safe supper dish to provide, it being particularly in request amongst ladies. 'Salmon' and 'lobster' appear in almost as many different forms as does chicken. Game pie is a very popular dish. Sandwiches of potted game, chicken, or lobster are invariably given, and every menu comprises jelly. Light French confectionery is supposed to put a finishing-touch to a well-arranged supper-table.

The wine is always a great feature at a ball-supper. Every man fancies himself to be a judge of wine, and many ladies imagine that their judgment may also be relied upon; but nevertheless there are both many men and women who cannot discriminate between gooseberry champagne and Irroy's 1864.

Champagne is always given at a ball-supper. Some ball-givers provide a variety of mineral water, apollinaris, etc. in addition to soda and selzer-water, which are drunk with champagne, sherry, or brandy. Brandy at 7s. per bottle is the quality usually given.

When a ball-supper is contracted for at so much a head, the confectioner engages to provide, in addition to the supper, all necessary plate, china, glass, tabling, flowers, and light refreshments, at a charge (not including wine) from 8s. 6d. to one guinea per head.

Party-Giving on Every Scale, ch. 5.

8

Ball-Room Etiquette

At a ball given in town a hostess should receive her guests at the head of the staircase, and at the door of the ball-room at a country-house ball. She should shake hands with each guest in the order of their arrival.

A lady and gentleman should not ascend the staircase or make their entrance into the ball-room arm in arm. The gentlemen usually enter the ball-room after the ladies of the party.

A ball is usually opened either by the hostess herself or by one of her daughters. Opening a ball simply signifies dancing in the first quadrille at the top of the room with a gentleman of the highest rank present.

The dances now in vogue are Quadrilles, Lancers, Valses, 'The Highland Schottische', 'The Highland Reel', and the Polka, which latter has taken the place so long occupied by the Galop. Country dances such as 'Sir Roger de Coverley', etc. are usually danced at private balls when given in the country, and often a London ball concludes with a 'cotillon', in which expensive presents are given.

Manners and Rules of Good Society, pp. 83-8.

9

'Invitations a la Valse'

Formerly it was the fashion for a young gentleman desirous of dancing with a young lady to say: 'May I have the pleasure of dancing with you ?', but the youth of the present day adopts a much more familiar style of address, and if ever so slightly acquainted with the young lady, he assumes a pleading tone and says, 'I hope you have kept a dance for me', or 'May I not dance something with you ?', or 'Won't you spare me a dance ?', or more familiarly he says 'Will you dance this ?', or 'Shall we take a turn ?'

To these different *'invitations à la valse'* a young lady no longer answers, 'I shall be very happy'. This phrase has disappeared in company with 'May I have the pleasure?' and she replies very practically, accordingly as to whether the applicant is in favour or not. 'Certainly,

I am not engaged for number five, nine, or thirteen', or 'I am afraid I have not one to spare except number fourteen, a quadrille', or 'I will give you a dance if you will come for it a little later, I am engaged for the next three dances', or 'Thank you, yes'.

To the question 'Are you engaged for this dance?' some foolish maidens reply that they do not think that they are engaged, at the same time being thoroughly aware that they are not, and the young men also are aware that the maidens are finessing, and averse to making the direct admission that they are in want of partners. A young lady with tact and aplomb escapes from this dilemma by replying with great readiness, 'I am very glad to say that I am not', which rejoinder is flattering to the young gentleman. . . .

Society Small Talk, by a Member of the Aristocracy (1879), pp. 101-2.

10

Garden Parties

Refreshments at large garden parties are invariably served indoors, but in the country they are sometimes served in a tent, or on tables placed under the trees. Rugs and Persian carpets are spread on the lawn, upon which seats are placed, so that should the grass be damp the guests need not fear taking cold.

Lawn-tennis is now generally played at garden parties, so much so that garden parties are often designated lawn-tennis parties.

In town and in the suburbs a military band is generally engaged to play from four to seven. Those who reside at a considerable distance from a town where a regiment is quartered fall back upon the band of the county militia, yoemanry cavalry, or local volunteers.

The refreshments indispensable at a garden party are tea and coffee, sherry and claret cup, cake and biscuits. Fruit and ices are given in addition when a saving of expense is not of paramount importance to the giver of the entertainment.

The quantity of claret cup drunk depends upon the number of gentlemen present, and also whether they are players of lawn-tennis, in which case there would probably be a run upon iced cups. In some remote counties the gentlemen at a garden party are represented by three or four young curates and two or three old gentlemen, while the ladies present muster from forty to fifty, in which case very little wine is drunk. When garden parties are held in or near London, or in the home counties, or in or near cathedral cities, university towns, garrison towns, etc. the numbers are more equal, and generally one third of the guests are gentlemen; a hostess when providing wine for a garden party naturally takes this into consideration.

Party-Giving on Every Scale, ch. 4.

II

At the Play

It is a piece of bad manners to enter the theatre late, disturbing the audience and annoying the players or singers. It is equally rude to leave before the entertainment is ended, unless the interval be chosen when nothing is going on.

Between the acts of a play the modern man thinks it his duty to himself to go out and have a drink and perhaps smoke a cigarette. But who shall say what golden opinions are won by those who refrain from acquiring the odour of tobacco, or whisky, while they are in the company of ladies in the heated atmosphere of a theatre?

Apart from the lady he is with and considerations connected with her, there is the inconvenience to which many of the audience are subjected by the passing in and out of so many. However, it is a recognized custom, so much so that a smoking *foyer* is attached to all the best theatres, and a warning bell is rung in it by the management a few minutes before the rising of the curtain.

Refreshments are frequently carried round by attendants to private boxes, and sometimes in the stalls as well. Should they appear, it is the duty of the gentleman of the party to ask the lady or ladies if they wish for any, and to pay for what is consumed. It is, however, a rare thing for ladies to eat or drink at the play.

The gentleman also pays for the programme at the few theatres where a charge is made.

Manners for Men (1898), by Mrs C. E. Humphry ('Madge' of *Truth*), pp. 96-102.

12

A Girl Needs a Chaperon

No sooner has a young lady left the schoolroom and dispensed with the chaperonage of the governess, than she requires the chaperonage of a married lady.

At country out-door gatherings, such as garden-parties, lawn-tennis-parties, archery-parties, and so on, the chaperonage is of comparatively slight nature, but at all other entertainments it is imperative that a young lady should be accompanied by a chaperon, whether it be a dinner or a dance, an afternoon tea or an evening assembly, a concert or ball, or theatre, etc.; and a young lady who attempts to evade this received rule would be considered unconventional and unused to the *convenances* prescribed by society.

The bias of many young ladies of the present day is to assert as much independence of action as opportunity offers, but any dereliction in this respect is noted to their disadvantage.

It is more especially at 'at homes', dances, and such, that an efficient chaperon is most needed, and the want of such most felt. By a good chaperon is meant a lady possessing a large circle of acquaintance, who is popular as well as good-natured—unremittingly good-natured throughout the whole evening in introducing the young lady under her care to those ladies of her acquaintance who are most in the habit of giving entertainments, and by introducing any gentleman to her whom she thinks would be likely to ask her to dance.

Manners and Rules of Good Society, pp. 209-11.

13

My Lady Nicotine

The habit of smoking in the dining-room has invaded all classes. Directly the ladies have left the dining-room, the silver cigarette-box and the dainty spirit lamp wherewith to light it are passed round. Ladies encourage and imitate the habit, and, being always anxious to please, willingly learn to take a puff at the odorous weed themselves. This condescension on their part has insensibly resulted in an acquired taste that bids fair to rival the habits of men.

A lurid fact which invests matrimony with fresh terrors! Only think of the expense of smoking for a couple! Think of the disadvantage under which a poor woman will lie, who can no longer reproach her spouse with his abominable extravagance in cigars! Think of the disappointment of the ardent lover when, pressing the lips of his adored one, he finds upon them the flavour of an inferior quality of tobacco! Ladies will surely not stop short at cigarettes; they will require shilling cigars, until eventually, perhaps, they may, from motives of economy, even take to the 'churchwarden'.

The mysteries of back-hair-brushing conclaves in the silence and seclusion of the night will be aggravated by the smell of tobacco issuing through the keyhole and under the door, while the dear girls themselves gravely discuss the respective merits of 'Bird's-eye', 'Cavendish', 'Turkish Latakia', and 'Irish Twist'. A man will hand his partner a cigarette as naturally as an ice, and the first present of the happy bridegroom must consist of a cigarette-case and a match-box!

LADY GREVILLE, *The Gentlewoman in Society* (1892), pp. 246-8.

A Bridal Dress of 1885

(c) DOMESTIC SERVANTS

Butler

In all establishments, from the largest to the smallest, the butler is the head of his department, and is answerable for the property placed under his charge, and for the proper performance of the duties of those under him, viz., the footman or footmen.

The plate chest is in his charge. It is his duty, every night before retiring to rest, to see that the plate in everyday use is carefully put away, and also to give it out in the morning to be cleaned. He also gives out plate used at dinner parties or balls, and sees that it is properly cleaned for use.

His next responsibility is the wine cellar. The cellar book is the check upon the butler as to the quantity of wine drunk in a given time. The master of every establishment keeps the keys of his wine cellars, and gives out so many dozen of wine for the consumption of the household. The butler's duty is to enter into the cellar book the amount of wine given out, and the number of bottles drunk per day.

It is the butler's duty to decant the wine for daily use, and to put away the decanters after every meal.

Where a valet is not kept, it is a butler's duty to valet his master; and when acting in capacity of a valet, he receives the left-off wardrobe of his master.

When two or three footmen are kept, a butler waits at breakfast, luncheon, tea, and dinner, and overlooks the arrangements for each meal.

During the afternoon it is a butler's duty to remain in the front hall in readiness to announce visitors. It is his duty throughout the day to see that everything is in its place and in order, in readiness for use in the drawing-room, morning-room, and library; the blinds up or down as the case may be, writing tables in due order, books rearranged, newspapers cut, aired, and folded for use, fires attended to by the footman, etc.

In households where one footman is kept, a large portion of the pantry work falls to the butler: he lays the breakfast table, waits at breakfast, and clears away the breakfast things: he assists in cleaning the plate and in attending to the lamps; he waits at luncheon, and when the footman has to go out with the carriage early in the afternoon, he clears away the luncheon and lays the dinner-table.

While the footman is out with the carriage, the butler answers the door, attends to the fires in the dining-room, drawing-rooms, and various sitting-rooms; and in the autumn and winter, and early spring, he closes the shutters in the sitting-rooms before the footman's return, and prepares the five-o'clock tea in readiness for the return of his mistress.

Footmen

The daily round of footmen's duties may be taken as follows:—

To rise at half-past six in the summer and seven in the winter; take coals to the sitting-room; clean the boots, trim the lamps, clean the plate; lay the breakfast table for the family; carry in the breakfast; wait at breakfast; remove the breakfast things; answer the door in the morning after 12 o'clock, take out notes if required; lay the luncheon table, take in the luncheon, wait at table, clear the table; wash the silver and glass used at luncheon; lay the dinner-table; go out with the carriage in the afternoon; answer the door to visitors; close the shutters in the sitting-rooms, attend to the fires therein throughout the day and evening; prepare and assist in carrying in the 5 o'clock tea, clear the table after tea, wash and put away the china; wait at dinner; clear the dinner-table, assist in putting away the plate, wash the glass and silver used at dinner and dessert; prepare and assist in carrying in the coffee to the dining-room; be in attendance in the front hall when dinner guests are leaving the house; attend to the requirements of the gentlemen in the smoking-room; attend to the lighting of the house, as soon as it is dusk, whether lighted with gas, lamps, or candles; clean, arrange, and have in readiness the flat silver candlesticks, before the dressing-bell rings in winter, and by 10 o'clock in summer; go out with the carriage when it is ordered in the evening; valet the young gentlemen of the family. Footmen are usually allowed two suits of livery a year.

Housemaid

The usual duties of a housemaid consist of:—to rise at six in summer and half-past six in winter; before breakfast to sweep and dust the drawing-room, dining-room, front hall, and other sitting-rooms; to clean the grates and light the fires; and where a lady's-maid or valet is not kept, she carries up the water for the baths for the family. After her own breakfast she makes the servants' beds, sweeps, dusts, and arranges the rooms, sweeps the front staircase and front hall.

She makes the best beds, and sweeps and dusts the rooms; cleans the grates, and lights the fires; when fires are kept up in the bedrooms during the day, it is her duty to attend to them, and to light them morning and evening, or when required; she prepares the bedrooms for the night, turns down the beds, fills the jugs with water, closes the curtains, takes up a can of hot water for each person.

After the family have gone down to dinner, she again makes the round of the bedrooms, and puts them in order; her last duty being to take up a can of hot water to each bedroom and dressing-room.

It is her duty to see, during the day, that each bedroom is supplied with soap, candles, clean towels, writing-paper, and all that is required for use.

Parlourmaid

A very large class of persons find it expedient to keep a parlourmaid rather than a man-servant; in watering-places, suburban towns, and even in town itself, persons with good incomes, but who live rather quietly than not, prefer to be waited upon by a parlour-maid, as many other services are rendered by her besides the actual parlour work.

Ladies who have not the support of a male relative in everyday life find it less trouble to keep their household in order when it is composed of female servants only, as a man-servant is proverbially inclined to take advantage of his position when there is no master to keep him in check.

The wages of a parlour-maid are not so high as those of a man-servant, and there is a further saving in the matter of finding clothes.

The most important of a parlour-maid's duties are the laying of the table for the meals of the family and waiting at table, answering the door and announcing visitors. Her further duties consist of getting-up the fine linen of the ladies of the family, and in assisting her mistress to dress, performing the duties of a lady's-maid as far as dressing is concerned, and in keeping her mistress's wardrobe in order, and all that relates to her wardrobe.

A parlour-maid wears a cotton gown, white apron and cap during the morning, and stuff gown with apron and cap in the afternoon; she is expected to do needlework for the house in the afternoon.

Lady's Maid

The duties of a lady's maid may be said to consist of the following:—

To bring up the hot water for her mistress in the morning and at various times of the day as required.

To bring her an early cup of tea.

To prepare her things for dressing.

To assist her in dressing.

To put her room in order after dressing.

To put out her things for walking, riding, and driving, both in the morning and afternoon.

To assist her in taking off her out-door attire.

To put in readiness all that her mistress may require for dressing in the evening.

To assist her to dress for dinner.

To put everything in order in her mistress's room before leaving it.

To sit up for her, and to assist her to undress on her return, and to carefully put away her jewels and everything connected with her toilette.

To keep her mistress's wardrobe in thorough repair, and to do all the dressmaking and millinery required of her.

To wash the lace and fine linen of her mistress.

These are the ostensible duties of a lady's maid, but there are many minor matters that in small households come within her province, such as dusting the china ornaments in the drawing-room, attending to the flowers in the drawing-room or in any of the sitting-rooms.

When ladies keep a pet dog or dogs, it is the duty of a lady's maid to attend to them; wash them, feed them, and take them out walking.

Cook

A first-class cook is not expected to be down until a few minutes before eight, in time for breakfast in the housekeeper's room. If she is housekeeper as well as cook, she makes and pours out the tea for the upper servants. After her own breakfast, she attends to and superintends the breakfast for the family. She makes out a menu for the day's dinner and luncheon on a slate according to the contents of the larder, and with due regard for variety.

Some mistresses have the slate brought to them by a footman at about eleven o'clock, and make any alteration they may think proper, and return it by him to the cook. Other mistresses have the slate brought to them by the cook, and consult with her respecting any change in the menu for the day. This is the most practical way of proceeding.

Some ladies stand very much in awe of their cooks, knowing that those who consider themselves to be thoroughly experienced will not brook fault-finding, or interference with their manner of cooking, and give notice on the smallest pretext. Thus, when ladies have a really good cook, they deal with her delicately, and are inclined to let her have her own way with regard to serving the dinner.

In town, the cook gives the necessary orders to the tradespeople who serve the house. The pastry, the jellies, the creams, the entrees are all made by her during the morning, and any dishes of this nature that are to be served at luncheon. After her own dinner, she dishes up the luncheon.

The afternoon is very much at the cook's disposal, except on the occasion of a dinner party, or when guests are staying in the house. Five to nine is always a very busy time; dishing up a large dinner is an arduous duty. When the dinner is served, the cook's duties for the day are over, and the remainder of the work is preformed by the kitchen-maids.

It is an understood thing that the cook has certain perquisites connected with her place, amongst others the dripping from the roast joints.

Valet

Valets are generally kept by single gentlemen and elderly gentlemen, and seldom by married men. Amongst the duties of a valet are:—

To brush his master's clothes; clean his top-boots, shooting, walking, and dress boots; carry up the water for his master's bath; put out his things for dressing; shave him, if necessary; assist him in dressing; pack and unpack his clothes when travelling; put out his master's things for dinner; carry up the hot water to his dressing-room.

To load for him when out shooting; stand behind his master's chair at dinner, and more especially to wait upon his master and the lady taken down to dinner by him; when at home he is expected to wait at his master's breakfast, and at the family luncheon and dinner; he attends to his master's wardrobe, and sees that everything is in repair and in order.

A valet to an elderly gentleman, besides performing these duties, renders any services that his master's health may require; such as sitting up late at night, carrying him up and down stairs during the day, when required to do so, or sleeping in his room at night, etc.

A valet is not a livery-servant; he does not receive an allowance for clothes, and his master's left-off clothes are given to him.

Wages

The tariff of wages paid to domestic servants is influenced in a great measure by the position of a master and mistress, and by the experience of the servant. Higher wages are given in town than in the country, and experienced servants ask higher wages than do inexperienced ones.

A butler receives from   £50 to £80 per annum
A footman receives from   £14 to £28 per annum
A professed cook receives from £50 to £70 per annum

A plain cook receives from	£16 to £30 per annum
A kitchen-maid receives from	£14 to £28 per annum
A scullery-maid receives from	£12 to £18 per annum
A housemaid receives from	£12 to £30 per annum
A lady's-maid receives from	£20 to £35 per annum
A head nurse receives from	£20 to £25 per annum
A nurserymaid receives from	£10 to £14 per annum

In some households, tea, sugar, beer, and washing are found; in others extra wages are allowed for these. When tea and sugar are allowanced, the usual quantity allowed to each servant is 1 lb. of tea per month, and 2 lbs. of loaf sugar, or money to this equivalent. When beer money is given, it varies from 1s. 6d. to 2s. 6d. per week; in some households the under female servants are allowed but 1s. per week.

Coachmen receive from 16s. to 25s. per week; in addition they are allowed rooms over the stables, or a cottage, rent free. Grooms receive from 10s. to 18s. per week.

The Servants' Practical Guide (1880).

'Making the pudding'

Girl's Own Paper (1885)

(d) DRESS AND THE TOILETTE

I

What a Lady Wears

A lady's morning dress should be simple and refined, and suited to the time of day. Lace, unless of a thick description, is not worn with morning attire: Honiton and Brussels would be quite out of place. Neither is much jewellery consistent; plain gold and silver ornaments are permissible, but never precious stones, except in rings.

When visiting at a friend's house the morning dress may be of a slightly superior style; for instance, a white embroidered dress may be worn where one of coloured cotton would be used at home, or a velveteen instead of a serge one.

Again, a dinner dress differs from that worn at a ball. Silks and satins, velvets and brocades, are the materials chosen, and trimmed with lace. The neck and arms are now generally covered, excepting at a specially 'full dress' dinner; the bodice is made high, but open in front, and the sleeves reach to the elbow.

Of late years young women have so arranged their hair that extra adornments have not been much in favour—a jewelled ornament placed according to fancy, a decorative comb, a bow of ribbon, arranged in the manner most becoming to the shape of the head or the style in which the hair is dressed, are employed. Older ladies wear caps composed of flowers, of feathers, or pearls, of fine lace or combinations of lace with one or more of the above-named.

In the ball-room nothing but complete full dress should be worn. For young people dresses of fabrics of those textures which do not look thick or heavy are chosen, such as surah silk, tulle, net, gauze, and the like, trimmed with lace and flowers. The bodice is made low, with

54

short sleeves; or cut open in front and at the back, with shoulder straps, and sleeves to the elbow.

The flowers worn on these occasions are generally artificial, because natural ones so soon fall to pieces from the heat of the room and the movements of the dancers.

The costume for paying calls when on foot may be light or dark, according to the season; but it must not be gay, and not have anything about it to attract attention. Carriage dress has much more licence. Handsome costumes, made of rich silken materials, flowery or feathery bonnets and lace sunshades, which would look quite out of place when walking, are suitable when driving.

For some years black gloves were universally worn at all times and seasons, and with every style of dress. Their place has been taken by tan-coloured gloves, which are worn with evening as well as with morning attire. All gloves are long, and are fastened by many buttons, from six on those worn out of doors to twenty on those worn with evening dress. Bracelets and bangles of gold or silver are worn over the glove.

The toilet for garden-parties, bazaars, flower shows, etc. is of a brighter, gayer fashion, and affords room for the display of much taste and elegance. Young women attire themselves in delicately tinted fine materials—materials which have a refinement, beauty, and softness characteristic of those whom they are designed to embellish, but quite distinctive from those worn in the ball-room. These costumes are made as effective and coquettish as possible—everything that will add to the gaiety, without passing the limits of morning attire, is permissible, and the whole is crowned by a bonnet or hat of like description.

The elder ladies should wear silks or some handsome material, richly trimmed with lace, and a foreign shawl or lace mantle, and bonnets, not hats, whether in town or country.

Costumes for picnics, excursions, and for seaside wear should be of a useful character. Yachting dresses are usually made of serge or tweed, as those materials are unspoilable by sea air and water, and at the same time possess warmth and durability.

The dresses worn by lawn-tennis players have various distinctive features. Wool should in some measure form the material, for health's sake, as a preventive of chills being taken; therefore cashmere, serge, and flannel are chosen. The bodice is usually made full, and the skirt is short, and not burdened with many frills and flounces. But prettiness and embellishments can be introduced—combinations of colours, bright ribbons, and various other adornments. A receptacle for the tennis balls is sometimes part of the player's costume. Its form can be that of a flat pocket, or a bag, suspended from the waist. Hats of every variety are worn, of all shapes and sizes.

Etiquette of Good Society (1893), ch. 6.

2

A Gentleman's Clothes

The questions that are asked me more often than any other are, 'What ought I to wear at my wedding?', and, 'What should the best man wear?'

If the wedding is in the summer, the best 'get up' consists of a grey frock-coat suit, silk hat, grey suède gloves, patent or glacé kid boots, light waistcoat, and rather dark grey tie. If the wedding is in the winter, you would wear a black frockcoat and waistcoat, grey striped trousers, glacé kid or patent boots, and grey suède or buckskin gloves. Lavender-coloured trousers to wear at weddings have gone out of fashion.

The same clothes would do equally well at any big function in town, and in summer you would wear the summer frockcoat at a garden party in town. You would wear similar clothes at most race meetings. On the river most men wear plain grey flannel coats and trousers, white or tan shoes. A similar get-up will do for the mornings at the seaside, or you can wear a knickerbocker suit. Don't wear a silk tie with tennis or boating flannels, or a cotton tie with a frockcoat. A white duck suit is a good suit to have at the seaside. The man who is economical will make the same knickerbocker suit do for cycling, golfing, and shooting. In this case the coat should be a Norfolk jacket. Some men like to wear a Norfolk jacket with a pair of grey flannel trousers. The two together make a good knockabout suit to be worn at places and on occasions when fashions don't matter.

When you are in town you mustn't appear in a lounge suit and a bowler after lunch; and of course, if you have any business appointment in the morning, you would wear a frock or morning coat with a silk hat. You may make an exception to these rules in the summer.

In August and September society people are not supposed to be in town, and therefore, if you happen to be in town, you can wear country clothes—a light thin lounge suit and a straw hat. If you are in town in August and September, you are supposed to be there only because you are passing through on your way to the country.

Don't wear thin button boots with a knickerbocker suit. Wear shoes or stout walking boots.

Don't wear tan boots or shoes with a black coat of any kind. Don't wear a bowler hat with a black morning coat. Don't wear a silk hat when you are wearing a navy blue jacket.

Of course, no gentleman ever wears a made-up tie.

A man shouldn't turn his trousers up unless there is mud out of doors, and he should take particular care to turn them down again before he enters the house. You see, when you turn your trousers up you collect a lot of mud and dirt in the turned-up portions, and hostesses have a kind of prejudice against having large portions of mud brought into the house.

Clothes and the Man: Hints on the Wearing and Caring of Clothes, by 'The Major' of *Today;* ch. 8 (1900).

3

Cycling Attire

Cycling has become one of the chief diversions of the day and one in which ladies now join. A lady's tricycling dress consists of a plain skirt, made sufficiently wide to allow the feet full play without causing them to draw up the dress by their action, and yet not so wide as to permit the skirt to hang in folds or flap in the wind. A Norfolk jacket, made to fit neatly but not tightly to the figure, cut low round the throat to allow the neck free action. Both skirt and jacket should be made of a woollen material, and one that is porous and of light weight. A soft silk handkerchief is worn round the neck, which will hide the absence of collar and brooch. Shoes, having firm but heavy soles, and a close-fitting soft hat made of the same material as the dress, complete the costume.

The dress of a gentleman is knickerbockers, and a short coat buttoned up the front; stockings ribbed and knitted of thick wool; shoes with stout soles; and a cap with peaks at the front and back, made like the suit, of porous woollen material, or an ordinary straw hat. A light silk handkerchief loosely tied round the neck should take the place of a stiff collar.

Etiquette of Good Society, ch. 18.

4

Dress for Motoring

(*a*) *For Ladies.* A warm gown should be adopted, made of a material that will not catch the dust, and it is also important to wear warm clothing under the gown; for unless such jerseys and bodices are worn, the wind penetrates, and it is quite impossible to avoid feeling chilled during a long day.

The best coats that I have seen for motor-car driving are some which come from Vienna, and are both cheap and comfortable. The fur employed for the lining is opossum, which is both light and thick; they are to be had of any length, they button up the front, are double breasted, and have two warm pockets placed crossways in front.

It is quite impossible to keep warm in a rapid motor journey except by using fur rugs, and they should be backed with leather, which mitigates the trouble of beating the dust out of them at the end of the day.

Difficult as it is to keep warm and fairly clean as regards the clothes which should be worn, the real problem is how to keep a hat on. The head must be warmly covered and the hat small, for anything large or wide offers too much resistance to the wind, and quickly gets blown off. After many experiments I am satisfied that the best head-dress for the motor-car is a Glengarry cap, pinned in one or two places to break the hard, straight outline, and to give a little height to it. It is light and warm, and with a long gauze veil, which covers not only the hat but comes over the ears, the wearer is as comfortable as possible. The material for making the veil must be not less than two yards long and three-quarters of a yard wide.

Glasses—not small dainty glasses but veritable goggles—are absolutely necessary, both for comfort and the preservation of the eyesight; they are not becoming, but then, appearance must be sacrificed if motor-driving is to be thoroughly enjoyed.

(*b*) *For Men.* Men frequently have their motor suits cut in the ordinary way, Norfolk jacket or short coat with trousers or breeches and stockings; but the coats are so made as to button round the wrist. Unless this precaution is taken it will be found that the cold air will blow up the sleeves, with the result that the hands, and the body generally, will be made very cold.

If the automobilist does not use a thick rug to protect his legs, gaiters should be worn with knickerbockers; and, if trousers are worn they should be bound tightly round the ankles when driving.

In the matter of overcoats, Englishmen seem to prefer a coat of Melton cloth lined with fur and fitted with a high, fur-lined collar. In the summer, when the weather is very hot, a great coat is sometimes unnecessary, except as a protection from dust. A light dust-coat will then be found useful. Capes should be avoided, as more than one bad accident has arisen from a cape blowing up in the driver's face and thus temporarily blinding him, with the result that he has driven his car into the ditch.

As to head-dress, the motor owner as a rule wears the same hat as he would wear for shooting, golfing, fishing, and other outdoor sports, viz. the cloth cap, or soft felt hat. Goggles, or glasses surrounded by silk or some other material, are almost indispensable.

(a) LADY JEUNE, (b) BARON DE ZUYLEN DE NYEVELT, President of the Automobile Club de France; *Motors and Motor-Driving*, ed. by Alfred Harmsworth (Lord Northcliffe) (1902), pp. 68-79.

5

Good Taste in Underclothes

Undergarments may be simple, but they should be as irreproachable as, or more so, than the dress, which even one spot disgraces. They should be as gracefully cut as possible, and if they can be cut out of very good material so much the better.

Happily, the taste for underclothing made of coloured surah silk or cambric has lost ground for some time back. Many women of refined tastes, indeed, never gave up white linen or cambric, or even simple calico, which can be so easily washed.

Chemises made of printed cambric, or pink, blue, and mauve surah, have this drawback—they cannot be thoroughly washed. Moreover, they are in somewhat doubtful taste.

A virtuous woman has a repugance to excessive luxury in her underclothing. She does not like too much lace or embroidery or ribbons and bows. She has them trimmed, of course, but with a certain sobriety which speaks in her favour; she likes them to be elegant, assuredly, so far as she can afford it, but she denies herself the abuse of and over-richness of trimming. She prefers comparatively simple underlinen, which there is no fear of washing, and which can be changed daily.

Coloured stockings begin to be less worn in summer, and only with shoes. With boots, we are coming back to white thread or cotton stockings.

All women who wear long stockings have for some time been in the habit of gartering them above the knee, and it is only in out-of-the-way country parts that to do this cords, tapes, and bits of string are sometimes used. The most humble servant-maid who is a little civilized buys elastic garters with buckles.

Garters should always be clean and fresh, never ragged or shabby. In America the garters do not match; a pair is composed of one yellow and the other black, or one yellow and the other blue, etc., but one of the two is always yellow: it is said that this brings good luck.

Everyone cannot bear a garter as tight as it should be. Their legs swell under pressure, and varicose veins form. In this case the stockings should be fastened to the stays by ribbons (suspenders). But accidents might happen; for if the ribbon, which must be well stretched to hold up the stocking, were to break, down comes the stocking over the heel! My advice is to wear at the same time a garter not at all tight, but sufficiently so to hold up the stocking, in case of accidents, until the damage can be repaired.

To wear the garter below the knee is against all rules of taste. If the chemise, the drawers, the little under-petticoat, and the slip-bodice could all be made to match, it would be in charmingly good taste. They should in that case be of fine nainsouk or fine cambric, with embroideries or valenciennes. The prettiest chemise is cut out either round or heart-shape. A ribbon run in tightens it a little round the shoulders. It is also buttoned on the shoulder. The neck and shoulders are edged with valenciennes or a light embroidery. The chemise must be neither too wide nor too long. It should not fill up needlessly either the stays or the drawers.

The night chemise should reach down to the feet and have long sleeves. It is trimmed with frills, embroideries, or lace, and is finished off with a large collar, falling to the shoulders in pleats. Ribbons are sometimes put in at the collar and cuffs. It is, of course, made of washing material.

BARONESS STAFFA, *The Lady's Dressing-Room* (1892), pp. 236-50.

6

My Lady's Corset

Detractors of the corset are quite right to blame the fools that deform their bodies and destroy their health to diminish their waists by an inch: an infinitesimal advantage, especially if we consider the price paid for it—compression of the vital organs, inconvenience in breathing, congestion of the face, restriction of the hips. (There are women who go so far as thus to imperil their powers of maternity.)

But, on the other hand, if the corset is only looked upon by woman as a support to her frail figure, it becomes useful. She will then have known how to give suppleness and elasticity enough to assure comfort as well as to allow of perfect liberty; that is to say, perfect grace and movement. The figure will undulate and balance itself like a sapling bending to the wind, and will no longer afflict us by recalling a knight in steel armour.

The corset is absolutely necessary for a very stout woman. It controls the exuberance of her bodice, and it is impossible for a fat woman to have any pretence to being well-dressed without it. She will not appear dressed at all.

The corset supports the petticoats, which would otherwise lay too heavily on the waist; and a very thin or even slight woman will have no style without its help. There will be something disjointed in her whole look, in the slightest of her movements.

The corset has yet one more good side. It serves as a support to the bust, the fibres of which would become distended; and it would soon fall too low if this kind of restraint did not keep it in its proper place.

The corset should only have bones in the back and front, unless the person it is for has lost her proper proportions, for in that case the sides must be supported as well.

Coutil is, in my opinion, too stiff a material of which to make a corset; satin, even cotton satin, is preferable, since we do not want armour; the most suitable material is chamois leather. There are already corsets of net for the summer, and corsets which can be enlarged as you like, and which follow the movements of breathing, thanks to the elastic sides with which they are provided; they are meant for weak and delicate women.

Short corsets are better than long ones, both for the sake of grace and comfort. If they are too high under the arms, they will make the shoulders appear too high. If they go down too low, they will elongate the body too much, the legs will appear shortened, and thus that happy harmony of proportion which constitutes true beauty will be destroyed.

The corset must be absolutely clean. A soiled corset is strong evidence of carelessness and lamentable want of neatness in the wearer. It should be preserved by a little petticoat body with short sleeves which can be sent to the wash the moment it begins to look soiled.

A white corset is the nicest of all, no matter what the material. I do not much like blue, pink, or mauve corsets; they soil as quickly as the white and are in less good taste. A black corset, it cannot be denied, is economical; it is easy to keep the white lining clean till the corset is quite worn out.

The Lady's Dressing-Room, pp. 238-45.

7

Dressing and Undressing

It is best to wash the face overnight, and not to expose the skin to the air after it has been wet. In the morning the face should be wiped with a fine towel, and an entire bath taken, followed by friction; or, if it is impossible to do this every day, all indispensable ablutions must be performed, and every care taken for necessary cleanliness.

The hair is then combed and arranged tidily, but usually dressed later. All depends, however, on the kind of life that is led. Those who go out early in the morning must have their hair dressed in good time. Those who busy themselves in their households must repair the disorder caused to their attire by the work they have been doing, when this work is done. They must get rid of the dust that may have settled on face, neck, and hair.

Those who work in their households, as well as those who only superintend them, should, on first getting up, dress themselves, with perfect neatness and care, as nicely as possible. It is as well to change the under-garments—stockings, petticoats, etc.—as well as the dress, when getting ready for the afternoon, whether to remain at home or to go out.

Undressing for the Night

Washing the face should be done at night. The hair should be well combed out, to free it from the dust of the day, and brushed with a soft brush. It is best to sleep with the head uncovered. Hair that is left free at night will be finer, more silky, and neater than if it is imprisoned in a cap.

Men should also brush their hair; and if they will take my advice, they will wear no night-cap till they are at least sixty. A bandanna always gives them a slightly ridiculous appearance.

Never put up directly, neither in drawers nor in cupboards, any of the clothes you take off. Open them out, or hang them up in an airy place for at least an hour. Then, after having brushed and folded them, put them by.

The clothes which cannot be washed should be occasionally hung out in the air for a day, and turned inside out.

The Lady's Dressing-Room, pp. 250–3.

8

A Touch of Powder

Sometimes it is necessary to powder the face, but it must be done artistically, and with a light hand. Nothing is so ugly as a face powdered like a Pierrot ready to grin.

The puff should be dipped into the powder with precaution, so as not to come out too full. Nor should it be wiped on the skin; it should barely touch the face, and that in a succession of small quick taps. The spectator should be left in doubt as to whether the skin is imperceptibly veiled by a thin cloud of powder, or whether it is the natural bloom. The effect then is pretty, especially under a veil.

I cannot advise blackening the lashes, in spite of the attraction it may lend to the eyes. All making-up so near to the precious organ of sight is doubly dangerous. If you wish to lengthen or darken your eyebrows, a solution of Chinese ink in rose-water is absolutely harmless. This is a secret of the harem.

The Lady's Dressing-Room, pp. 94, 100-1, 173-4.

9

A Sensible Girl's Trousseau

A really sensible girl will not spend much money on her trousseau, though I have heard it said that, as the trousseau is one of the few things a girl can raise money for, a girl who has no *dot* (dowry) should furnish her wardrobe plentifully, especially with underclothes.

Already possessing a few clothes for her back, she actually requires for her trousseau: 3 nightdresses, silk, cotton, or woollen, as desired; 4 to 6 shifts, or combinations; 8 pairs of stockings—3 woollen, 3 black silk or Lisle thread, and a couple of pairs of white silk or lace for evening wear; 2 corsets; 2 summer vests, 4 winter; 3 white petticoats—2 good and one handsome (other petticoats according to habit); 2 evening bodices or slips (camisoles are best), and 2 coloured woollen, or 6 linen bodices; 6 pairs of boots and shoes, for bad weather and bright, day wear and evening and fireside slippers; one dressing-gown; one toilet jacket of flannel; 12 collars, or a few yards of frilling; 12 towels; at least two dozen handkerchiefs—12 for common use, say 12 finer, and a few lace ones besides are as well—plenty will be wanted, not only for colds in the head, but even, perhaps, who knows ?—for tears; cuffs and gloves as required; last, but not least, nice handsome travelling trunks and a well-fitted dressing-bag to pack them all in.

MRS HAWEIS, *The Art of Housekeeping* (1889), pp. 48–9.

IO

Wedding Finery

The dress of a young bride is made of soft-textured silk or satin or brocade, trimmed with flowers and rich white lace, and a large veil of the same description of lace as that on the dress. A wreath of white flowers is worn under the veil, white gloves and shoes, and a bouquet composed entirely of white flowers. Any great display of jewellery is in bad taste. A set of pearls looks well, or something of the same plain and simple character.

There is more variety in bridesmaids' dresses than in that of a bride.

Mrs Loftie, 'The Dining Room' (1878)

3. 'Children's corner' in the
dining-room

Fireside reflections

Mrs Orrinsmith, 'The Drawing Room' (1878)

E. F. Bailey-Denton, 'Handbook of House Sanitation'

A picturesque costume is often chosen which combines two colours, or is made entirely of one shade. The hats or bonnets are often composed of the same material as the dress, or else that which trims it. Sometimes veils of plain tulle are worn, and wreaths take the place of bonnets. All the bridesmaids are dressed alike, and their bouquets are composed of coloured flowers.

The older guests should choose some handsome, rich material, and have it trimmed with white or black lace. Over their shoulders should be worn a lace mantle or one of silk or satin, and their millinery trimmed with feathers and flowers. Morning attire is proper for gentlemen.

Etiquette of Good Society, ch. 6.

II

Funereal Garb

Until recently it has been the general custom to supply crape scarfs and long crape hat-bands to the mourners, and silk scarfs and hat-bands, as well as gloves, to the friends, officiating clergymen, and bearers. At funerals of children and young girls these scarfs were either of white silk, or of black silk tied with white ribbon. These special habiliments are now very rarely exhibited and are rapidly falling into disuse.

The dress of the chief mourners is, for ladies, woollen materials trimmed with crape, and for gentleman, black suit and ties, black kid gloves, and a band of black cloth round the hat.

12

Widow's Weeds

The regulation period for a widow's mourning is two years. Of this period crape should be worn for one year and nine months—for the first twelve months the dress should be entirely covered with crape, and for the remaining three months trimmed with crape; during the last three months black without crape should be worn. After two years, half-mourning is prescribed.

The widow's cap should be worn for a year and a day. Lawn cuffs and collars should be worn during the crape period.

Widowers should wear mourning for the same period as widows, but they usually enter society much sooner. A widow is not expected to enter into society under twelve months, and during that time she should neither accept invitations nor issue them.

Manners and Rules of Good Society, pp. 223-6.

CHAPTER 2

LIFE AND LABOUR IN LONDON

Charles Booth's 'Grand Inquest'

In the crypt of St Paul's Cathedral in London theretis a memorial tablet to 'Charles Booth, merchant shipowner. Born 1840. Died 1916.' The inscription continues: 'Through his long life he had at heart the welfare of his fellow citizens, and believing that exact knowledge of realities is the foundation of all reform, he dedicated himself to the examination of the social, industrial, and religious condition of the people of London. Those who knew him loved him and drew inspiration from the energy of his leadership and the originality of his mind.'

Born at Liverpool into a family of merchants and shipowners, Liberal or Radical in politics and Unitarians in religion, Booth was educated at a secondary day school in Liverpool and then as a youth entered the offices of the shipping firm of Lamport & Holt. In 1862 he joined his brother Alfred in launching what developed into the Booth Shipping Company. The business made rapid progress, and when it was decided to open a branch in London Charles Booth moved south to take charge.

On settling in London he began to take a deep interest in social problems. As a young man he had been an enthusiastic Radical, but as the years passed he moved steadily towards the right, and eventually joined the Unionists. Anything in the nature of Socialism left thim cold, although he was on easy terms with some of the Socialist pioneers, including H. M. Hyndman of the Social Democratic Federation. But he was not really interested in politics. He was a highly successful business man, a 'captain of industry' indeed, and as his wife (she was Mary Macaulay, a niece of the historian) wrote in the modest memoir of her husband that was published in 1918, 'those who imagined that a business life must be dull, wanting in the interest and charm attending political, literary, or scientific pursuits, filled him with amazement'. He was a firm supporter of the Capitalist system, and looked upon the profit motive as an efficient and very necessary regulator. He could see nothing in the least disreputable in making money.

All the same, like many another excellent Victorian, he was persuaded that the possession of great wealth brought with it great responsibilities. He was increasingly worried about the 'state of the poor', and eagerly looked for ways and means of improving their hard lot. But the more earnestly he sought the more nonplussed he became. As his wife puts it,

'Opinions the most diverse were expressed, remedies of the most contradictory nature were proposed'. Nowhere could he get a clear answer to the questions that perturbed his mind. 'Who are the people of England? How do they really live? What do they really want? Do they want what is good, and if so, how is it to be given to them?'

In those middle 1880s the thing that oppressed him most was a 'sense of helplessness', and this found expression in a paper that he read before the Royal Statistical Society in May 1887 on 'The Condition and Occupations of the People of the Tower Hamlets', the district more generally known as the East End of London. The wage-earners (he argued) were helpless to regulate or obtain the value of their work, the employers could operate only within the limits of the competitive system, the rich were unable to relieve want without at the same time stimulating its sources, and the legislature was helpless because the bounds of successful interference by Act of Parliament were closely circumscribed. Out of these feelings of helplessness sprang socialistic theories, 'passionate suggestions' that were contrary to man's nature and neglected all the fundamental facts of human existence.

Then he went on to explain how, in his opinion, this sense of helplessness might be relieved. 'The problems of human life must be better stated. The *à priori* reasoning of political economy, orthodox and unorthodox alike, fails from want of reality. At its base are a series of assumptions very imperfectly connected with the observed facts of life. We need to begin with a true picture of the modern industrial organism, the interchange of service, the exercise of faculty, the demands and satisfaction of desire. It is the possibility of such a picture as this that I wish to suggest . . .'

A lively discussion followed the reading of his paper, and Booth was left in no doubt that if he wanted to see such a picture as he had in mind, then he must make it himself. This is what he now set out to do, and the result was *The Life and Labour of the People in London*, which in its final, definitive form, published 1902-3, extends over seventeen volumes.

From first to last, Booth was in full charge of the project, and he paid for it out of his own pocket. The inquiry was directed along two fronts, one concerned with the conditions under which the people lived and the other the conditions under which they worked. But there was no strict division between the two, and Booth hoped that the double method would provide a check upon the results of each.

The first volume appeared in 1889, and dealt with East London, an area comprising the Tower Hamlets with an extension into Hackney and with a population of rather more than 900,000—about a quarter of the population of the Metropolis as a whole. The reason why Booth chose this particular area was, as he stated it, because 'it is supposed to contain the most destitute population in England, and to be, as it were, the focus of the problems of poverty in the midst of wealth, which is troubling the minds and hearts of so many people'.

The basis of the inquiry was the Census of 1881, but the information this supplied was of course mainly statistical, and Booth realized that this must be supplemented by the personal observation of individual cases. With this end in view he instituted a method of interviewing that is not the least of his contributions to sociological science.

Equipped with notebooks and pencils, he and a small body of helpers proceeded to interview a host of people in all walks of life—school-teachers and sanitary inspectors, ministers of religion and social workers, medical officers of health, superintendents of 'model dwellings' and rent-collectors, district visitors, and, most knowledgeable of all, the attendance officers in the employ of the London School Board.

Every street in the area was visited, and every house in every street. The condition of each family living there was carefully investigated and noted down. Furthermore, Booth had maps prepared of each district, on which the character of each street was indicated in colours, from red indicating the well-to-do, through pink, purple, light blue, dark blue, down to black, which indicated the black spots where dwelt the people of the lowest class, the very poor, vicious and semi-criminal.

The first volume was followed by others dealing with the rest of the metropolitan area, although not in quite the same exhaustive detail. The complete work comprises, as already stated, seventeen volumes: four under the heading of 'Poverty', five of 'Industry', seven of 'Religious Influences' (a somewhat misleadingly restrictive title), and a final volume of 'Notes on Social Influences and Conclusion'. Altogether they contain getting on for six thousand pages, and making a selection from so vast a material cannot but prove a daunting task. However, it is hoped that the 'documents' given in this chapter are fairly representative of the tremendous whole, besides comprising most of what is specially interesting and valuable when looked at from the 'human angle'.

In his latter years Booth was a principal advocate of Old Age Pensions, and he lived long enough to see his proposal of a pension of 5s. a week to be paid out of the national exchequer to all persons in poor circumstances over the age of 65, carried into effect by Asquith's Liberal government in 1908. But his most enduring monument is the work under review. We may well agree with Mrs Sidney Webb (who as a young woman was proud to serve as 'an industrious apprentice' on his staff of investigators) that Booth's 'grand inquest into the conditions of life and labour of the four million inhabitants of the richest city in the world' seems 'to stand out as a landmark alike in social politics and in economic science'.

(*a*) CLASS AND CIRCUMSTANCE IN THE EAST END

[Booth opened his inquiry with an investigation into the 'life and labour' of the inhabitants of the East End of London—an area comprising Shoreditch, Bethnal Green, Whitechapel, St George's-in-the-East, Stepney, Mile End Old Town, and Poplar, together with the parish of Hackney. He divided the people into Eight Classes according to 'means and position'.]

A, the lowest class, consists of some occasional labourers, street-sellers, loafers, criminals and semi-criminals, together with inmates of common lodging-houses and the lowest class of streets. With these ought to be counted the homeless outcasts who on any given night find shelter where they can.

Their life is the life of savages, with vicissitudes of extreme hardship and occasional excess. Their food is of the coarsest description, and their only luxury is drink. It is not easy to say how they live; the living is picked up, and what is got is frequently shared.

From these come the battered figures who slouch through the streets, and play the beggar or the bully, or help to foul the record of the unemployed; these are the worst class of corner men who hang round the door of public-houses, the young men who spring forward on any chance to earn a copper, the ready materials of disorder when occasion serves. They render no useful service, they create no wealth; more often they destroy it. They degrade whatever they touch, and as individuals are perhaps incapable of improvement . . . I do not mean to say that there are not individuals of every sort to be found in the mass. Those who are able to wash the mud may find some gems in it. There are, at any rate, some very piteous cases.

Class B—casual earnings—very poor. In East London the largest field for casual labour is at the Docks; indeed, there is no other important field. The labourers of Class B do not, on the average, get as much as three days' work a week, but it is doubtful if many of them could or would work full time for long together if they had the opportunity. From whatever section Class B is drawn, except the sections of poor women, there will be found many of them who from shiftlessness, helplessness, idleness, or drink, are inevitably poor.

The ideal of such persons is to work when they like and play when they like; these it is who are rightly called the 'leisure class' amongst the poor—leisure bounded very closely by the pressure of want but habitual to the extent of second nature. They cannot stand the regularity and dulness of civilized existence, and find the excitement they need in the life of the streets, or at home as spectators of or participators in some highly coloured domestic scene.

Class C—intermittent earnings—are more than any others the victims of competition, and on them falls with particular severity the weight of recurrent depressions of trade. Stevedores and waterside porters may secure only one or two days' work in a week, labourers in the building trade only eight or nine months' work in the year.

There will be many of the irregularly employed who could not keep a permanent job if they had it . . . They are a somewhat helpless class, not belonging to any trade society, and for the most part without natural leaders or organization.

In this class the women usually work or seek for work when the men have none; they do charing, or washing, or needlework for very little money; they bring no particular skill or persistent effort to what they do, and the work done is of slight value.

Class D—small regular earnings. The men are the better end of the casual dock and waterside labour, those having directly or indirectly a preference for employment. The rest are the men who are in regular work all the year round at a wage not exceeding 21s. a week, including factory, dock, and warehouse labourers, carmen, messengers, porters, etc.

Of the whole section none can be said to rise above poverty, unless by the earnings of the children, nor are many to be classed as very poor. What they have comes in regularly, and except in times of sickness in the family, actual want rarely presses, unless the wife drinks. As a general rule these men have a hard struggle to make ends meet, but they are, as a body, decent, steady men, paying their way and bringing up their children respectably.

In the whole class the women work a good deal to eke out the men's earnings, and the children begin to make more than they cost when free from school: the sons go as van boys, errand boys, etc., and the daughters into daily service, or into factories, or help the mother with whatever she has in hand.

The comfort of their homes depends, even more than in other classes, on a good wife. Thrift of the 'make-the-most-of-everything' kind is what is needed, and in very many cases must be present, or it would be impossible to keep up so respectable an appearance on so small an income.

Class E, regular standard earnings. These are a large proportion of the artisans and most other regular wage earners. I also include here, as having equal means, the best class of street sellers and general dealers, a large proportion of the small shopkeepers, the best off amongst the home manufacturers, and some of the small employers. This is by far the largest class of the population under review, adding up to over 42 per cent. Few of them are *very poor*, and the bulk can, and do, lead independent lives, and possess fairly comfortable homes.

As a rule, the wives do not work, but the children all do; the boys commonly following the father, the girls taking to local trades, or going out into service.

The men are connected with almost every form of industry, and include in particular carmen, porters and messengers, warehousemen, permanent dock labourers, stevedores, and many others. [They] take readily any gratuities which fall in their way, but against anything which could be called charity their pride rises stiffly. This class is the recognized field of all forms of co-operation and combination, and I believe, and am glad to believe, that it holds its future in its own hands. No body of men deserves more consideration.

Class F, higher class labour, and the best paid of the artisans, together with others of equal means and position; [they] earn certainly more than 30s., and up to 45s. or 50s. Besides foremen are included City warehousemen of the better class, and first-hand lightermen; they are usually paid for responsibility, and are men of very good character and much intelligence.

This is not a large section of the people, but it is a distinct and very honourable one. These men are the non-commissioned officers of the industrial army. They have nothing to do with the planning or direction (properly so called) of business operations; their work is confined to superintendence. They supply no initiative, and having no responsibility of this kind do not share in profits; but their services are very valuable, and their pay enables them to lead reasonably comfortable lives. No large business could be conducted without such men as its pillars of support, and their loyalty and devotion to those whom they serve is very noteworthy.

Their sons take places as clerks, and their daughters get employment in first-class shops or places of business; if the wives work at all, they either keep a shop, or employ girls at laundry work or at dressmaking.

Class G, lower middle class. Shopkeepers and small employers, clerks, etc., and subordinate professional men. A hard-working, sober, energetic class.

Class H, upper middle class. All above G are here lumped together, and may be shortly defined as the servant-keeping class. Of these more than two-thirds are to be found in Hackney.

Grouping the Classes together, A, B, C, and D are the classes of poverty sinking into want, and add up to about 35 per cent of the population; while E, F, G, and H are the classes in comfort rising to affluence, and add up to 65 per cent.

Life and Labour of the People in London, Poverty, vol. I, ch. 2.

(b) LONDON LIFE

I

Down Whitechapel Way

London is the great centre in England of the foreign resident population, and Whitechapel is the great centre of the foreign population in London. It is not the least interesting of the features that make the Whitechapel Road the most varied and interesting in England, that amid the crowds that jostle each other on the pavement, or gather in eager groups round the flaring lights of the costermonger's barrow, the fancy shows, and the shooting saloons of the great trunk artery of East London, the observant wanderer may note the high cheekbones and thickened lips of the Russian or Polish Jew, the darker complexion and unmistakable nose of his Austrian co-religionist, and here and there, perhaps, a group of men with dusky faces and Eastern attire, who have wandered up from the docks, along the Commercial Road, and are piloting themselves timidly among the unaccustomed crowds, their scarlet fez caps and flowing robes adding a dash of colour and a flavour of orientalism to the busy scene.

Or if we wander down into the maze of streets and quaint waterside nooks of Shadwell High Street and Ratcliff Highway, we may chance to find John Chinaman leaning against the shop-door, or ministering to the wants of his Asiatic customers. If we step inside, and take care not to alarm him, we may find entrance to an opium den, where some twenty or thirty Celestials or Malays are dreaming over their pipes.

The neighbourhood of Limehouse Walk is perhaps the best, or worst, place to find these haunts, but the halo of romance that once hung around them from associations of Edwin Drood has] well-nigh faded since the den from which the great master of description [Charles

74

Dickens] drew the materials for his picture of opium-smoking in his last romance, has been improved away to make room for a new Board School.

Life and Labour of the People in London, Poverty, vol. 1, pp. 543-4.

2

Hoxton's Oliver Twists

Hoxton is the leading criminal quarter of London, and indeed of all England; and it is easy to see how pleasantly central and suitable a position it occupies for nefarious projects; so that it might be not inaptly described as the 'fence' between rich and poor. 'Wall off Hoxton', it is said, 'and nine-tenths of the criminals of London would be walled off', but in saying this a certain class of the criminals of London only was referred to and the proportion is doubtless exaggerated.

Of professional thieves there are two distinct kinds: those who live from day to day by the more casual kind of depredations, and those who lie low while making elaborate plans for some great haul. The latter may maintain a life of apparent respectability, pursuing ostensibly some regular calling, and they bring to bear upon their operations much forethought and some skill. They perhaps have had the training of a carpenter, a blacksmith, or a locksmith. They live the life of the lower middle class.

The number of first-class burglars is said to be very small; with most, daring takes the place of skill. But in playing their game against society, what is regarded as unnecessary violence is avoided as a rule. The relations of these men with the police are curious, regulated by certain rules of the game, which provide the rough outline of a code of what is regarded as fair and unfair. Violence is a breach of these rules, or sometimes the result of their breach by the other party, but if 'fairly' taken no ill-will is borne.

These men are generally known to the police, and so are the receivers into whose hands they play. Gold or silver stolen anywhere in London comes, it is said, at once to this quarter, and is promptly consigned to the melting-pot. Jewellery is broken up; watches are 'rechristened'. The 'fences' or receivers of stolen goods are of all grades, and serve every sort of thief; and in Hoxton thieves of every kind seem to be represented.

As in the days of Oliver Twist, the old thieves teach the young. I should suppose that, given some natural capacity in this direction, the very atmosphere of Hoxton would breed handy lads for this business, but it is so much an art that it is said that the supply of young thieves depends on this unindentured form of apprenticeship. I do not know whether the professors are actuated by benevolence only; it would almost seem so; or whether, as one good turn deserves another, the young can sometimes help the old. No doubt in burglaries a boy is often useful.

One of the most notorious developments of juvenile crime has been that of bands of young boys, called after this or that street and making themselves the terror of the neighbourhood. Of these gangs, and their fierce quarrels among themselves, turning on the favour of the girls who consort with them, we have heard strange accounts. One of our informants, a schoolmaster, speaks of the terror exercised by the leaders of these boys over their followers. Sitting safe at home the follower hears the whistle and turns pale, but obeys the summons. It sounds romantic and absurd, but I believe it to be no more than the truth.

Life and Labour, etc., 3rd series, vol. 2, pp. 111-15.

3

Bargains in Bermondsey

The stalls and shops that line the streets (in the neighbourhood of the Bermondsey New Road) were extremely busy from 6 o'clock till midnight on Saturday, and busy again with a poorer class of customer on Sunday morning. The buyers on Saturday included many poor figures, but the majority looked hearty and happy enough. The butchers were selling good pieces of meat freely, the greengrocers doing an active trade in new potatoes (it was June 2nd), and in green gooseberries and green peas, as well as cabbage and rhubarb. Many who had bought lamb bought mint.

Girls crowded round the stall of summer hats and artificial flowers, picking out what they fancied—'Sixpence-halfpenny and two-pence, eight-and-a-half the lot', remains in my mind as the summing up of a bargain for a white chip hat and some white tulle with which to trim it—but most of the girls bought artificial flowers, and were extremely particular about shades of colour.

Opposite was the usual scene of the sale of second-hand female underclothing, the surrounding crowd consisting of the poorest middle-aged women—mothers. It is an almost silent trade, for not a word passes beyond the naming of the price. The garment is sold or not sold, and if not sold goes back on to the rising heap and another is held up to view. The boot shops are a remarkable sight. It takes time to buy boots: you have to try them on; and the customers wait their turns, seated in rows, till served. It takes money, too. Shops selling women's clothes were also crowded with those waiting to be served. Nor did the purchasers seem to be of poorer class as the night drew on, except that there was the usual sight of the buying of cooked food.

It is remarkable that, except at the cookshops, where slices of pork or pudding are sold to be carried home in paper, there are here no places where anything to eat can be had. Such coffee-shops as there are had closed for the night. Supper is not what these shops aim to supply. That service is taken by the stall on wheels, which has its accustomed pitch, and remains available till the small hours, and by it is done very well. Coffee, tea, hard-boiled eggs, bread and butter, cake; all quite good; fully as good as at the coffee-shops; but to be eaten hastily, standing.

Life and Labour, etc., 3rd Series, vol. 4, pp. 188-9.

4

A Good Word for the Police

Nearly everyone speaks well of the police. Even if some think them not sufficiently a terror to evil doers, it is admitted that the line taken is a matter of policy, and is no doubt dictated from headquarters. At any rate, it is generally assumed that the men are advised not to make trouble. They do their duty, and take hard knocks and broken heads as all in the day's work when they have occasionally to strive with the fierce Irishry of Devons Road. They may not interfere as much as some desire with prostitutes in the streets near the docks and elsewhere; they may be content merely to frighten boys found playing pitch and toss in some quiet court; or may shut their eyes to minor infringements of the licensing acts or to the betting that goes on in all directions; but those who demand more stringent action admit that it would be difficult to go so far beyond public opinion as would be necessary to enforce the strict letter of the law, and that to attempt this would not only require a greatly increased number of police, but would run the risk of disturbing the happy relations which exist between police and people.

Life and Labour, etc., 3rd Series, vol. 1, p. 52.

5

The Factory Girl as She Really Is

By the 'factory girl' is meant the lower grade of factory workers who may be found in comparatively small numbers in box, brush, and cap factories; who are in the majority in jam factories; and who hold almost undisputed sway in the rope and match factories.

The 'factory girl' generally earns from 7s. to 11s.—rarely more, for the very good reason, in many cases, that she does not want more. She can be recognized on ordinary days by the freedom of her walk, the numbers of her friends, and the shrillness of her laugh. On Saturday evenings and Sunday afternoons she will be found promenading up and down the Bow Road, arm in arm with two or three other girls, sometimes with a young man, but not nearly so frequently as might be imagined.

On those occasions she is adorned and decked out, not so much for conquest as for her own personal delight and pleasure, and for the admiration of her fellow women. She wears a gorgeous plush hat with as many large ostrich feathers to match as her funds will run to—bright ruby or scarlet preferred. Like all the working women in the East End, she wears good tidy boots on all occasions, perhaps with high heels, but generally suitable for walking, although a little higher perhaps than those adopted by the Rational Dress Society. She goes to penny gaffs [low theatres] if nothing better is offered her; she revels in the thrilling performances at the Paragon or the music-halls; and only too often she can be seen drinking in the public-house with a young man with whom she may or may not have been previously acquainted.

[Factory girls] are often the daughters of dock labourers or other irregularly employed workmen, frequently of drunkards. They have been brought up in stifling rooms, with scanty food, in the midst of births and deaths, year after year. They have been accustomed to ups and downs; one week they have been on the verge of starvation, another they have shared in a 'blow-out'. They have learnt to hate monotony, to love drink, to use bad language as their mother tongue, and to be true to a friend in distress. They care nothing for appearances, and have no desire to mix with any but their equals. . . .

On the whole, these girls, outside their homes, lead a healthy, active life. They do not over-exert themselves at the factory. They rise early and have plenty of open-air exercise, both on their way to and from the factory and in their evening walks. They are rough, boisterous, outspoken, warm-hearted, honest working girls. Their standard of morality is very low, so low that to many they may seem to have none at all: and yet the very tolerance of evil that is shown by the girls who so willingly subscribe for a companion who has 'got into trouble' may be one reason why these girls have such a repugnance to the worst forms of immorality.

Their great enemy is drink; the love of it is the curse they have inherited, which later on, when they are no longer factory girls, but dock labourers' wives, will drag them down to the lowest level, and will be transmitted to the few of their children who survive. They are nearly all destined to be mothers, and they are almost all entirely ignorant of any domestic accomplishments.

MISS CLARA E. COLLET; *Life and Labour*, etc., Poverty, vol. 4, pp. 322-6.

6

What They Spend Their Money On

The standard of dress amongst young people [in the East End of London] is rising fast; clothing, like other things, is cheap; but whilst more is obtained for the money it is also the case that more money is spent. Scent, for instance, is extensively sold in small bottles at a low price, and girls very generally wear jewellery of some sort. The smoking of cigarettes and cheap cigars has also become general in recent years, and among young men a clay pipe is rarely seen. There are few who do not possess a watch.

There appears also to be an extraordinary abundance of doctors, explained by the success that has attended cheap fees. To make a large income in this way, and drive a pair of horses, seems to have been quite possible, and though the business is perhaps now overdone it is still profitable.

Door-step canvassers of all kinds thrive. There is evidently a good deal of money to be picked up in various ways. Betting agents carry on their lucrative trade very openly. A favourite local amusement is whippet racing, the whippet being a small greyhound; the races often take place on the Bow running ground, and thus give an opportunity for some betting combined with a breath of fresh air.

An enormous business, too, is done in excursions for the day by train and brake. Some of these excursions are arranged for the men working for some particular employer, others by the members of some club or society, and others again are set on foot by some publican or caterer at so much a head for all who like to go. For such purposes there is always plenty of money.

Amidst all this ready expenditure of money on dress, or drink, or pleasure, there appears to be little that leaves any very permanent results in acquisition of other than temporary benefits. Such actual saving as we hear of is for the sunny rather than the rainy day. Insurance against death and to cover funeral expenses is indeed general, and maintained almost as a first charge upon income, and membership in solid Friendly Societies, providing substantially for sickness as well as death, is fairly common, but we are told that the bulk of the population has nothing laid by.

It is, however, possible, that there may be more than is known; men do not advertise their savings, and a rather high standard of home life, involving accumulations of some kind, is suggested by the appeal of a purveyor of musical instruments on the hire system, who advertises on every wall 'What is home without a piano?'

Life and Labour, etc., 3rd Series, vol. i, pp. 12-16.

7

Bluebell Trophies

On a fine Sunday evening at the end of May . . . The bicycles were a sight coming back with country trophies, mostly branches of hawthorn in blossom, across their handle-bars. One had a large bunch of bluebells.

Life and Labour, etc., 3rd series, vol. i, p. 252.

8

East End Morals

While there is not much prostitution here [the Docks area of London's East End] there is, perhaps in place of it, a good deal of loose morality. With the lowest classes pre-marital relations are very common, perhaps even usual. Amongst the girls themselves nothing is thought of it if no consequences result; and very little even if they do, should marriage follow, and more pity than reprobation if it does not.

As a rule, the young people, after a few experiments, pair off and then are faithful, and usually end by marrying. It is noted by the clergy who marry them, how often both the addresses given are from the same house. It is observed also that it is nearly always the young woman who puts up the banns; not unfrequently she does not know the man's full name.

This peculiar code of morality is independent of recognised law, and an embarrassment to religion, but it is intelligent enough and not unpractical in its way, and those teachers of religion who come in closest contact with the people are the most forward in recognizing that the word 'vice' is inapplicable to the irregular relations that result, whether it be before or after the legal marriage; though they would probably cling (in religious desperation) to the appellation of 'sin'.

I do not know exactly how far upwards in the social scale this view of sexual morality extends, but I believe it to constitute one of the clearest lines of demarcation between upper and lower in the working class. I do not suppose that young men of the better working class are more virtuous than those of the classes above, or than their talk among themselves would indicate; on the other hand, the girls, though not ignorant of evil, are full of pride, and a fall from the paths of virtue is a very serious matter for their families and themselves; serious enough to bring very great pressure on the man concerned, who is most likely to be well known. In such cases, however, a prompt marriage may probably hide all.

It is girls of their own class that the young men run after, and with whom, if at all, the Lotharios among them will boast of their successes. But equality of class is a great safeguard, and the free and honourable terms of companionship, under a very definite code of rules, between those who are recognized as 'keeping company', are in favour of virtue, and are made more effective by the early age at which marriage is possible and usual. And it may be pointed out, that while the pressure of the consequences of previous relations leads in some cases to the most undesirably early marriages between mere boys and girls, the non-postponement of marriage brought about by the general freedom of courtship, carries with it many social advantages.

Life and Labour, etc., 3rd Series, vol. 1, pp. 55-6.

9

Common Lodging Houses

There is no legal definition of a common lodging-house, but it may be roughly defined to be a house in which beds are let out for the night or by the week, in rooms where three or more persons not belonging to the same family may sleep at the same time.

A proportion of those who make their home in the common lodging-houses do so of necessity, driven thereto by poverty, the victims of misfortune, or of irregularity or slackness of work. But many others voluntarily adopt this method of life; amongst them are men earning good wages—artisans, for instance, from the Midlands or the North—who seek a temporary abode while fulfilling engagements to work for short periods at a distance from their family or friends. Some again find it convenient to be able to shift their quarters at short notice and to preserve a stricter incognito than would be compatible with ordinary family life.

In houses such as we are concerned with, the kitchen is the common living room and provides the attraction of free social intercourse. A bright coke fire is kept burning night and day for cooking and general use. The furniture, strong and of the roughest description, consists of a long table occupying the centre of the room, with wooden benches on either side, and perhaps a few common chairs in addition. The cooking apparatus provided is of the simplest kind. A few frying-pans or grid-irons serve in turn to prepare for table, herring, saveloy, rashers, steak, or other form of food belonging to a succession of guests.

Of crockery there is next to none: a few old jam pots will often be the only provision for tea and coffee. The teapots are usually provided, but smaller articles, such as cutlery, are too portable to be used in common, and clasp knives will be produced from the pocket; spoons are not always thought of, and we have ample illustration of the fact that fingers were made before forks, whilst an old newspaper will often supply the want of a plate.

Seated on and around the tables are to be seen groups of men engaged in games of chance or skill with dice or cards of an ancient appearance, or in recounting anecdotes too often ill-fitted for polite ears, varied with song, dance, and discussion—political or theological—while beer, gin, and tobacco abound.

As the evening wears on, or morning approaches, the occupants drop off one by one to the sleeping rooms. These are usually well-ventilated, and contain rows of small iron bedsteads, arranged as in hospital wards, only closer together. The bedsteads are provided with mattress, rug or blanket, and sometimes also with sheets, which are changed once a week. Sometimes about the premises, oftenest in an outside shed, there is a supply of water, washing tubs, and towels for general use, and other conveniences are generally adequate.

The prices vary from 3d. to 6d. a night, the most usual charge being 4d. Payment is required in advance, but some credit will be given to well-known customers who can be trusted to pay as circumstances permit. Weekly payment secures a reduction, equal usually to one night or 'Sunday free'.

Any person able to pay can obtain a night's lodging, no question is asked, and names are not taken. A man may lodge for years in a house and only be know to the landlord or his 'deputy' by the number of the bed he occupies or a nickname given by the other lodgers.

The landlord undertakes no responsibility for the safety of a lodger's clothing or other property, unless specially deposited with him, and everything brought into the house is at the owner's risk. A man must be very sharp to remain long in such places without being the victim of some petty theft, and it sometimes happens that people are robbed of all their clothing while asleep in bed.

While there are among the inhabitants of these houses many who never do an honest day's work of any kind, but live by gambling, thieving, or fraud, spending their lives alternately in the common lodging-house and the gaol, there are also a considerable number who excite our utmost pity—poor 'derelicts of humanity' who, from sheer inability, whether bodily or mental, cannot work, of if they attempt to work are worse than useless. These would seem to spend their lives interchangeably between the common lodging-house, the night shelter, the casual wards, and the workhouse.

The common lodging-houses for females only would appear to be almost entirely occupied by women of the lowest class—thieves, prostitutes, and beggars, with a very small proportion of casual earners such as crossing-sweepers, basket-hawkers, charwomen, and washerwomen. With regard to the houses for 'married couples' the less said the better—for the most part they are simply houses of accommodation.

In common lodging-houses social distinctions are recognised and even rigidly adhered to. The class divisions in this lowest society follow much the same lines as are to be found in the world outside. Though bearing all alike the stamp of poverty and suffering, the one as often as the other under the misfortune of detected crime, a man of education or literary attainments will hold himself far above the casual labourer or handicraftsman, and a broken-down clerk or shop assistant would hesitate to frequent the company of common beggars.

Life and Labour, etc., Poverty, vol. 1, pp. 205-14.

10

Round the Clock in a 'Model Dwelling'

Life in 'Buildings', we may say, depends more on the class of inhabitants than on structural arrangements. It is curious, on the principle of 'like to like', how quickly a Building forms for itself a certain character—Jews' Buildings, rowdy Buildings, genteel Buildings, etc., all being estimated as such by public opinion. Racial prejudices keep the Christians apart from the Jews, and a taste for cleanliness or for quietness determines folk who can afford to indulge it to spend a little more on rent for the sake of mixing with those who are 'particular', and who 'keep themselves to themselves'.

T. Buildings, where I lived for a year, is a pretty red brick building, with five storeys of tenements, two sides of a square, and enclosing a good-sized asphalted court. My dwelling consisted of two tiny rooms, about 9 feet square, opening into one another. The front door, with its separate number and knocker, opens out of the front room into a common open balcony; and the back door out of the back room into a tiny private balcony, about a yard or so square, leading to the sink, etc. These little balconies are often turned to good use with flower boxes and hanging baskets, and one woman had rigged up a pigeon house, and kept pigeons very successfully there.

Each tenement is complete in itself, except for the want of a tap; to fetch water the tenants have to take their buckets to a common tap on each balcony.

Though so small, the rooms are fresh and very clean, brightly coloured and painted once every year. The asphalted court provides a large and safe playground for the children, and the flat roof is utilized for washhouses and a drying ground. Each tenant is bound in turn to clean and whiten a part of the balcony and stairs, and each in turn on their fixed day enjoys the use of a washhouse and the roof to dry clothes.

These common rights and duties lead, of course, to endless contention. (I may quote the remarks of a neighbour on the ferocity of the combatants on a washing-day dispute: 'Why, they'd tear you to pieces;

bull-dogs I call 'em.') In the summer T. Buildings was very pretty, with the red bricks and white stairs and balconies, and flowers in most of the windows. . . .

A short sketch of an average day in T. Buildings will give some idea of the way of life.

At 5 o'clock in the morning I hear the tenant overhead, Mr A., getting up for his day's work. His wife, who does a little dressmaking when she can get it from her neighbours, was up late last night (I heard her sewing-machine going till 1 o'clock), so he does not disturb her. He is a carman at the Goods Depot of a Railway Company, and has to be there at 6 o'clock, so he is not long getting his breakfast of bread and butter. But before he has done I hear a child cry; then the sound of a sleepy voice, Mrs A., recommending a sip of tea and a crust for the baby. The man, I suppose, carries out the order, for the crying ceases, and then I hear his steps as he goes downstairs.

At 8 o'clock there is a good deal of scraping and raking on the other side of the wall. This means that my neighbour, Mrs B., an old woman partly supported by her dead husband's savings, partly by the earnings of two grown-up daughters, is raking out and cleaning her stove. Then the door is opened, the dust is thrown down the dust-shoot. and a conversation is very audibly carried on by two female voices.

Among other topics, is the favourite one of Mrs A.'s laziness in the morning—though Mrs B. knows perfectly well that Mrs A. has been up late at work, having indeed repeatedly complained of the noise of the sewing-machine at night; and though Mrs C. openly avows that she will not say anything against Mrs A., as she has always been very nice to her.

At half-past eight I hear the eldest child of the A. family lighting the fire and dressing her two little boys for school.

With the departure of the children there is a lull. At ten Mrs A. gets up, and at eleven she sallies out to make sundry purchases. Before she goes, however, Mrs A. has a bright gossip on her threshold with Mrs C, a tram-conductor's wife, who has looked in to return the head of a loaf borrowed on the previous Saturday night. In the dialogue, which lasts more than five minutes, I hear Mrs B.'s name repeated a good many times, and catch also the phrase 'spiteful old cat', and I believe that Mrs B.'s remarks at 8 o'clock are now being repeated with Mrs C.'s artistic variations.

Soon after twelve there is a great hubbub of children's laughter and shouting in the courtyard under my window. The children have returned from school and they seem to have a good deal of fun together till we begin to hear the mothers calling them in to dinner.

In the afternoon a certain torpor falls upon the Buildings, only broken by the jingling cans and cat-calls of the afternoon milk-boys. But this is the favourite time for the women to call upon one another, and I can catch various fragments of conversation relating to the bad turn Mrs D.'s illness is taking, to the uncalled for visit of the curate to a lady who dislikes curates, to the shocking temper of little Maggie (Mrs C.'s child) who is reputed to be the tease and torment of all the children in the place.

Looking out of the window I do not see the unhappy Maggie, but find myself watching instead a spirited game of cricket between four girls on one side and three boys on the other. The wickets are chalked up against the wall, and a soft ball is used. The game, however, collapses, for the boys, who are smaller than their opponents, refuse to go on, saying, 'it isn't fair', and the girls retire triumphant, but disgusted.

At 6 o'clock a row in the street calls a load of the inhabitants out on to the balconies, where we can look down exactly as from boxes in a theatre on to the stage. The parties to the quarrel are a man and his wife in a distinctly lower walk of life (like all the inhabitants of houses in the street) than any of the tenants of the buildings. They are eventually separated after much 'old English' on both sides. The general impression among the spectators is in favour of the man, but the incident is soon forgotten.

Very soon after, various savoury smells begin to float out on to the landings. The favourite meal of the day, the 'tea', is being prepared against the husband's return. All is comparative peace and harmony, the children's hands are washed, the room is tidied, and the cloth laid. The A.'s have sprats, as I have good reason to know. Mrs A. is aware of my partiality for this fish, and in a neighbourly spirit sends me in a plateful by her most careful child, from whom I learn that Mrs D. is much worse and wandering in her head, and that 'mother is going to sit up with her'. Mrs D.'s husband is a night watchman, so he is at hand by day to look after her, and the neighbours are taking turns to nurse her at night.

In the evening some of the men go out to the neighbouring 'Club' and sing songs or talk politics, one or two drop into the bar of the favourite 'pub', but the majority simply stay at home with the wife and children. Mr A., the carman, is essentially a family man, and he makes a point of going through some gymnastic tricks with his boys and putting them to bed. Occasionally he receives a visit from a mate, but this is rare; and generally he retires not later than 9.30. Mr C., the tram-conductor, has a liking for the *Star*, and reads aloud striking passages after tea. . . .

'A Lady Resident', in *Life and Labour*, etc., Poverty, vol. 3, pp. 37-41

II

Board Schools and the Children in Them

Among the public buildings of the Metropolis the London Board Schools occupy a conspicuous place. As befits their purpose, they are uniformly handsome, commodious, and for the most part substantial and well arranged. The health and convenience of both children and teachers have been carefully considered. Taken as a whole, they may be said fairly to represent the high-water-mark of the public conscience in its relation to the education of the children of the people.

A Board School is commonly arranged in three storeys, corresponding to the three departments, boys, girls, and infants, each storey having an entrance and playground of its own.

When an 'infant' is three years old it may be sent to an elementary school; and mothers of the poorer class are often glad to have a child out of the way and looked after during school hours at the cost of a penny a week. At five the law requires it to attend. At seven it ranks as a boy or girl, and is promoted accordingly.

An infant department under the London School Board usually contains from 300 to 500 children, distributed according to age or ability, in classes of 40 or 50, up to 60 each. Some of the classes are in separate rooms; others are two or three together in a larger one, each with a teacher to itself. The 'babies', i.e. children under five, have a gallery of their own, with little benches comfortably fitted, rising one behind the other, so that every pair of eyes has the teacher full in view.

An infant class, even in a school of the lowest grade, is a pleasant sight, always provided that there is a bright capable head teacher who puts her heart into her work, and inspires her assistants with her own energy and cheerfulness. The busy contented little faces that we see around us tell plainly enough that school is a place to be happy and comfortable in, more so, in many cases, than the children are or can be in their wretched homes.

In all but the very worst localities, however, the majority of the parents are fairly decent folk, working when they can, and doing their best for their children, however poor that best may be. Even as regards the poorest and most neglected homes, we find the children in the infant classes reflect the vice or poverty of the parents less than those in the upper departments. The 'slum' mother, as a rule, will spend herself over the little ones, toiling for their bread, and delighting to dress and deck them out.

Still, in all poor schools we shall find many whose puny and sickly looks show too clearly that they are either feebly born, or are living under unwholesome and bad conditions at home. Usually such children come either from drinking homes, or from those where the family has over-run the means of subsistence, and the over-worn mother must herself often work for the children's bread before she has it to give to them.

I have known a woman of this class present herself at the door of an infant school with a couple of slices of bread, begging that her children might be allowed to eat it at once, as she had bought it with money earned since they went breakfastless to school.

At the first glance it might seem that not much could be done in the way of education, with a school full of such children of seven years old and under. If they are kept in order, taught the rudiments of cleanliness and good behaviour, and can learn to make pot-hooks, and read words of one syllable, the little girls to hold a needle too, all without too many tears by the way, that is as much, some would say, as can reasonably be expected.

Our London Board infant children would laugh at a curriculum like that. They have Kinder-garten, object-lessons, Swedish-drill, and action-songs; none of them requiring tears at all, though serving admirably to develop both the little bodies and the brains as well. Also at seven the Code requires that they shall be ready for examination in Standard 1, this being a kind of 'matriculation examination', undergone by infants on entering a boys' or girls' department. It includes reading from books containing words of more than one syllable, spelling, writing, arithmetic as far as addition, subtraction, and half the multiplication table, singing by note as well as by ear, needlework for girls, and either drawing or needlework for boys.

'They need a great deal of encouragement'

The problems of neglect and poverty come more distinctly into view when we pass from the infants' to the upper departments of a school of this class. In the boys' department, which we enter first, we find the head teacher busy with a class of Standard 1, dull and backward children, who require the most skilled teaching that the school possesses, to coach them up to examination point. A sorry group they are; fifteen or twenty of them; failures from the infants, or boys just 'run in' by the attendance officers from the streets, who may never have been in a school before. One or two are tidy-looking boys; one has a clean washed face, and a white collar on. The rest are ragged, ill-kept, and squalid in appearance. Some are filthily dirty, others sickly looking, with sore eyes and unwholesome aspect. One or two seem hopelessly dull, almost vacant. Another, a little scare-crow fellow, alert and sharp, with a pair of black eyes twinkling restlessly around as if he were meditating escape, had made his own living, we are told, in the streets before the officer ran him in.

'They need a great deal of encouragement', the teacher tells us cheerfully; 'but some of them are beginning to make a start. They come cleaner than they did; and that is a great step towards civilization.'

But this is the lowest circle in the mount of toil; and as we rise through the standards, things improve. In schools of this class the lower standards are always the worst. . . . After Standards III and IV, a marked improvement is apparent. We see a freer sprinkling of 'clean collar boys', less sickliness and squalor, less evidence of under-feeding or neglect at home.

A London child who has passed the fourth standard is free from school at thirteen years of age. The dull and sickly, the idle and irregular, reach the barrier and leave; their parents hurrying them off to work the moment legal release is possible. The brighter or more regular children, on whom the training of the school has told, or who come from the more respectable homes, move on into Standards V or VI. The sixth standard boys, to whom the teacher introduces us with honest pride, open-faced, intelligent-looking lads, the crown of his toil, whom he has carried through all the stages of their school career, count up to only 6 per cent of the whole. In some schools it is not more than 2 or 3 per cent.

'Never no time to play'

In the girls' department it is the same. Everywhere we are met by tokens of penury and bad conditions at home. Children are pointed out to us stunted in growth, with faces old beyond their years, burdened out of school with the whole charge of the wretched little home. 'Never no time to play', as one of them explains. . . . Even the youngest of these girls, we find, has often to wash and dress and feed the baby, cook the father's dinner when the mother is at work, and 'clean up' the single room in which the family live.

One step in advance, however, has recently been taken. In every London Board School the older girls learn cookery. A fair number of the children have been to the cookery centre. All are fond of it. Their faces brighten the moment it is spoken of. Some of them, the tidier ones with decent mothers, are proud to tell that they have made at home the things they learned at the classes. Shepherd's pie, rock cakes, and Irish stew, seem popular attempts. All declare that their dish turned out well; with the addition, usually, that 'father ate it'.

Many things are taught at these cookery centres besides cookery—cleanliness, neatness, precision, despatch. The observing faculties are brought into play, the latent womanliness developed. All these girls get to something that they can understand and be interested in, and which works into their scheme of life.

Passing now to schools of the upper grade, we are conscious of distinct advance. A more inspiriting and satisfactory sight can hardly be desired than that presented by a London elementary school such as may be seen in every workmen's suburb, or planted where the better paid trades abound. The great bulk of the children are wholesome, bright-looking, well-fed, well-clad, eager for notice, 'smart', and full of life.

MARY C. TABOR, *Life and Labour, etc.*, Poverty, vol. 3, pp. 205-34.

12

What is Toynbee Hall?

What Toynbee Hall is will be best understood if we record how it came to be. Its inception followed on the appointment of Canon Barnett [1844-1913] to the living of St Jude's [Whitechapel]. Under his guidance, and that of Mrs Barnett, who has tendered constant assistance to her husband's work, this small East-End parish became a centre not only of great activity, but also of thought. Intimate relations with Dr Jowett [of Balliol College, Oxford] and with several of the remarkable men who came under his influence, led to their paying visits to St Jude's, and the idea of a University Settlement in East London gradually took form.

Of all these young men Arnold Toynbee, though in some respects a visionary, stood out as having the most suggestive and sympathetic mind. His death in the Spring of 1883, even more than his life, helped to clinch the purpose of the rest, and it was decided to associate the new settlement, opened at the end of 1884, with his name. It has never connected itself with any political party or with any religious school. The key-note has been freedom of individual thought, and, as a corollary of this, corporate action on all controversial issues has been carefully avoided.

The direct and expressed objects were to 'provide education and the means of recreation and enjoyment' for the people; 'to inquire into the condition of the poor and to consider and advance plans calculated to promote their welfare', and thus thought and sympathy were to be brought to bear upon the condition of life in a working-class and poor neighbourhood. In a great variety of ways these objects have been attained, but indirectly also the influence exercised by the settlement has been very considerable. As pioneer settlement its advice is continually sought and its experience consulted; strangers desiring to study the problems of povery, of industry, and of crowded City life, are hospitably entertained, and are helped in their researches by the residents, some of whom are themselves ever on the same quest.

Moreover, Toynbee has gradually formed traditions, and through them has acquired a widely-recognised, and very persistent individuality of its own. In essence, perhaps, there was nothing very original in the fundamental principles adopted, which were merely 'a new phase' of 'neighbourliness and goodwill', an expression of very simple forms of 'civic duty', re-emphasizing the claims of old and valuable ideas. People, however, were roused to think that some new discovery had been made as to the way in which social obligations could be met, and thus these ideas have often come to be associated with Toynbee Hall in the public mind, with the result that perhaps its greatest achievement lies in the fact that it has caused many people in many parts of the world to consider and seek to think out and apply these ideas afresh for themselves.

Toynbee Hall, in addition to carrying on its work of organising classes, lectures and conferences, fostering educational societies and social clubs, providing concerts and entertainments, and affording a centre where 'East End' and 'West End' can enjoy a common hospitality, and where working class leaders first obtained social recognition, has also been connected with all local efforts made for improved administration whether in Local Government and the Poor Law, in school management, or in the guidance of charity in assisting the poor.

Life and Labour, etc., 3rd Series, vol. 2, pp. 55-8.

13

A Pleasant Corner in Walthamstow

Bright Street . . . a street chiefly of the better class of working-people. . . . It is a pleasant street, and in summer time the fresh green trees and tidy little gardens, not to mention window gardens, line each side; our parish flower shows with useful inexpensive prizes are a great incentive to the latter. Several married policemen live here, and it is seldom you come across a house inhabited by more than one family. There are also many postmen—family men—who carry on little trades in their spare hours when 'off duty', chiefly 'boot-repairing', alias 'cobbling'.

Those whom their wives call 'city clerks' live here too, with real drawing-rooms in front—bay windows filled with flowers and lace curtains, antimacassars tied on every chair with coloured ribbon, and a centre-table with the children's prize school books ranged cross-ways all round.

Three or four little general shops intersect the houses, and at the further end a few larger shops, greengrocers, pork and sausage, and a second-hand clothes establishment. A quietly-conducted public-house at the corner end. One house has been turned into a dispensary, presided over by a 6d. Doctor, with a very long name and numbers of letters following it. Bright red blinds printed in white inform the residents of the hours of consultation and draw attention to the moderate charges, viz. 'A Bottle of Medicine and Advice for 6d'.

Life and Labour, etc., Poverty, vol. 1, 267–8, 271.

14

Saturday Night in Woolwich

From Shooter's Hill on bicycle at 10 p.m.; all dark and quiet till New Road was reached; there the crowd began. Many soldiers in uniform, shops all open, and booths on west side of street leading to the market-place.

Men, women, and children all good-humoured and well-dressed, out for marketing and to see the fun or for a promenade simply; and all young. Children, from babies in arms to ten years old, husbands and wives and fathers and mothers, between twenty and thirty-five; hardly a grey hair or an old face amongst them all.

A few soldiers, almost tipsy, at the corner of the New Road and Thomas Street, a small crowd watching them and listening to the nigger minstrels playing outside the public-house. In the market itself there was greater seriousness. Most were coming away with their purchases in large paper parcels, but a good number were still buying, and the market-place was full. The man never carried the parcels, except where the woman had a child in her arms, and not always then. The men, in caps and bowler hats, wore collars, and a few had black coats. The women in bonnets and cloaks, not quite in their best, but, like the men, evidently dressed for the occasion. Two or three labourers in their working clothes were the exception.

Chief interest centred round the butchers' stalls, but some were doing a good business in flowers and bedding-out plants. From the market the flow of the crowd was towards Powis and Hare Streets, where the best shops are for drapery, grocery, cheese and fruit. Fair strawberries were selling at 8d. a pound, good cherries at 6d. The crowd was good-tempered and sober, and out more for promenade than business. Such business as was done was inside the shops. Boot and shoe shops were best lighted and made the best show; after them came the public-houses.

Thence to the streets which comprise the 'Dust-hole'. I found them quiet and dark, there seemed to be few people in the lodging-house kitchens, and not many in the beer-house. Most doors were open; smell of dirt in the air, dark filthy stains on the pavement on either side, and a man asleep, drunk. Figures emerged suddenly from dark corners and disappeared again as mysteriously as they had come.

Returned shortly after closing-time (i.e. 12.10). There was then more life in the streets; the occupants of the public-houses had just been turned out. They stood in groups round the open floors. There was no quarrelling—no noise. Occasionally a voice would rise, but it never went so far as a row.

In the market everyone was packing up and going off with barrows and pony carts. One joint, which had been 6d., was now offered at 3d. per lb. The last pieces were being sold off. Only the poorest were buying now. Then back past the barracks, seeing a good number of soldiers who could only just walk. So on past the Common to Shooter's Hill, where, in a small patch of wood, was a nightingale singing loudly and being answered by another in the Crown Woods on the south side of the hill. It is thanks to the execrable train service that nightingales still sing, and pheasants are still preserved, and the bluebells carpet the woods within twelve miles of St Paul's. (May 27, 1900.)

Life and Labour, etc., 3rd Series, vol. 5, pp. 145-6.

15

Saucy Doings on Peckham Rye

The Peckham Rye Band has a long record. Now the band consists of forty performers. All wear black coats and tall hats, and make an imposing show. Immediately round the bandstand is the customary enclosure, asphalted and filled with chairs, with room for 1500 people. Admission, including the use of a chair, costs a penny, and practically every seat was taken.

When the music stopped at 9 o'clock the great mass of the people drifted slowly away, but for a quarter of an hour or so a certain amount of noisy play was noticeable in the immediate vicinity of the bandstand, the noise invariably coming from young men and young women or boys and girls. The proceedings were very juvenile. There was a good deal of running and squealing; some embracing and kissing; but not very much excitement, and the girls who were run after seemed to have come for the purpose. Some were too young, both boys and girls, to be allowed to go loose in this way. Others were 'grown up'.

One of the latter, a girl of perhaps twenty, was caught in a momentary whirl of the crowd, and seized by a man to be embraced roughly and kissed. No sooner was she released, than another man, apparently thinking she was fair game, repeated the process, and then, hot, flushed, but hardly disconcerted, the girl rejoined her companions, consisting of a second girl and two young men. She had, apparently, some words of protest on her lips, but all the consolation she received from her swain, who seemed to have accepted the proceedings with a kind of grumpy calmness, was the remark, 'You shouldn't be so d — d saucy'. He seemed to have hit off the situation, not only as it affected his own companion but a good many others round about: on the one side, d — d sauciness; on the other, responsive rudeness.

Life and Labour, etc., 3rd Series, vol. 6, pp. 193-5.

16

Hammersmith Streets

It was the Saturday in Holy Week, between 9.30 and 11.30. From Uxbridge Road up Prince's Road: street empty: no life; along St Catherine's Road, asphalt messy, but not very dirty; most doors open, no light in any of the passages; figures standing about, young men and young women, some bare-armed women gossiping; occasional lights in upper windows; many windows open, although it was cold; no noise.

Up St Clement's Road, many children about; along Crescent Street, the beerhouse at the corner full; more women than men inside; much talking but no drunkenness; hatless women, with white aprons, rough hair and bare arms, and with shawls round their shoulders. As they met the cold air coming out, two of them seemed at first to realize that they had taken too much, and clutched at one another's shawls for support. Many women in the beerhouse in Crescent Street, and in those at either end of Bangor Street. Men here were coming home full, sullen, solitary, addressed by no one and speaking to no one.

At St Anne's Road and Latimer Road the first brawl, between a man and a woman—both drunk, but kept apart and sent home with great tact by a policeman; the man would have gone quietly, but the woman would persist in calling him names.

In St Anne's Road three young women of laundry type, singing, arm-in-arm, reeling, noisily drunk; one with a small baby in her arms. Then into Norland Road, another woman drunk and noisy and a few men equally drunk, but quiet, lurching homewards; one woman, in a drunken torpor, sitting on the pavement propped against the wall. In this road there were shops and a few costers, but no demand except for winkles.

Into the Uxbridge Road and then higher to Hammersmith Broadway, and west along King Street. This is the great market street of West London; tram-lines down centre, costers' barrows and kerbstone sellers. The street full from side to side with people—men, women, and children; a few sightseers, but the majority buyers, well-to-do artisans with their families. More trade done with the shops than the barrows; some demand for penny toys and sweets. Women, old and young, all had sweets obvious in their mouths. There was none of the shouting of the ordinary market street. Butchers were very busy, and hardly had time to cry 'Buy, buy, buy'. Fair meat sold for 4d. a pound, scraps 3d.; 6d. a pound for joints. Fowls 1s. 3d. and 1s. 6d. Watercress ½d. per bundle. The quiet, the amount of business done, and the well-dressed appearance of the buyers were the main feature. Everyone seemed to know exactly what they wanted and to get it. After purchasing, one turn down the street and then home was the rule.

Life and Labour, etc., 3rd Series, vol. 3, pp. 191-2.

17

Vice at Victoria

South Pimlico: between Victoria Station and Lupus Street: the whole district swarms with prostitutes. The streets near Victoria Station are their home parade; the small hotels in Vauxhall Bridge Road their houses of accommodation, and the (adjoining) streets their dwelling-place.

These young women usually room together and are satisfactory as lodgers. If they ply their trade altogether away from their abodes litlle can be said, and with regard to their way of life, an eye is shut. Even if the good rule that maintains the respectability of the home is broken, if hansoms drive up at night, it is difficult for the authorities to take action as long as the neighbours make no complaint. And where there is so much of this kind of vice—in a number of streets every third house is said to be affected by it—public opinion becomes lax.

Life and Labour, etc., 3rd Series, vol. 3, pp. 87–8.

Illustrated London News (1895)

5. London after dark

In the gallery:
Christmas Pantomime at
Drury Lane

Illustrated London News (1893)

6. A cookery class in a London Board School

A dinner table à la 'Mrs Beeton'

(c) PROFESSIONAL PEOPLE

I

Religion

Of the ministers of religion enumerated in London at the 1891 Census, the clergy of the Established Church largely outnumbered those connected with other bodies. Their parochial organization by which the whole area is divided into parishes, each under the control of an incumbent, gives them unique advantages in dealing with the huge population, and this combination of numbers and organization makes the Established Church one of the most powerful factors in the local life of the Metropolis.

Of the 2205 clergymen returned, about 1650 are engaged in parochial work as incumbents or curates; the remaining 550 occupy other church offices, are chaplains of institutions, are engaged in teaching or are connected with some of the numerous religious societies, having their headquarters in London.

None can be termed poor in the sense the word is applied to the labouring population. Their incomes have, indeed, a wide range: those of the more fortunate equalling that of a cabinet minister, whilst some curates may not receive more than £90 a year. The duties to be performed are no less variable: in some thickly populated parishes the demands upon the time of the clergy are incessant, whilst in others, such as some of the City parishes, the duties are almost nominal, only necessitating the holding of a few services each week, which may be, and often is, done by deputy.

Passing to other religious bodies, there were 370 Roman Catholic priests and 832 dissenting ministers returned. Their social condition and incomes have also a wide range, although stipends do not rise so

D   97

high as in the Established Church, and the number at the lower end of the scale is proportionately greater. Of the dissenting congregations, the Wesleyans, Baptists, and Congregationalists are numerically the most important. The Wesleyan Methodist Church is governed by a Conference, which meets yearly. It accepts and ordains ministers, and appoints them to their circuits, the circuit usually consisting of several chapels in adjoining neighbourhoods. Houses are provided for the ministers in the circuits, and special provision is made for the education of their children and for old age. With Baptists and Congregationalists the appointment of the minister rests with the members of the church which he serves and the stipend depends upon the size and comparative wealth of the congregation. Consequently the amounts paid vary greatly and are at times very low; and the cases are not few in which the minister obtains his living in some other calling, receiving only a nominal sum for his ministrations.

The stipends of London Presbyterian ministers range from £76 to £1500 per annum, the majority receiving £350 to £500.

Corresponding to the wage-earning class in other walks of life are the 2651 persons (1208 men and 1443 women) returned as missionary, scripture-reader, district visitor, or Bible-women. The duties of these men and women are similar. Their lives are spent amongst the poor, visiting from house to house, holding meetings in mission-rooms, often a transformed shop, parlour, or kitchen, or even a disused loft. In this way they come in constant and direct contact with the poverty, wretchedness, and suffering ever present amongst the dwellers in our poor streets, and are frequently the almoners of the charity that as continuously seeks to alleviate their condition.

Salvation Army officers, usually two, in charge of a station have no fixed income. From the collections taken at the meetings they must pay the local expenses and send 10 per cent. of the amounts received to head-quarters. The remainder is available for the maintenance of the officers; but their weekly allowance must not exceed the following amounts:- unmarried men—captains 18s., lieutenants 16s.; unmarried women—captains 15s., lieutenants 12s.; married couples 27s., with 1s. a week extra for each child. Not infrequently the balance is insufficient to provide this pittance, in which case the officers should apply to head-quarters for whatever is necessary. As a rule they prefer to go without rather than become chargeable to the central fund.

As a whole those engaged in the subordinate service of religion compare very favourably with those occupying a similar financial position in other walks of life. They are careful, steady and temperate as a rule, the majority being total abstainers. Obtaining a better return for their money, the homes and general appearance of these people are equal to those of persons whose incomes are considerably larger.

Life and Labour, etc., Industry, vol. 4, pp. 191-4.

2

The Law

London seems the natural home of barristers, solicitors, and law clerks, and the majority of those who live in London are London born. Their headquarters are the Inns of Court and Chancery Lane, at the junction of the City and the West End, with the Courts of Justice in their midst, and a large proportion of the legal business of the whole country, contentious and non-contentious alike, is here transacted.

The factories of the law are noiseless, and many a passer-by is tempted to turn aside from the roaring streams of traffic in Holborn and the Strand into the quiet backwaters formed by the courts and gardens of Gray's Inn, Lincoln's Inn, and the Temple, where the barristers' chambers are to be found.

Solicitors are more scattered. A number of large firms have their offices in the City, and there are a good many also in the West End proper, some of high repute and active in 'family business', and others, especially in the streets off Bond Street and Regent's Street, who do business for tradesmen and moneylenders, and choose this position in order to be near their clients.

The preliminary education for both branches of the profession is expensive, and men who seek to enter them, especially as barristers, must be in a position to live on their own means for some years, or else must pick up a living in the by-paths of literature, for it is usually long before they can pay their way out of their professional earnings. The reward comes later, or may not come at all, but, if it comes, the years of earning are usually prolonged. Lawyers are not past their work until well advanced in life.

The higher branches of clerks from which solicitors are usually recruited, start by being 'articled', i.e. apprenticed to a practising solicitor. They are of higher social standing than those who work their way up from boyhood, and the distinction between 'articled' and 'unarticled' clerks in a solicitor's office is a fairly sharp one.

Unarticled clerks receive much the same pay as those employed in commerce. Starting as boys at 7s. or 8s. a week they reach 28s. to 40s., and may eventually become managing or confidential clerks at from £150 to £400 per annum. It is open to them, if they pass three qualifying examinations, and can afford to pay the fees, to become solicitors on their own account. Not many do this. As clerks their work is hard and closely sustained. In addition to the clerks, a large office will usually have two or three cashiers, rent collectors, and shorthand writers.

Barristers' clerks have more leisure. They start when fourteen or fifteen years of age under a 'senior' clerk. Between the ages of seventeen and twenty-one the boys earn 15s. to 18s. and call themselves 'junior clerks'. After a year or two at this they begin to look for a position as 'only' clerk, and in this capacity may serve four or five young men who have been lately called to the bar, and are setting up for themselves in chambers. For the clerk as well as his master there is a fee with every brief. Young barristers have but little remunerative work, and the clerk, who as soon as he becomes a chief or only clerk is properly entitled to nothing beyond the regular fees, demands a guarantee that the sum paid him shall not be less than, it may be, £70 to £100. Clerks to barristers in fair practice earn from £200 to £400 a year. The incomes of the chief clerks to barristers in the largest practice would run up to £800 or £1000, or even more. It is roughly calculated that clerks' fees are from 5 to 8 per cent of their employers' earnings. In return for this they keep the fee book, and act as intermediary between barrister and solicitor with respect to the amount of fee that will be accepted, since etiquette forbids the barrister to do this for himself. They also arrange the times of conferences, and have many other duties of a semi-confidential nature. Amiability, tact and honesty are the qualities in greatest demand.

Office hours are from 10 a.m. to 6 or 7 p.m. or to 4 or 5 p.m. on Saturdays, excepting in the long vacation, when the hours are shorter if, indeed, the chambers are not shut up altogether.

If his master is made a judge of the High Court the clerk receives a fixed salary of £400, but should he be made judge of an inferior court, or in any case at his death, the clerk must find a new employer, and sometimes has to make an entirely fresh start. This is a risk which every barrister's clerk has to run. The tenure of employment under a firm, as with solicitors, is very different.

Life and Labour, etc., Industry, vol. 4, pp. 72–4.

3

Medicine

In the West End of London the representatives of medicine and dentistry are found in their greatest numbers in the neighbourhood of Harley Street and Hanover Square. Over the remaining districts they are scattered fairly evenly, though dentists have a traditional home in St Martin's Lane and Ludgate Hill, and all seem to give preference to houses situated in a square, or at the corner of a street. In a square the light is better and there is greater quiet, while a corner house has the counterbalancing advantages of greater prominence and the convenience of a side-door into the surgery.

For all medical men a course of training extending over five years, and the successful passing of sundry examinations, forms a necessary prelude to their careers as practising physicians or surgeons.

The prospects of success for the young men in this profession may be judged from the table given below. This table is taken from the reports (unpublished) of St Bartholomew's Hospital. In it Sir James Paget traces the careers of one thousand of his pupils over a period of fifteen years, dating from their entrance to the hospital at which he was a lecturer. Of the thousand

23	achieved distinguished success.
66	„ considerable success.
507	„ fair success.
124	„ very limited success.
56	failed entirely.
96	left the profession.
87	died within 12 years of commencing practice.
41	died during pupilage.

1000

Those are classed as having achieved distinguished success who gained and maintained leading practices in counties or large towns, or held important public offices, etc. Considerable success is ascribed to those who gained good practices, or more than ordinary esteem and influence in society. Fair success to those who acquired a moderate practice—enough to live with—or ordinary public appointments. Very limited success, to those who were not in moderately good practice nor likely to obtain it.

Of the fifty-six failures, twenty-five were idle or dissipated and intemperate.

Of the ninety-six who left the profession, 'thirteen while pupils left or were expelled in disgrace, and three were wisely removed by their friends. Of the remaining eighty, one while still a pupil and one after beginning practice, retired on private means, too rich to need to work; four after beginning practice had to leave in disgrace—one of them was rather sinned against than sinning; another, who had been a good student, speculated in mines, lost money, forged, and is in prison; three became actors, of whom two are in obscurity and one is well esteemed in genteel comedy; four entered the army with commissions, one after and three before obtaining a diploma for practice; three pupils enlisted as privates, and one of these distinguished himself by courage and good conduct sufficiently to win a commission; one while a pupil, left for the bar and has succeeded; five after passing took orders in the Church of England, two in the Church of Rome; ten pupils, and as many after having begun practice, left for different forms of mercantile life at home or in the colonies; three pupils and six young practitioners took to farming. The remaining twenty-seven left the profession for various pursuits which need not be specified, unless to say that three became homeopathic practitioners, but took to that class no repute for either wisdom or working power.' If we deduct the loss by death (which agrees with the general average mortality of males over nineteen years of age) and those who, after leaving the profession, succeeded in some other way, the proportion of failures and even of those whose success was 'very limited' is certainly not large.

A practitioner, especially if he has a surgery attached to his house, generally employs one or two assistants, who may either be resident or non-resident, and qualified or unqualified. These men may be spoken of as wage-earners, and are paid £60 to £100 per year if qualified, and £30 to £60 when unqualified, as resident indoor assistants. Outdoor assistants usually have their rooms found for them by the principal, and earn £80 to £150 when qualified, and £50 to £80 if unqualified.

Life and Labour, etc., Industry, vol. 4, pp. 80-3.

4

Hospital Nurses

In no walk of life has the desire of certain women for independence and usefulness outside their homes found on the whole a more satisfactory expression than in the adoption of the profession of hospital nurse. The census at each decade shows an increase in the numbers of women so employed.

All classes are drawn upon to satisfy the demand. Many are ladies by birth and education and many belong to the upper servant class. Daughters of clergymen, military and naval officers, of doctors, of farmers, of tradesmen and artisans are found side by side in all the great metropolitan hospitals. Many of those who would formerly have sought places as music teachers or nursery governesses have been absorbed in this way.

Great numbers apply every year to be taken on as nurses. One matron told us that last year (1895) she had 2500 applications. Candidates must as a rule be not less than twenty-three years of age, and have special qualifications. Among other things stated on the printed papers usually given to them it is not uncommon to read, 'You are required to be punctual, quiet and orderly, cleanly and neat, methodical and active, patient, cheerful, and kindly, careful and trustworthy.' ('With wings' might well be added.) Inquiries are also made and references given as to former life, and if these are satisfactory an interview with the matron follows, after which the candidate is finally rejected or accepted as a probationer for one to three months on the understanding that if she is suitable she will then contract to remain in the service of the hospital for from one to three years.

The period of hospital training considered necessary to produce a fully qualified nurse is most generally stated to be three years. In practice this varies. Some hospitals grant a certificate after one or two years, and others after three or four. In the same way, the length of time necessary for promotion within the hospital is uncertain. Nurses, it is said, are born and not made. In some places, a probationer may after a year be promoted to the post of sister over the heads of staff-nurses who have been working for a much longer time. In others, the post of sister is reserved for ladies by birth and education only.

Daily round in a London hospital. At one of the largest of the Metropolitan General Hospitals, a nurse on day-duty is usually called at

5.45 or 6 a.m.; she has a breakfast of ham and eggs, coffee, etc., and then enters the wards at 7. For about two hours in the morning both night and day nurses are on duty together, and the time is spent in sweeping the wards, washing the patients and preparing them for and serving them with their breakfasts. Between 9 and 10.30 a.m. twenty minutes or half an hour is allowed off for nurses to tidy themselves and take a lunch of bread and milk in summer or of soup in winter. After this they are on duty until about 1, when they go in two relays to dinner. This is the chief meal of the day, and consists of soup and meat and pudding or cheese, with beer or milk to drink. In some hospitals a nurse must sit at table for half an hour, whether she is eating or no, for the sake of her digestion; while in others she is free as soon as she has finished.

Then follows a long spell in the wards, interrupted only by tea, taken usually in the wards, until 8.30 or 9.30, when, after telling the night-nurses about the new patients, or any changes in the condition of those of the day before, she goes off to a supper of cold meat and vegetables. Finally, she must be in bed with her light out by half-past ten.

The day is not always so long, for the afternoon is often broken by rest and recreation for from two to four hours once, twice, or thrice a week, and some hospitals grant this amount of leave regularly every day. In addition, a whole day once a month, and an evening once a fortnight is not unusual, while the yearly holidays are for three or four weeks.

A night nurse starts by having breakfast between 8 and 9 p.m. Luncheon, which she cooks for herself at whatever hour she likes during the night, generally consists of something savoury to tempt the palate; and she takes her dinner when she comes off in the morning.

Sisters have no night duty, though they may be called up in emergencies. They are the official mouthpieces of the nurses, through whom complaints are made to the matron, and they receive the orders of the visiting physicians and surgeons as they make their rounds, and are responsible for their fulfilment. They organize the nursing of the ward and prepare each day a written report on the cases before them. As a rule, they come on duty at 8 a.m., and go off at 8 or 10 p.m. Their chief meal is dinner at 7 or 8 p.m., which they have with the whole body of hospital sisters together. Their other meals are often prepared and served by the wardmaids in the rooms in which they live and sleep—situated generally at one end of the ward or wards under their supervision. In the matter of leave and holidays they are allowed rather more than that given to staff nurses.

Probationers in their first year may be paid from £8 to £12, or sometimes are not paid at all. They rise to about £30 in their third year. Staff nurses commence at something between £22 and £30, and rise to £26 or £40 in the third year. Sisters may receive as much as £60 or

£80, but the more usual salary varies between £32 and £50. In addition to these sums, a uniform consisting of about three cotton dresses with caps and aprons is allowed, and about 2s. per week for washing.

The higher posts of assistant matron or superintendent are remunerated with a salary of from £35 to £60, while the head matron may receive anything from £70 to £150, depending upon the size of the hospital, or up to £200 or £250 in the larger and richer of the general hospitals.

In point of money the earnings of the nurse compare favourably with those of the daily governess and the upper domestic servant, while her social rank is distinctly superior to that of the latter. The prospects of marriage are also better, because of the constant contact into which she is brought with the students and their teachers in the course of her duties. Moreover, the uniform is most becoming to its wearers. So the profession has attractions of its own, which weigh in the balance against its undoubted hardships.

Life and Labour, etc., Industry, vol. 4, pp. 87-102.

5

Theatre, Music Hall, and Ballet

At the bottom of the scale [of actors] there is the 'general utility man' who has only a walking part and does not open his mouth more than once or twice in the evening. He owes his name to the fact that he is supposed to be able to fill a small part whenever his services may be required. There is also the 'walking lady'. Then there are 'heavy business' or villain's parts, and 'low comedian's' parts and 'juvenile's', which last are the 'minor lover' parts.

What is known as the stock company system has of late years given place more and more to the system of touring companies and of long runs. In the former system, the bond of union which holds a company together is local; it is the theatre to which they are attached, with its repertory of plays in which they are all versed, and which they represent in succession at brief intervals. In the latter system, the bond is not the place but the piece which the company has been formed to represent, whether in one given locality, or in a succession of localities.

The old stock company system has been credited with possessing greater merit as a school of acting than the system now in vogue. The frequent change of the plays put on the stage gave the actor more opportunity of developing his powers than he can have in a single character, to the exclusive representation of which he is bound for several months, or even for a year or two.

Some scope for training is, however, still afforded by the custom of 'under-studies'. These are young actors who study a major part in addition to their own in order to be able to serve as a substitute in case of need. And it is not unusual for actors to take dramatic pupils.

The chief methods of obtaining engagements are (1) by advertising, (2) through an agent, (3) applying directly to the management. Agents charge commissions varying between 5 and 10 per cent on the first fortnight's salary.

The remuneration of actors varies immensely. From 30s. to £4 or £5 a week is as accurate an estimate as can be given for the ordinary run.

Music Halls

Music halls appeal to a far larger class of pleasure seekers than theatres. Prices are not so high, and the entertainment provided does not, as a rule, demand an undivided attention. You can smoke and drink at your ease while the entertainment is going on, for a ledge fixed at the back of the seat of the man in front of you serves as a table on which to place your glass; and you may arrive late or go away early and be blessed by the management for doing so.

Hence the 'halls' are especially favoured by young men. But by no means exclusively so, for in the East End of London and South of the Thames, many will take their wives and children or sweethearts with them to pass a happy evening.

The great difference between an actor in a theatre and a music hall 'artiste' is that whereas the first has his part provided for him, the second has to depend upon his own individual efforts and abilities. Even in 'sketches'—such as the 'Burlesque sketch', the 'Negro sketch', the 'Comic knock-about sketch', the 'Sensational sketch', the 'Romantic sketch', the 'Pantomime sketch', and Comedy—music hall artistes bring their own company and their own piece, and the manager of the hall has nothing to do but to mount it in the matter of scenery.

The great advantage of music-hall work lies in the possibility of fulfilling engagements, or 'turns' as they are called, at two or three places in one evening. Performances usually last from 7.45 p.m. to 11.30, and even a little later, and the number of turns offered to the public during these hours varies between ten and thirty. The worst paid turn is the first, and the best are those between 9.30 and 11 p.m. Some men manage four turns in an evening, i.e. four separate performances in four different places.

The yearly income of men on the music-hall stage was put by one who was conversant with all branches of the profession at, £150 to £400 for third-rate men, £400 to £700 for second-rate men, and £1000 to £3000 for first-rate men.

Ballet

The salaries of the highest grade of ballet dancers range from five guineas a week to £20. The majority of these are foreigners, because it is said that the English girl will not train with sufficient assiduity to reach perfection. Next to them come the 'front eight' of the ballet dancers proper, then the middle rows, and lastly the back rows and 'extras'.

A dancer's position in the rows is determined by her proficiency and personal appearance. The back rows are composed of the beginners, the *passées*, and the unskilled. So long as a dancer retains the necessary amount of agility, she can remain on the boards well on into middle life; mother and daughter have danced in the same ballet before now. The dresser's art is quite equal to supplying the necessary appearance of youth.

Those who are skilful enough and fortunate enough to get into the *corps de ballet* of a house such as the Alhambra or Empire have pretty regular employment all the year round, but a great number can only obtain temporary engagements at pantomime time or other busy seasons. At other times they go on tour in the country, live with their parents (who are usually of the working class), or turn dress-makers or needlewomen, or have recourse to less reputable modes of obtaining a livelihood.

The front row of a regular ballet receives 30s. to 35s. for a week of seven or less performances. In pantomime time the favoured few in the front line may be able to count on 40s. per week for evening performances, and during the Christmas run of a popular piece will earn £3 a week of twelve performances for six or eight weeks. In the second row, where appearance is not of so much importance, not more than half that sum is earned, while the 'extra ladies', as the members of the back row are usually termed, will make something between 12s. 6d. and 18s. per week.

Girls who do dressmaking or are milliners or even domestic servants in the summer, often turn to the ballet in winter.

In reckoning the earnings of a ballet dancer we must remember that she has generally to find her own tights and shoes. Lisle thread or spun silk tights may be had for 8s. or 10s., but really good silk tights cost from 15s. 6d. to 21s. Shoes cost from 2s. 6d. to 5s., and last three or four weeks; this, however, depends very much on the condition of the flooring, and on the wearer's step, a heavy tread wearing out the shoes sooner than a light one.

Life and Labour, etc., Industry, vol. 4, pp. 129-39.

. 6

Artists' Models

Artists' models sometimes have been and often become ballet-girls. The regular pay for models whether for face or figure is 7s. for a whole day, including two meals, and 3s. 6d. or 5s. for half a day. At the Royal Academy they receive a good deal more—54s. a week—but their engagement at these rates does not last for more than one month, because the custom is for each visiting academician to bring a model with him for his term as a lecturer.

Male models are very frequently Italians, and the profession runs in families.

Female models as such lead a pleasant life, and in the end often marry one or other of those to whom they have been sitting. Those of them who are not fortunate enough to do this not infrequently end by going on the stage.

Life and Labour, etc., Industry, vol. 4, p. 133.

7

Fleet Street Journalists

London, as the headquarters of English journalism, has for its centre the locality of Fleet Street. Within a half-mile radius of this thorough-fare are produced the great bulk of the two thousand periodicals which are issued from London printing offices, more than five hundred of them being daily or weekly newspapers and journals.

In the office of a first-class morning newspaper, the business of the day will usually commence in the commercial department between 9 and 10 a.m., the manager arriving at about the latter hour. The first task will be the opening and reading of letters, of which there is invariably a large assortment, covering a wide range of topics and dating from many quarters. More particularly is this the case on Monday mornings, Sunday being not unnaturally the day chosen by unofficial correspondents who desire to invoke the powerful assistance of the press.

These communications being disposed of, with the aid of telegraph, telephone, and shorthand clerk, or consigned to the editorial or other departments (including the waste-paper basket), the manager has usually a number of callers to see; and, in a general oversight of all departments, finds a variety of matters needing attention. It is part of his business to engage all members of the staff, and to assign the daily duties of reporters, correspondents, etc. Foreign and special correspondents receive from him their commissions and act under his instructions, he orders all plant and machinery, signs cheques, and is generally consulted in matters connected with the management of the different departments. Business ceases at about 6 p.m. in the office of the manager, he being, for practical purposes, succeeded by the editor, whose work has then not long begun.

For the policy to be followed by the newspaper, as well as for the general accuracy of its contents, the editor is responsible, and with him rests the ultimate decision as to what shall or shall not appear. To conduct his paper on lines which shall be at once sound and popular, winning the approval of many and, so far as possible, giving offence to none, is no easy task. An editor must be able to express on the spur of the moment views on all public questions, and requires a wide knowledge of men and things, as well as good judgment and great tact.

The editor reaches his office at about four in the afternoon, and is followed by some of his contributors or assistants, with whom he talks over and arranges the subjects of tomorrow's leaders, special articles, notes, etc., often reserving to himself some portion of the work and allotting the remainder.

By 7 p.m. the principal sub-editor, foreign-editor, and their half-dozen or so assistants have reached the office. The sub-editor is mainly responsible for the news department, and on him it largely depends whether or no the paper is made interesting and readable. Apart from the demands of the advertisement manager and of the editor in respect to leaders, etc., the 'sub' has generally a pretty free hand in the filling up of the columns of the newspaper, and must see that the tit-bits of news—particularly if of an exclusive character—receive due prominence, that the headings are 'taking' or sensational, and that nothing important is omitted.

Commencing with the mass of telegrams from 'our own' or 'our special' correspondents, news agencies, etc., which are awaiting attention, he and his staff proceed to decipher, arrange, and get them into proper shape for the compositor, following on or dealing concurrently with law and police reports, city news, and accounts of the morning's meetings. As fast as these are disposed of, fresh batches of 'copy' pour in from parliamentary and other reporters, district correspondents, and many other sources, and have similarly to be dealt with, the stream continuing to flow with brief intervals until, at midnight, the editor receives from the master printer his nightly statement of the quantity of 'matter' already in type.

Not unusually the statement shows that the amount of still available space is very limited, if not entirely exhausted, and henceforward only the most important items, and those perhaps in a very condensed form, find their way into print. Sometimes even these measures will not suffice, and then the sub-editors must overhaul the reports already in proof, condensing or rewriting in accordance with the exigencies of space. Clipping, pruning and revising, toning down the adjectives of some, or the too poetic phrases of others, correcting errors of grammar, and steering clear, if it be in any way feasible, of the far-reaching and exceedingly stringent libel laws, the sub-editor and his staff continue at work till 2 a.m. or thereabouts, when, having seen the last belated paragraph safely on its way to the composing room, they are free to follow the example of their chief (who has probably preceded them by about half an hour), and, donning hat and coat, wend their way homewards through the quiet of early dawn, leaving to others the final stages of printing and publication.

Of reporters there will be from about six to ten on the ordinary staff of a morning paper, exlusive of a few ladies, who are of special use in reporting Court functions and other fashionable gatherings in which the mysteries of women's dress have to be noted and commented upon.

In the Press Gallery of the House of Commons there are during the height of the Session about 120 reporters, each paper having a staff varying from sixteen to six or seven, in addition to writers of parliamentary leaders, notes, etc. Acting under the direction of the chief reporter, they each in turn take a spell at reporting, and in the intervals transcribe their notes into longhand, or whilst waiting, beguile the time with smoke, chat, light refreshments, games, etc., in the comfortable rooms which are reserved for their use within the precincts of the 'House'.

On a newspaper such as we have described, editor and manager will be both highly paid, salaries usually ranging from £1000 to £2000, and rising in exceptional cases much higher than this; whilst assistant editors will get from £500 to £1000, sub-editors £400 to £600, and reporters £200 to £500. Members of the parliamentary staff receive from five guineas to eight guineas a week.

On morning papers of a secondary class, and on the evening and general weekly papers, the staff is much smaller, and rates of pay are on the whole from half to two-thirds of those prevailing on the leading morning journals.

There are several agencies which keep a special staff for supplying news to the London and Provincial Press; and there are a considerable number of men who make a somewhat precarious living by acting as scouts to the army of regular journalists, picking up odd items of police or other news, attending fires, inquests, etc., and who are paid at the rate of 1d. or 1½d. per printed line by the papers which accept their contributions.

Life and Labour, etc., Industry, vol. 4, pp. 150-6.

8

Cricket 'Pros'

Cricketers, especially first-class men, may be ranked among the lowest paid of all professional men.

Professional cricketers receive a regular wage of 30s. to 40s. per week during the season, and in fine weather can double the sum by the tips given by those to whom they bowl at practice-nets. The Marylebone Club offers £4 to players in winning matches of two or three days at Lord's, and £3 10s. if the match is lost. If the match is away from home the 'pro' is given £5 or £6 for two or three-day matches (out of which he must pay his expenses), and £2 plus expenses in one-day matches. Umpires are paid £2 per match of two or three days and expenses, whether at Lord's or away, and £1 with expenses for one-day games.

At the Oval the rates are much the same, but the Surrey Club allows its employees a retaining wage of 20s. and a few 30s. during the winter, while the M.C.C. does not.

For big fixtures like the 'Gentlemen v. Players', etc., 'pros' are given £10 and the umpire £5.

The season lasts from the beginning of May until the end of August. In winter cricketers are sometimes retailers of games requisites. Often they return to the trade—boot-making, or whatever it may be—to which they belong, and sometimes keep a public-house. After a number of years' service, it is usual for large clubs to initiate a match in which the gate-money and subscriptions are given over to the men benefited.

Life and Labour, etc., Industry, vol. 4, pp. 146-7.

(d) A ROUND OF TRADESMEN

I

Drapers

———

Drapers' shops vary in style—low, medium and high class—according to the customers for whose wants they cater, or more roughly according to the neighbourhood in which they are situated. Walworth is as much above Bermondsey New Road as Lewisham or Holloway would consider themselves above Walworth; and a widening gulf separates these from shops in Kensington, in Oxford Street and in Regent Street. But it is more to our purpose, as affecting the conditions of employment, to classify shops according to their size, viz. large, medium and small.

Small shops are those in which only the draper and his family and perhaps one assistant are engaged; shops of medium size, those where the employer himself lives on the premises, and where the number of assistants is not too great for personal relations to exist between employer and employed; and large shops are those huge modern establishments where the numbers employed range from 50 to 1500 or 2000. In such as these the personal relation necessarily is lost; everything is done by rule, and the business is a huge machine working more or less perfectly on prescribed lines from which no deviation is permitted.

Hours of Work. The day's work in a large draper's shop begins at 7 or 7.30, when the porters come, followed shortly by a number of junior assistants and apprentices, known as the 'squadding' party, who dust and prepare the shop. An hour later the other assistants arrive and the early party go to breakfast. The dressing of the windows is then proceeded with, and may take as much as two or three hours to complete, but by 10 or 11 at latest all are in their places behind the counters, and from then till 1 o'clock is the busiest part of the day in City and West

End shops. Closing time is 6 or 7 in winter, and an hour later in summer.

In establishments of medium size—to be found mostly in the suburbs—the assistants do not tidy their shops overnight, for such shops remain open later, not closing their door before 9 or 10, and often having late customers who once in must be served. In these shops the busiest part of the day is from 7.30 to closing time, especially on Saturday.

In small shops attended to by the draper and his family, the hours are often longer but the conditions are less irksome. The family lives in the room at the back of the shop, emerging when wanted. If there is an assistant at all, she will be a young girl, living at her own home and paid a few shillings a week for her services. In the morning an occasional customer may drop in, and in the dinner-hour children come for cottons and needles or other small articles. In the evening business becomes more lively.

In first-class shops the hours of the men may be stated at from 59 to 70, and for the women from 56 to 67 per week. In medium-sized shops the total hours will be from 71 to 76, and in some places even more. Quite small shops, opening early and late, have no quotable hours of work.

Excepting the married men, nearly all the assistants live on the premises, or in lodging-houses controlled by the employers. The food, as a rule is plain but good. The men have mostly single beds—two, three, or four to a room. The girls not infrequently sleep two in a bed, and sometimes as many as six to a room.

Wages. When out of his apprenticeship or period of probation a young man will receive £15 or £20 a year, or in low-class houses perhaps only £12. The rate of pay rises gradually to £40 or £50 for assistants behind the counter, and situations of shopwalker or buyer are the prizes of the profession. The salaries of shopwalkers range from £70 to £120 in the lower class trade, and amount to £150 or £200 in large stores or West End houses, and those of buyers are about half as much more, rising to £300 and more. Buyers seldom live on the premises; shopwalkers may or may not, and are paid more or less accordingly.

Young women begin at £10 or £20 and rise to £40. Few prize situations are open to them, and the greater number do not get beyond £20 or £30. They pass on to matrimony. With women as with men the larger and better shops pay the most.

In addition to salary, 'premiums', or commissions upon the sales effected, are given in all except a few high-class houses, where the custom is regarded unfavourably as leading assistants to press goods upon unwilling customers; such firms give commissions only to the heads of departments on the general results.

Rules, etc. Every establishment has its code of rules, and these in large houses are very numerous, covering every detail of shop and house life—many of them, perhaps, necessary, but others of a trivial, and, one would think, vexatious character, difficult to remember, and still more difficult to rigorously observe. They are usually enforced by a system of fines, such as 1d. to 6d. for being late in the morning, proportioned to the number of minutes lost; 6d. to 1s. for being late in coming in at night; 2s. 6d. for not coming in at all; an equally heavy penalty for allowing a customer to go away unserved without informing the shop-walker. Then there are a series of fines for offences against cleanliness—such as for bringing blacking into the bedrooms. Fines are usually deducted from the premiums earned, and are devoted to the library, or towards paying the doctor's bill.

With shops which close early on Saturday it is usual for assistants to spend Sunday away with friends, or at their homes, returning on Sunday night. Some firms even expect those who sleep on the premises to be out all day Sunday, which is very hard on such as have no friends near.

Health. The long hours worked, combined with long standing, have a very deterimental effect upon drapers' assistants, causing anaemia and a general deterioration of health, which renders them an easy prey to indigestion, constipation, and kindred maladies.

Some of the evil effects might be lessened by the general provision of seats for assistants, so that when not actually engaged with a customer they could take a few minutes' rest. Unfortunately seats behind the counter are only provided in a small minority of shops, and even in these establishments they are seldom used. As one employer said, 'It is necessary that they should always appear busy, even if not much business is being done; this is one of the great arts of the trade'.

G. E. ARKELL, *Life and Labour, etc.*, Industry, vol. 3, pp. 68-70.

2

Tailors

Outfitters and tailors' salesmen form a numerous body, and are quite distinct from the men who make the garments. The business is divided into two branches: the 'bespoke' and the ready-made or 'R.M.' trade, as the latter is familiarly called.

The division tends to become more sharply defined. A person wishing clothes made to order will usually not go to a shop selling ready-made goods, nor will purchasers of ready-made clothes go to a bespoke tailor, although the latter often keeps a small stock of ready-made clothing to accommodate customers, and the former frequently advertises his goods as 'made to measure'.

In large establishments salesmen are known as first, second, third, and so on, and, by a tacit understanding, the first or senior salesman has a prior right to serve customers.

The hours of work are those usual in shops. In the City and West End 8.30 a.m. to 7.30 p.m., whilst in the suburbs the closing time is two hours later. A few salesmen live on their employers' premises, but to do this is unusual, and is becoming still more so. Some employers, however, continue to provide dinner and tea for their assistants, so that they may be always within call should their services be needed.

Remuneration is by salary and commission. The salary may be anything from 20s. to 60s. or 80s. per week, the higher sums being only paid by the best firms. In ordinary houses 30s. to 35s. a week is usual, the latter being considered a good wage.

The commission, called 'B.Y.' (an abbreviation of the word bounty) adds 5s. or more to each man's earnings, the amount varying according to the house and the opportunities of the salesman. This commission may be a fixed sum on each suit, but more frequently varies according to the material, being greatest on goods that the firm wishes to sell quickly, the amount being marked on the ticket attached to the roll of cloth. In this way old patterns are disposed of and the stock kept fresh and unsoiled.

When a man becomes first salesman, his ambition is to start business on his own account, and to do this he must have a cutter. Thus the usual plan is for a cutter and a salesman to combine in starting a new business. Should the salesman not be able to do this, his prospects become distinctly worse as age advances, and when he reaches fifty he has little chance of obtaining a new situation if thrown out of work.

Life and Labour, etc., Industry, vol. 3, pp. 11-12.

3

Hosiers

A linendraper will sometimes call himself also a hosier, but it is in ladies' hosiery mostly that he deals, and the term 'hosier' is almost exclusively applied in the trade to the dealers in ties, socks, etc., for men's wear. To this is added the trade of shirt-makers.

The assistants are almost invariably men. Youths are taken as apprentices for three or four years, a premium of £30 or £40 being paid for the shorter period. These youths are boarded and lodged, and, if a premium is paid, may receive a small weekly stipend, equal in amount to the return of the premium at the end of the period. When out of their apprenticeship, if they continue to live in the house, the young men earn about £20 a year; but if, as is becoming more general, they lodge elsewhere, a weekly wage of about 16s. is paid. In addition, commission on sales is given, which may amount to 5s. for juniors, rising to 15s. per week for first salesmen.

As a rule, hosiers stand aloof from the Early Closing movement, and it is evident that their interests are somewhat different from those of drapers. The business depends more on chance customers, to whom the sight of the shop recalls some want, or whose fancy is attracted by some article in the window. The longer the shop is open where men may pass, the more trade is likely to be done, and thus the hours are long. These shops usually open at 8.30, and remain open till 10 p.m., even 11 or 12 on Saturday. The hours in the West End are shorter, for their customers do not often pass after 8 o'clock. Some of the City shops have adopted early closing on Saturday—basing their action, no doubt, on a similar calculation.

Life and Labour, etc., Industry, vol. 3, pp. 80-1.

4

Hatters

Fifty or sixty years ago the beaver hatters regarded with some scorn the manufacture of the new-fangled silk hat, but soon were obliged either to leave the trade or adopt what was accepted by the public as an improvement. Today silk nap is in its turn giving way to felt.

Silk hat manufacture is a declining trade. It is still, however, a rule that men should wear a fashionable hat; but recent times have led to some of them, painfully aware of the incongruity of a good hat and shabby clothes, to wear a 'bowler'.

The manufacture of silk hats is concentrated to a great extent in the neighbourhood of Blackfriars Road. Felt hatting is of minor importance in London, the chief seat of the manufacture being at Denton in Lancashire and Stockport in Cheshire. All the hats so extensively advertised at 3s. 6d. and 3s. 9d., and by a few enterprising men as 'Our splendid 2s. 6d. hat', are manufactured in the Provinces. St Albans is the chief centre for men's straw hats, and Luton for ladies'. Caps, whether for bicycling, golf or travelling, are chiefly made in the Jewish workshops of East London, although these feel keenly the competition of Manchester. Even caps bearing the names of well-known hatters are made in Whitechapel.

Several of the London factories have one or more retail shops. Salesmen enter the shops as boys, and learn to block and iron a hat, and when promoted to the counter, should be able to take the shape of a customer's head if necessary. The hours of work in West End shops are from 9 to 7; in other localities rather longer.

Life and Labour, etc., Industry, vol. 3, pp. 26-38.

5

Bakers

In London, and also in many provincial towns, the baker of bread turns night into day. He works for long hours in an almost tropical temperature, and inhales the gas-laden air of a bakehouse, often small and ill-ventilated, and very generally placed below the level of the ground.

The average hours in London are 70 or 80 per week, but some men are employed for fully 90 or even 100 hours. The work is not absolutely continuous. In the process of preparing the sponge or dough, there are periods of waiting while the ferment acts. One operation may be alternated with another, or the time filled up in the moulding of the loaves, or in the hurrying forward of a batch of rolls, but nevertheless there are times when the men may sit and smoke or even sleep awhile, trusting to the foremen or first hand to rouse them when fermentation has gone far enough, or when the oven doors are opened.

Subject to local dfferences, the wages for 'foremen' and 'first' hands are 35s. to 50s. a week, for 'second' hands 25s. to 35s., and for 'third' hands 22s. to 32s., with allowances of bread and flour in each case.

That the men at present, in many cases, suffer in health there seems little doubt. Behind the floury whiteness of their work-a-day face lies too often the pallor of ill-health. They lack energy. The masters complain of stupidity and lack of interest in their work; they say that the men 'have no ambition'. The trade union officials find them apathetic, and therefore poor material for their purpose; and in despair turn to legislation to find a cure for the bad conditions under which so many of their men live.

Life and Labour, etc., Industry, vol. 4, pp. 144-58.

6

Dairymen

In Kelly's London Directory for 1895, 1450 dairymen are enumerated, of whom, judging by their names, not less than 529 are of Welsh extraction. The name Jones appears in the list 103 times, Davies or Davis 83, Evans 63, Williams 38, Morgan 36, Jenkins 30, Edwards 29, Lewis 22 times, and so on through Griffiths, Hughes, Lloyd, Owen, Price, Rees, Thomas, etc. The Welsh are a clannish people, and no doubt their numbers in the milk trade have been greatly swelled by the immigration of friends and relations of the original founders of businesses.

Earnings. Of the men employed in the London dairies, the vast proportion are milk-carriers, though in large businesses there are in addition managers of branches, foremen of rounds, and a few men employed in making butter.

Managers are paid from 30s. to 60s. a week, with a house or rooms rent free. In most cases they have, in addition, milk, eggs, and butter for their own consumption. Round foremen receive from 30s. to 35s. a week, and as a rule get a commission on each new customer they obtain. The wages of carriers range from 20s. to 26s. a week. Those who drive a cart are usually paid 1s. more than those who wheel a 'pram'; their duties, however, are somewhat harder, as they generally have to attend to their horse and cart. In addition to the fixed wage, a commission is always paid of from 2s. to 4s. for each new customer who takes a quart a day.

Wages and commission, however, seldom represent the whole earnings of the milk-carrier; there is no doubt that by sundry illegitimate means he too often helps himself. In one way or another the earnings of the carriers average 33s. a week; those who are abnormally dishonest make more for a time; but short measure, or an unusual excess of water in the milk is likely in the end to rouse the anger of a long-suffering public, and to lead to complaints to the master, who in his own interest as well as that of the customer will dismiss his peccant carrier.

Hours of work. In the wholesale trade work begins habitually at 4 o'clock [a.m.]; the man ought to be finished not later than 5 p.m. In the retail trade work begins an hour later, and lasts with intervals till 6 or 7 o'clock [in the evening]. In most businesses each man has to do three rounds, the second round—when eggs and butter are taken as well as milk—being called 'the pudding round'.

Both in wholesale and retail trade, the actual hours vary to some extent for each man. When once the men leave the dairy they are almost free from supervision, and can, within certain limits, get through their work as fast or as slowly as they please; one man will spend a good deal of time in gossiping, another, perhaps, cannot resist the temptation of an occasional halt for liquid refreshment.

The great grievance of carriers and cowmen is the necessity for working every day in the year. There is hardly any other trade in which the work is so continuous. The cowman must do his milking every day, and the carrier must work his round at least twice every day, from one year's end to another.

The grievance is not an easy one to remedy. The best-intentioned cow can only yield a certain quantity of milk at each milking, and even were it possible to forestall the supplies so as to send out in the morning the whole of the milk required for the day, a double quantity could not well be delivered in one round. That the public would ever consent to curtail their supply, though but for one day in the week, is not at all likely. In no trade, perhaps, is the demand of the consumer more imperative. Man's wants may be disregarded, but in this case it is the women and children who are to be considered, and above all, the voice of the baby, which would make itself heard.

General condition of the trade. The sale of milk has increased, and is increasing quite out of proportion to the growth of population, but the cutting of the price has made it difficult for the dairyman to earn a profit unless he works on a large scale, or adopts methods of trading which, if not actually dishonest, are not such as his customers would be likely to approve.

The practice of 'washing' or watering the milk, though still very prevalent, is less common than it was. At one time certain members of the trade boasted of their ability to make one churn do the work of three. Those 'good old days' are gone; inspectors are more numerous and more active than they were, and the risk of prosecution for selling watered milk is very great. But though 'washing' has declined thousands of gallons are sold daily as pure milk, which have undergone a great deterioration in their progress from the cow to the consumer. The practice of abstracting some portion of the cream, or of mixing separated with whole milk, is increasingly prevalent.

Another objectionable custom is the colouring of the milk. The public, or some portion of it, prefer a yellow liquid. As the vast majority of cows persist in yielding white milk, the dairyman has been obliged to call in art to remedy the deficiencies of nature. The added matter is said to be anatto, a harmless vegetable substance.

Life and Labour, etc., Industry, vol. 3, pp. 173-84.

7

Butchers

Butchers in the strict sense of the word, i.e. men who kill their own meat, are a rapidly decreasing class.

Wages throughout the retail trade vary greatly. Head shopmen or managers earn from 30s. to 70s. a week; assistants from 15s. to 30s.; boys from 7s. to 14s. Slaughtermen are paid at the same rate as other assistants, but have some perquisites, such as the blood and bladder, from which, in some shops, they make as much as 8s. or 10s. a week. The men are nearly always boarded, and in most cases lodge in the house; if they sleep out they are usually allowed an additional wage of from 3s. to 5s. There appears, however, to be a growing tendency for men both to lodge and board out.

Hours, except in the West End, are from 6 or 7 a.m. to 8 or 9 p.m. on Tuesday, Wednesday, Thursday, and Friday, and till 12 p.m. on Saturday. Most butchers now close at 5 on Monday. Half an hour is allowed for breakfast and an hour for dinner; tea is usually taken in the shop. In the West End the hours are from 8 to 8.

Except in the West End, again, the trade is not seasonal; there, during the London season, extra men are generally engaged, but they are never skilled butchers, and do nothing except serve in the shop and go round with the carts. During the slack season the regular men usually take a compulsory holiday of a month or, in some cases, two months each.

As to dress, the men buy their own. Jean smocks cost from 8s. to 15s. each; and those made of serge, from 23s. to 30s. Aprons cost about 4s. each. A man will probably require two smocks and two aprons in a year.

Life and Labour, etc., Industry, vol. 3, pp. 201-2.

8

Grocers

Originally a grocer was a tradesman who sold little else but tea, coffee, cocoa, sugar and spices; his tendency to entrench to some extent on the provinces of other trades is no doubt of long standing, but it is only under the stress of competition with 'the stores' that he has gradually extended his business until it now embraces a number of trades which were at one time totally distinct; two indeed, those of the Italian warehouseman, and the tallow chandler, seem now to have no separate existence.

The Italian warehouseman sold only foreign produce, such as macaroni, olive oil, sardines, etc.; his trade is now merged with that of the grocer. The tallow chandler dealt mainly in soap and candles, articles which are now sold only by grocers or oil and colourmen.

Other trades, such as that of the provision dealer, the cheese-monger, and the oil and colourman, are still separately carried on, but there is much overlapping between them and the grocer, while nearly all the prominent men combine these various businesses under one or it may be many roofs, for grocers and oil and colourmen have a number of branch establishments more commonly than the members of any other trade.

The change in the character of the articles supplied—as for instance, the production of preserved milk and canned vegetables and meats, and the supply of pickles and preserves, formerly made at home—and altogether an amazing extension in the requisites of household consumption, has had a great influence on the development of the grocer's business. The wine licences also had an effect.

In a trade so large and, as far as labour is concerned, so unorganized, there is, naturally, great diversity of wage, but the general scale of remuneration appears to be as follows: The manager of a branch shop gets from 30s. to 60s. a week, with board and lodging; a first-counterman from 24s. to 35s. or from 14s. to 25s. with board and lodging; a second-counterman from 20s. to 25s., or from 10s. to 16s. with board and lodging. Though probably the majority of grocers' assistants still live in, there is a growing tendency to rebel against the custom.

Men have to buy aprons for themselves at a cost of from 1s. to 2s. each, and will require from three to six a year. They are also obliged to wear several clean shirts a week, which involves an expenditure of not less than 1s. a week for washing.

Excepting in high-class businesses in the West End, the hours are very long. The almost universal time of opening is 8 a.m. The usual closing hour for the first four days of the week is 9 or 9.30. On Fridays few shops close before 10.30 or 11. and on Saturday the usual hour is 12.

In spite of the long hours, the trade does not appear to be unhealthy; there is little reason why men should not work on to a good old age, yet a grocers' assistant who is elderly is exceedingly rare. This is due partly to the fact that most masters prefer that their men should live on the premises, and therefore avoid those who are married; but the chief cause which drives men out of the trade early in life is the preference of customers for youth. Some, when too old for the retail, get work in the wholesale trade, but the majority seem to turn to travelling or canvassing, a field of labour for which they are usually well qualified, as they are better educated and socially of a higher class than all other shop employees, except drapers' assistants.

Life and Labour, etc., Industry, vol. 3, pp. 216-20.

9

Greengrocers

Few men lead a harder life than a master greengrocer, at all events when, as most of them are, he is in a small way of business. He must be at [Covent Garden] market not later than 4 a.m., and on most days he is at work till 10 or 10.30 p.m., and on Saturdays till 1 or 1.30 a.m. His assistants have somewhat shorter hours; one of them at least will be required for market work; in summer he will begin at 3 a.m., and finish about 6 p.m.; in winter his day's work will, perhaps, be two hours shorter. He reaches home from market about 8 a.m., and spends the remainder of his time in soliciting orders or delivering goods, and in attending to the horses. The shop salesmen work, as a rule, the same hours as grocers, though, perhaps, if anything, a little longer.

The wages of assistants vary from 20s. to 30s. a week. Men have nothing to buy except aprons, at a cost of about 5s. a year.

The busy time is during the 'soft fruit season', for about three months from the end of May, and at this period most masters require extra hands, while additional help may also be needed on Saturdays and at Christmas. As the work is quite unskilled, those who are taken on at times of stress are seldom greengrocers, but for the most part men who do not seek regular work.

Among shopkeepers, greengrocers stand low in the social scale; the work is hard and rough; both masters and men are, as a rule, poorly educated; no other business can be started with so small a capital, and little skill or knowledge of any kind is required.

Life and Labour, etc., Industry, vol. 3, pp. 226-7.

10

Coalmen

Coal for household use comes by rail chiefly from the Midland Counties, the trucks containing it being shunted into sidings at various convenient points and there unloaded and reloaded for delivery.

The recognized rate for delivering coal is 7d. per ton, and a carman will usually do six to eight tons (three or four loads of two tons each) in a day. A shilling a day is paid for driving the horse, and one penny for watering it, and sometimes the carman gets a little for attending to his horses.

A story is told of a well-known firm having, in answer to a complaint from a prim lady customer as to muddy boots and insolence, sent a letter in which they regretted they 'had not been able to secure the services of a gentleman to do the work'. It is, indeed, very far from a genteel occupation—hard, dirty, often stifling and exhausting—and as is the work, so are the men—rough of manner and tongue. They eat well and, as a rule, drink heavily, swallowing their 'two or three tons' (or eightpences) a day, and their four or five half-pints before breakfast. Usually a 'score' is run up at a neighbouring tavern, so that such money as can be spared from the home—and often unfortunately a good deal more—is mortgaged to the publican before it is earned.

With all this, however, the coalie has qualities which commend themselves to our race. Sturdy and independent, the men stand by each other through good or ill report, readily admitting their failings while doing little to remedy them.

Life and Labour, etc., Industry, vol. 3, pp. 431-44.

II

Undertakers

Undertaking is a seasonal trade, and the busy time is, as would be expected, from November until April, though a sudden rush may come at any time on the advent of cold winds or fogs. What undertakers prefer is a good steady death-rate. Fluctuations annoy them, for any sharp rise in the rate is sure to be followed by a period of slackness. For instance, the influenza epidemic greatly overworked the trade in the years 1891 to 1893. The weaker members of the community were swept away, and, as a consequence, there is now a reaction, and this year (1894) has been one of the worst ever experienced in the annals of undertakers. This decrease in volume of business is also partly due to better sanitation; and the autumnal rise in the death-rate, which was known to the trade as the 'Plum Season', is now a thing of the past.

There is no regular apprenticeship [to undertaking], and though but little skill is needed, there is not much temptation for outsiders to enter the trade. Fathers generally bring up their sons to this business, which, when all is said, is one that habit can only partially rob of its unpleasantness, and which at times is replete with horror.

The proverbial jollity of undertakers' men is not so marked now as formerly. They must be steady men, we are told—'the master's reputation depends on it'. Such jollity as still survives is no doubt due to the natural reaction from the sad, and sometimes dreadful, scenes with which they are brought in contact, or to the levity which, with all of us, creeps in upon or succeeds a sustained effort after gravity of demeanour, animated, perhaps, by the gifts of customers and a share of the funeral hospitalities.

Coffins are made by 'coffin-makers', who belong to this industry only, and do not overlap with either carpenters or cabinet-makers. No great degree of skill is required, and the men working for an undertaker are often chosen for other qualities than an intimate knowledge of their craft. Thus it is more important to have a strong, presentable man, with a good suit of black clothes of his own, than a highly skilled workman. And further, respectful and, if possible, sympathetic manners, are especially necessary; for future orders depend much on the satisfaction of present customers and their consequent recommendation.

Coffin-makers often accompany the funeral to the grave as attendants, but in large establishments there is a special and permanent staff of men who, when not so employed, are made useful as carriage-washers and grooms.

Coffins are mostly made of oak or elm, and into them shells are sometimes fitted, which may be either of wood or lead, but the latter is very little used now.

In other respects also funerals now involve less expense and pomp than formerly, and, as a rule, the poor pay proportionately rather more for show than do the rich. Plumed hearses are no longer used, except, it is said, by costermongers and chimney-sweeps, and others upon whom ancient custom has a very strong hold. Crape and long silk scarves used formerly to be provided for all the mourners by the undertaker. This expense is never incurred now, and 'mutes' are very rarely seen. On the other hand, flowers, now so usual, were not then thought of. They would have been considered Popish. They, however, are not supplied by the undertaker.

Again, burials on Sunday are now very rare, and this has prevented many men, altogether outside the business, from taking on this work as an extra. Many a young shop assistant was formerly not unwilling to take a Sunday outing in the suburbs, even though he had to get there on a hearse.

There seems to be no importation of coffins ready made from abroad. Sometimes those who die in foreign lands are sent over to be buried in England, but the superstition of sailors prevents their being shipped in anything possessing the outward shape of a coffin; they come instead in cases as pianofortes, or as 'specimens in natural history'.

Life and Labour, etc., Industry, vol. I, pp. 205-9.

(e) PUBLIC SERVICE

I

Soldiers of the Queen

Many people would smile incredulously if told that London is a military centre, and yet nearly ten thousand troops are constantly quartered there, and it contains within its bounds that huge establishment which Englishmen often term *the* Arsenal.

The ordinary daily life of the soldier is divided into three parts: general and field drills occupy his morning, detail drills or stable duties fill a great part of the afternoon, whilst his evenings are mostly given to social, domestic or barrack-room life. The actual duties depend much upon the branch of the service, and the heaviest work falls to men in the Royal Artillery and the Army Service Corps.

In summer the routine of an artilleryman's day is as follows: Reveille sounds at 5.30 a.m.; at 6 a.m. he goes to the stables, where grooming and feeding his horse occupies him until breakfast at 7 a.m. Drill lasts from 8.30 to 11; from 11.30 until about 12.30 is spent in the stables, and at 12.45 dinner is served. At 2 o'clock drivers return to the stables once more and gunners go to carbine drill. From 3 to 4.45 the men are free; some go out, others rest, but most have some little duties to perform, and in nearly every barrack-room three or four men may be seen seated on their cots cleaning their equipment. At 5 p.m. the bugle sounds for stables, and at 6 o'clock tea is ready. Except those employed as guards and pickets the men are free after tea until the time for turning in, and this may be deferred until midnight if a pass be obtained.

In other branches of the service the general routine is similar, with variations caused by particular duties.

Sunday is an off-day; with few exceptions the men are free for the day after attending the morning Church parade.

His official duties finished, little restraint is placed upon the soldier in his leisure moments, whether afternoon or evening. He generally leaves the barrack-room as soon as possible, these apartments being usually dull and cheerless. The men must 'either sit on their cots or on wooden forms. No chairs are provided. In most barracks, however, there are recreation rooms, provided with billiard tables and other amusements; reading-rooms supplied with newspapers and periodicals of various kinds, and regimental libraries to the use of which a small monthly subscription entitles a man.

Outside his barracks the soldier, stationed in London, has a wide choice in the disposal of his leisure. There is always a theatre or music hall within easy reach. Nor are other allurements wanting. The public-houses near the barracks are arranged with an eye to his tastes (at a well-known soldiers' house in Woolwich, all the barmaids wear red blouses); civilians ready to stand treat are often to be found, whilst if a soldier has any money in his pocket, there are dangerous friends, both male and female, who will help him to spend it. To counteract such attractions, Institutes, Homes and Clubs of various kinds have been opened by religious bodies and private individuals.

Pay and Allowances. With some exceptions amongst the officers, pay in the Army is reckoned per day. On joining the Service, the pay of the private ranges upward from a minimum of 1s. a day in infantry regiments. The Foot Guards commence at 1s. 1d., Engineers 1s. 1½s., Army Service Corps, Ordnance Store Corps, and Medical Staff Corps, 1s. 2d., Royal Artillery 1s. 2½d. and the Household Cavalry at 1s. 9d. a day.

In addition, every soldier is provided with clothing, quarters, bedding, fuel and light, a daily ration of ¾ lb. of meat and 1 lb. of bread, and, when required, medical attendance. The expenses which may in our times be called necessary, but which are borne by the soldiers, are for groceries and vegetables, washing and haircutting. For groceries and vegetables, 3d. to 4d. a day is deducted from his pay, and a halfpenny or a penny for washing.

The young soldier can thus reckon positively upon a net weekly sum which amounts to not less than 4s. 4½d. in the Foot Guards, 5s. 3d. in the Artillery, and 9s. 0½d. in the Life Guards. The sum seems very small, but when he has become an efficient soldier, a well-conducted man's income is augmented by additional allowances known as 'Good Conduct', 'Extra-duty', 'Working', and in certain cases, 'Corps' pay.

For non-commissioned officers the rates of pay are: lance corporals or acting bombardiers, 1s. 3d. to 1s. 9d. a day; corporals, bombardiers and second corporals, 1s. 8d. to 2s. 8d. a day; lance-sergeants, 2s. to

2s. 4d. a day; sergeants, 2s. 4d. to 3s. 3d. a day; colour-sergeants, 3s. to 3s. 4d. a day; and staff sergeants from 3s. 6d. to 5s. a day. Men holding warrant rank as sergeant-majors receive 5s. to 6s. a day.

Pensions. Men permitted to re-engage, in order to complete twenty-one years with the colours, become entitled to a pension varying according to rank and length of service.

Family life. For a soldier to marry is not an offence against military law, but the proportion of men in each regiment who may belong to the married establishment is fixed, and the authorities will not recognize wives of men married 'off the strength'. The regulations permit all warrant officers and most non-commissioned officers of the rank of sergeant to marry; below that rank the number on the married roll in each corps varies from 3 to 7 per cent.

When the private has obtained his place on the roll, he is entitled to a room in the married quarters, an allowance of coal (120 lb. a week in winter and 80 lb. in summer), as well as light. He may also draw his daily ration of bread and meat. Thus, if a guardsman, he is provided with lodging, rations, fuel and light, and 8s. 2d. a week in money.

The position of a man marrying without permission is very different. His official status in the regiment is precisely the same as that of his bachelor comrades. Be he ever so careful, he cannot, unless he has good conduct badges, give his wife more than 5s. 3d. a week. Unfortunately, the number of men married off the roll is considerable, and especially so in regiments quartered in London. Often the wife is or was a domestic servant. She may retain her situation for some time after marriage, but sooner or later she has to leave it and a room is taken within a short distance of the barracks, the rent of which will absorb a large part of the man's money. Here the woman commences a difficult struggle to support herself; and if children are born, the family soon seeks charity, or the woman is tempted to have recourse to prostitution for a livelihood.

Life and Labour, etc., Industry, vol. 4, pp. 58-66.

2

London Policemen

The Metropolitan police force was established in 1829, as was also the City police. These two organizations divide the London area between them. The City police, numbering 1018, are responsible for the City 'and its liberties'; and the Metropolitan police, with 15,216 men, under-

An operation at
ring Cross
ital

Cassells' 'Living
London' (1906)

'Lost in London'

Illustrated London
News (1888), British
Museum Photo

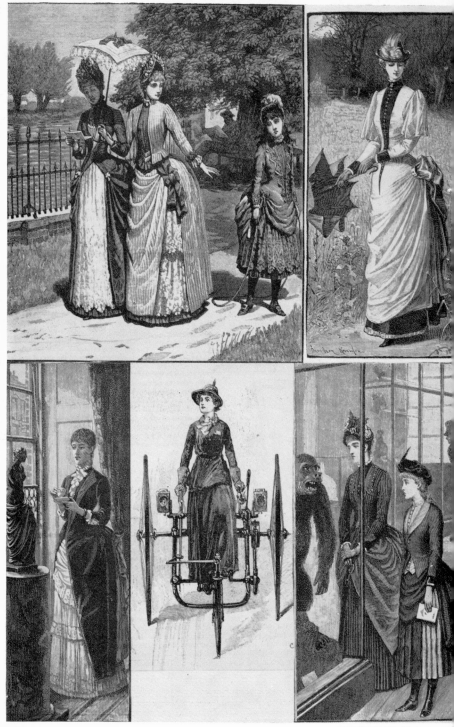

8. Fashionable attire for 'Forsyte' ladies

takes the surrounding district within a radius of fifteen miles from Charing Cross.

A policeman is liable to duty at any time in the twenty-four hours, but the time spent regularly on his beat is only eight hours out of the twenty-four, being either two watches of four hours in the daytime, between 6 a.m. and 10 p.m., or one period of eight hours in the night, between 10 p.m. and 6 a.m. Night and day duty are shared in rotation.

The hours on beat do not by any means include all the time ordinarily occupied, as a constable has to attend the court as required, and is expected to work up his cases, and on extraordinary occasions, when a larger force than usual is needed in the streets, he may be kept on duty for many extra hours.

The policeman's work varies greatly according to the district in which he is stationed. In a suburban neighbourhood, except for occasional disturbances, the duties are not heavy, but tedious, and the prolonged walking, even at the regulation pace, is wearying to the feet, The ordinary policeman must constantly perambulate his beat, visiting every street and entry. At night he examines the fastenings of windows and doors, marks entrances so that he can tell whether they have been visited in the interval of his round, and walking silently in the shadows of the houses comes upon the belated pedestrian with startling suddenness.

In busy neighbourhoods the strain is greater, especially upon those engaged in regulating vehicular traffic, for whom special reliefs are found necessary. 'When in doubt ask a policeman' is a rule largely adopted by visitors to the Metropolis, and, bombarded by a series of not always coherent questions, the London constable almost invariably succeeds in giving courteous replies.

In addition to their primary duties—the prevention of crime and the detection of offenders—the police have been charged with the enforcement of special laws and other obligations for which their widespread organization and exact local knowledge fit them. They deliver magistrates' orders and serve summonses. The Licensing department examines and licenses hackney carriages, omnibuses and tramcars, and issues the licences to the drivers and conductors. Nearly 30,000 articles left in these vehicles during 1894 were dealt with by the Lost Property Office. They have to see that public-houses are properly conducted during the day and closed during the prohibited hours; that bicycle lamps are lighted at the proper time and kept alight; they have to look after stray and unmuzzled dogs, and to assist sheriffs' officers and county court bailiffs. Additional duties are imposed under the Public Health Act, the Explosives Act, the Pedlars, the Gun Licence, the Contagious

Diseases (Animals), the Vagrancy, and other statutes too numerous to mention.

Neither Sundays nor other public holidays are times of rest for the police, but on Sundays the number of men is reduced. One day off in fourteen is allowed, and after twelve months' service in the Metropolitan and eighteen months' in the City police, sergeants and constables have a week or ten days, and inspectors two or three weeks' leave annually.

Pay and allowances. The scale of pay is higher in the City than with the Metropolitan police and was raised for both forces in 1890. In the City the pay for constables begins at 25s. and rises gradually till it reaches 36s. 3d. at the end of six years. Sergeants commence with 41s. 5d. and rise to 45s. 3d. For inspectors 57s. 6d. is the minimum. In the Metropolitan force the pay at first is 24s. and rises to 32s. in eight years. Sergeants start at 34s and rise to 40s. Station sergeants begin at 45s. Inspectors begin at 56s.

In addition to their nominal wages, various allowances increase the real earnings of the police. All are supplied with uniform clothing and boots, or a money allowance instead. Men living in the stations receive a small allowance of coals. Special duties also carry extra pay. Men employed at public buildings, etc., receive about 1s. a day and those engaged in regulating the street traffic 1s. to 2s. 6d. a week in addition to their regular money. Superannuation also must be counted as a benefit, for the deduction of (at most) 2½ per cent from their wages does not nearly provide the pension of two-thirds pay which the men are entitled after twenty-six years' service.

Other legitimate though unrecognized emoluments come in return for occasional services rendered, as for instance that of calling workmen in the morning.

Candidates must be under 27 years of age, and, if married, must not have more than two children when joining. The standard of height is 5 ft. 9 in., and the medical test is very strict; more than half the applicants failing to pass the doctor. The army provides a good proportion of the men. The bulk of police recruits, however, are countrymen, straight from rural employment, to whom the wages offered appear wealth.

Except as regards the City, policemen have to live in the district they serve, and are obliged to find respectable quarters as best they can, paying often dearly. A few of the married men live at the stations, and most of the single ones are accommodated in what are called 'section houses', otherwise, in the more crowded parts of London, the choice is almost limited to the better class of block dwellings.

Section houses are attacked to the principal London stations, at which the men pay a small sum weekly for lodging, and find their own food. The larger houses have reading and recreation rooms, and are supplied with a library and even billiard tables. Everything necessary for vigorous physical exercise is provided.

Besides diseases resulting form exposure, such as bronchitis and rheumatism, their occupation renders the police exceptionally liable to accidents and malicious injuries. One shilling a day is deducted in case of absence from duty owing to sickness, and the amount credited to the pension fund. There is no deduction from pay in case of absence due to injury while on duty.

Life and Labour, etc., Industry, vol. 4, pp. 47-54.

3

Civil Servants

The first point, perhaps, to notice with regard to the civil servant is that he is on the whole better off than the majority of workers in private employment whose position can be compared with his. In saying this, we do not wish to imply that his salary or wages are necessarily higher than are paid for a similar class of work in the outside world; in some few cases they may be less; but the civil servant enjoys contingent advantages such as fall to the lot of few other members of the community.

Not only does he work for a master whose business is subject to no vicissitudes of fortune, but his security of tenure is far greater than that of the servant of a private employer. The private trader is obviously much more directly interested in the efficiency of his servants than the head of a Government department; and there is a still stronger reason which militates against the dismissal of a civil servant, and that is that heads of departments have always before them the fear that pressure may be brought to bear by Members of Parliament. The result is that a Government department is certainly more long-suffering than a private employer, and dismissal is not likely to result except from flagrant and repeated misconduct, or from the grossest incompetence.

But an advantage which the civil servant enjoys, perhaps even more important then security of tenure, is regularity of employment. For him there are no seasons of slackness; he is free from the hateful necessity of hunting for a job, and however small his income he knows to a penny what it is and will be, and can arrange his life accordingly; while even old age has less terror for him than for other workers, from the knowledge that at the end of his career there is a pension awaiting him.

It should, however, perhaps be noticed in this connection that the civil servant is to some extent a picked man. In almost every case he is subject to an examination, either physical, educational, or both, nor can his appointment be confirmed until his character has undergone investigation and probation; he is expected, moreover, to keep up an appearance of respectability, whatever the grade to which he belongs. This fact, that civil servants are perhaps rather superior in attainments and physique to the average man, may account to some extent for their spirit of discontent; in the lower ranks a considerable proportion of the men are probably intellectually superior to the class from which they have sprung, and in many cases it is possible that they are too highly educated to do very willingly the mechanical work which falls to their lot.

Clerical Establishment.—Clerks are divided into Upper division clerks, Second division clerks, abstractors, boy clerks, and boy copyists.

Upper division clerks are on scales of salaries which vary much in different offices; in every office, however, they are divided into three classes. In the Treasury, the most highly paid office, the salaries are:

Third class	£200, rising by annual increments of £20 to £600			
Second ,,	£700,	,,	,,	£25 to £900
First ,,	£1000,	,,	,,	£50 to £1200.

In the majority of offices the scale is from £150 (by annual increments of £15, £20 and £25) to £800.

It should be noticed that private secretaryships, with extra remuneration, are open to first division clerks, and that promotion does not necessarily stop at the highest point of the scale, as staff appointments with salaries up to £2000 are often filled from their ranks.

Second division clerks are divided into a lower and a higher grade. The scale of salary for the lower grade is:

£70 by annual increments of £5			to £100	
£100	,,	,,	£7.10s. to £190	
£190	,,	,,	£10	to £250

In the higher grade the salary is £250, increasing by £10 annually to £350. Second division clerks are eligible for promotion to the upper division after eight years' service. The number of second division clerks is almost 3000, of whom the vastly larger proportion are in London.

Abstractors, sometimes called assistant or supplementary clerks: this class includes all survivors of the large body of men who were once called writers or copyists. The salary is £80, increasing by £2 10s. yearly to £150.

Boy clerks are paid 14s. a week, rising by 1s. a week each year. Boy clerks are not retained as such in the service after completing their twentieth year, but many of them pass into the second division. Boy copyists are paid at the rate of 4d. per hour, with an addition of ½d. per hour at the end of each year of approved service.

The hours of clerks are with a few exceptions seven a day, with a half-holiday every other Saturday.

The *Inland Revenue* officers most largely represented in London are: Collectors, with salaries from £500 to £800; Supervisors, £250 to £400; Officers, 1st class £180 to £250, 2nd class £115 to £160; Assistants of Excise, £50 to £80; Surveyors of Taxes, with salaries from £200 to £600.

Post Office. The most important bodies of men in the Post-office (under the numerous higher officials whose salaries range from £150 to £2000) are: Overseers, 40s. a week to 68s.; sorters, 18s. to 56s.; postmen, (*a*) Head postmen, 32s. to 38s. (*b*) Town postmen, 18s. to 34s. (*c*) Suburban postmen, 18s. to 32s. Postmen receive a boot allowance of £1 1s. a year, and a stripe and 1s. extra pay a week is given for each five years of good conduct up to fifteen.

It should be noticed that the senior postmen on each round who are engaged in the delivery of letters make a considerable sum by Christmas boxes, the amount received varying from about £3 to £15 per head.

There are in the Post-office 409 female clerks on salaries from £65 to £190, and 160 female sorters with salaries from 12s. to 30s. a week.

Life and Labour, etc., Industry, vol. 4, pp. 10-21.

4

Elementary School Teachers

Young people who desire to become elementary teachers have to undergo a long and arduous course of preparation. The preliminary requisites are good health and moral character and satisfactory proof of having passed Standards V or VI of the Elementary Code. Candidates may be required to serve a short period of probation, and then, if accepted, commence a four years' apprenticeship as pupil teachers. At the end of this period they enter for the Queen's Scholarship examinations, and if they pass sufficiently high in the list, they are eligible to go to a training college.

These colleges are all in private hands, being managed either by societies connected with the different denominations or by unsectarian bodies. A Government grant is paid averaging about £100 for men and £75 for women, in addition to which an entrance fee ranging from ten to twenty-five guineas is charged. In return, the students are provided with tuition, board and lodging, etc., but usually have to find their own books and personal expenses. After two years at college (occasionally extended to three years in cases of special merit), the young teacher passes the certificate examination in either the first, second, or third class, and then serves a probationary period of eighteen months in one and the same elementary school. Following this, if the inspector's report be favourable, the probationer receives a parchment certificate; and finally, at the end of about eight years of preparation, emerges as a fully qualified teacher.

In order to become head teachers, candidates must, in the case of the London School Board and of some of the voluntary schools, have received a collegiate training, and almost invariably, in the case of London schools, they must have passed in either the first or second divisions.

Duties and Remuneration. The schools are open for instruction usually on five days in the week between the hours of 9 a.m. and 12.30 p.m., and 2 p.m. and 4.30 p.m., but these hours may be extended by a quarter or half an hour for the treatment of backward or refractory children. Assistants have each the charge of a class, whilst the head teachers have the care of the whole school, and in the smaller schools sometimes take a class also. There are generally six or seven weeks' holiday in the year, viz. a fortnight at Christmas, one week at Easter, and three or four weeks from about the middle of July.

Pupil teachers in London Board Schools, after serving the probationary period, commence at a salary of 5s. a week for boys and 3s. for girls, rising in the third and fourth year to 12s. and 14s. for boys, and to 8s. for girls. The regular engagement starts at £95 for men and £85 for women, rising after two years' service to £105 and £90 respectively. From this point the men's salaries increase by annual increments of £5 to a maximum of £155, which is further augmented to £165 on their becoming head assistant teachers. Women rise by £3 a year to £125, or £135 as head assistants. The remuneration of head teachers varies according to department and number of scholars: masters of boys or mixed departments, £150 to £400; mistresses of girls or mixed departments, £120 to £150; mistresses of infants' departments, £120 to £240.

Life and Labour, etc., Industry, vol. 4, pp. 162-9.

5

Municipal Service

Municipal officers are well above the line of poverty. As showing what is evidently about the ordinary rate of remuneration we give the salaries of all the officials of one vestry [the unit of local government in London, outside the City, until the establishment of municipal boroughs by the London Government Act of 1899] with 97,845 population:

Vestry clerk, £450
Medical officer of health £450
Surveyor, £450
Assistant clerk, £190
Accounts clerk £200
First office clerk, £170
Second office clerk, £135
Third office clerk, £110
Assistant surveyor, £200
Surveyor's clerk, £140
Junior clerk, £85
Senior sanitary inspector, £170 with uniform
Foreman of roads, £170 with residence, gas, etc.
Sanitary inspector, £130 with uniform
Wharf superintendent, £150
Board attendant and official messenger, 42s. a week
Hall keeper, £110 with residence, uniform, etc.
Assistant hall keeper, 38s. per week with uniform.

Collectors of rates and taxes are paid by a commission on the sum collected, and we find that the earnings of twelve collectors in a representative London parish ranged from £222 13s. 3d. to £341 17s., but of these all but two earned over £310.

Included under municipal officers are firemen. In the London Fire Brigade the Chief Officer receives £900 with house and allowances valued at £200 a year. Firemen receive from £1 6s. to £1 17s. 6d. a week. All officers are given their uniform and receive pensions on retirement. It may be noted that London firemen are recruited entirely from sailors, who must have spent at least two or three years on a sailing ship.

Life and Labour, etc., Industry, vol. 4, pp. 21-5.

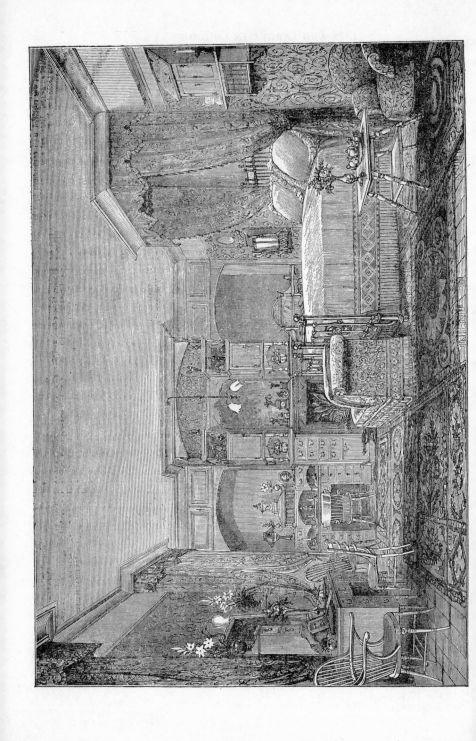

CHAPTER 3

YORK'S WAGE-EARNING POPULATION

[Although on a much smaller scale, Seebohm Rowntree's *Poverty: A Study of Town Life*, first published in 1901, may rank with Charles Booth's *Life and Labour of the People in London* as a pioneering effort in social investigation.

Benjamin Seebohm Rowntree—Seebohm was his mother's maiden name—was born in York in 1871, the son of Joseph Rowntree, who with his brother Isaac had not long before launched the cocoa and chocolate making business which was to give the family name a worldwide significance. The Rowntrees were Quakers, and Seebohm was educated at the Quaker school at Bootham, whence he proceeded in 1887 to Owen's College, Manchester. Two years later he joined the family firm in York. Shortly afterwards the works were moved from their cramped old premises in the city to a new site on the outskirts. At that time there were about 900 employees, but before the close of the century they numbered a couple of thousand, and within the next ten years that number was doubled.

From the outset Seebohm took a deep personal interest in the welfare of the staff, he pioneered a number of improvements in the way the business was carried on, and throughout strove to apply his Quaker religious principles allied with a progressive Liberalism. When in 1897 the firm was converted into a limited libability company he joined the Board, and on his father's death in 1925 he followed him in the chairmanship, which post he held until 1941.

Inspired by Booth's great work, Rowntree embarked on a similar investigation in York in the spring of 1899, and it was completed by the September following. Some of the information was obtained by voluntary helpers, 'district visitors', clergymen, and others, but the bulk was obtained by an investigator in his employ who went systematically from house to house. The final result showed that 20,302 persons (27·84 per cent) of the population of York were living in poverty—7,230 persons (9·9 per cent) in 'primary' poverty, i.e. in families whose total earnings were insufficient to obtain the minimum necessaries for the maintenance of merely physical existence, and 13,072 (17.93 per cent) in 'secondary' poverty, i.e. in families whose total earnings would have been sufficient for the maintenance of merely physical efficiency were it not that some portion of it was absorbed in other expenditure, either useful or wasteful.

E*

It was shown that for a family of father, mother, and three children, the minimum weekly expenditure upon which physical efficiency could be maintained in York was 21s. 8d.

This 27·84 per cent in York compared with Booth's 30·7 per cent of Londoners living in poverty, but, all things considered, Rowntree was fairly justified in claiming that the proportions were 'practically the same'.

'Rowntree' thus supplemented 'Booth', and the two together went a long way towards destroying Victorian complacency with the way things were going. So far from the state of the poor getting steadily better, so that grinding poverty might erelong become a thing of the past, it was now demonstrated that there was a hard core of destitution and misery which defied all the efforts of private benevolence, and was likely to continue as a portent and a challenge. Rowntree devoted the rest of his life to answering that challenge. He advocated a great extension of State action, and through his many writings he became a 'founding father' of the Welfare State. He died in 1954.]

My object in undertaking the investigation detailed in this volume was, if possible, to throw some light upon the conditions which govern the life of the wage-earning classes in provincial towns, and especially upon the problems of poverty . . . Having satisfied myself that the conditions of life obtaining in my native city of York were not exceptional, and that they might be taken as fairly representative of the conditions existing in many, if not most, of our provincial towns, I decided to undertake a detailed investigation into the social and economic conditions of the wage-earning classes in that city . . . to try to obtain information regarding the housing, occupation, and earnings of every wage-earning family, together with the number and age of the children in each family. These particulars, obtained in the autumn of 1899, extended to 11,560 families living in 388 streets and comprising a population of 46,754 [out of a total estimated population of 75,812] . . .

Any classification of families according to income must be an arbitrary one. I have adopted a method which is similar in some respects to that adopted by Mr Charles Booth in his *Life and Labour of the People in London* . . . The population is divided into seven classes as follows: Class A, Total Family Income under 18s. for a moderate family (a family consisting of father, mother, and from two to four children). Class B, Total Family Income 18s. and under 21s. Class C, Total Family Income 21s. and under 30s. Class D, Total Family Income over 30s. Class E, Domestic Servants. Class F, Servant-keeping. Class G, Persons in Public Institutions.

Class A [1957 persons in 656 families, constituting 2·6 per cent of the total population] comprises the poorest people in the city . . . Their weekly earnings amount in the aggregate to £274 11s. 6d. Out of this sum, £68 13s. 4½d. is paid for rent, leaving £205 18s. 1½d. with which to provide food, clothing, fuel, and all other necessaries . . . The poverty of the Class is rendered apparent when it is stated that it would cost £227 15s. 8d. to provide *food alone* for these people for one week, according to the diet allowed to paupers in York workhouse. . . . The poverty of the members of Class A is indeed such that probably the bulk of them would be driven into the workhouse, were it not that their meagre earnings are eked out by charity, either public or private.

Families which are, from any cause, in particularly hard straits, are often helped by those in circumstances but little better than their own. There is much of this mutual helpfulness among the very poor. In cases of illness neighbours will almost always come in and render assistance, by cleaning the house, nursing, and often bringing some little delicacy which they think the patient would 'fancy'. In some districts also it is a common practice, on the death of a child, for one of the neighbours to go round the neighbourhood to collect coppers towards defraying the cost of the funeral.

Members of Class A do not live in any one particular district, but are found scattered almost all over the working parts of the city. Wherever a house or a room is to be had for a low rental, either on account of dilapidation or dampness, or from any other cause, it is eagerly taken up by a member of this Class. Many of these houses and rooms, hidden away in dark and narrow streets, are indeed miserable dwellings.

The food of these people is totally inadequate . . . consisting largely of a dreary succession of bread, dripping, and tea; bread and butter and tea; bacon, bread, and coffee, with only a little butcher's meat, and none of the extras and but little of the variety which serves to make meals interesting and appetising . . .

The clothing is often as inadequate as the food; this is notably the case amongst the uncomplaining poor, who receive few gifts of clothing, their clean and tidy appearance not suggesting that although the exterior garments are tidy, the under garments are totally inadequate to keep out the cold.

Few people spend all their days in Class A. It is nevertheless a class into which the poor are at any time liable to sink should misfortune overtake them, such as continued lack of work, or the death or illness of the chief wage-earner. The families who are in it because the wage-earner is out of work will rise above it when work is found, unless physique and *morale* have been ruined by the period of economic stress. Many families too will rise above it when the children begin to earn money.

But the old people, who have no children growing up, must remain in the class until they die, or enter the workhouse.

Class B [4492 persons in 983 families, 5·9 per cent of total population] consists chiefly of unskilled labourers and their families, and although their standard of living is a degree better than that of Class A, there is, nevertheless, a large amount of poverty among them.

Practically the whole of this class are living either in a state of actual poverty—by this is meant that their total earnings are insufficient to supply adequate food, clothing, and shelter for the maintenance of merely physical health—or so near to that state that they are liable to sink into it at any moment. They live constantly from hand to mouth. So long as the wage-earner is in work the family manages to get along, but a week's illness or lack of work means short rations, or running into debt, or more often both of these. Extraordinary expenditure, such as the purchase of a piece of furniture, is met by reducing the sum spent on food. As a rule, in such cases it is the wife and sometimes the children who have to forego a portion of their food—the importance of maintaining the strength of the wage-earner is recognized, and he obtains his ordinary share.

'If there's anything extra to buy, such as a pair of boots for one of the children', a woman (in Class B) told one of my investigators, 'me and the children goes without dinner—or mebbe only 'as a cup o' tea and a bit o' bread, but Jim (her husband) ollers takes 'is dinner to work, and I give it 'im as usual; he never knows we go without, and I never tells 'im.'

Let us take the case of a woman whom we will call Mrs Smith, an excellent housewife, with a steady husband and three children at home. Her house is scrupulously clean and tidy. Mr Smith is in regular work and earns 20s. per week. He keep 2s. a week for himself, and hands over 18s. to his wife. Out of his two shillings Mr Smith spends 1d. per day on beer, 3d. a week on tobacco, puts 3d. into the children's savings-box, and clothes himself out of the remainder. One new dress, Mrs Smith tells us, will last for years. For everyday wear she buys some old dress at a jumble sale for a few shillings. Old garments, cast off by some wealthier family, are sometimes bought from the ragman for a few coppers; or perhaps they are not paid for in cash, but some older rags and a few bones are given in exchange for them. Garments so purchased are carefully taken to pieces, washed, and made up into clothes for the children. Mrs Smith said that she once bought a pair of old curtains from the ragman for 3d. She cut out the worn parts and then made curtains and short blinds from the remainder sufficient for all the windows in her house. She regularly pays 6d. a week for sick club, 4d. for life insurance, and 3d. per week into the clothing club held in connection with her church. On being requested to do so, she kept detailed accounts of her total income and expenditure during two months. Her 18s. is usually spent as follows:

	s.	d.
Food (five persons)	11	0
Rent	3	2
Coal and light	2	0
Soap, etc.		5
Sick club		6
Life insurance		4
Clothing club		3
	17	8

It was obvious that with such a normal expenditure there was no appreciable sum available for 'extras'. 'Then how do you do, Mrs Smith', my investigator asked, 'when you have to meet any extraordinary expenditure, such as a new dress, or a pair of boots?' 'Well, as a rule', was the answer, 'we 'ave to get it out of the food money and go short; but I never let Smith suffer—'e 'as to go to work, and must be kept up, yer know! And then Smith 'as ollers been very good to me. When I want a new pair of shoes, or anythink, 'e 'elps me out of 'is pocket money, and we haven't to pinch the food so much.'

The families belonging to Class B are distributed all over the working-class districts of the city. They inhabit, as a rule, the cheapest houses they can obtain, excepting the very cheap and dilapidated houses occupied by Class A. Their houses seldom have more than two bedrooms, the total number of rooms usually varying from two to four. Many of the houses are overcrowded, and a large proportion are old and without modern sanitary conveniences. Often there is no scullery, and the pantry consists of an unventilated cupboard under the stairs. In many cases the water-tap and privy have to be shared with several other houses. The average sum paid for rent by families in this class is 3s. 7½d., which is equal to 18·4 per cent of the average family income ...

The pawnshop often plays an important part in the lives of the people in Class B, but especially is this true of those who live in the slums, where the stream of people coming to the pawnshop on Monday morning is a characteristic sight. The children are sent off with the weekly bundle early on that day, and a number of them may sometimes be seen sitting on the steps outside the pawnshop door waiting for it to open. Once the habit of pawning has been formed, it is difficult to break. Some families pawn their Sunday clothes regularly every Monday, and redeem them as regularly on the following Saturday night when the week's wages have been received.

Many of those now in Class B will rise into a higher class as soon as their children begin to earn money, possibly to sink back again, however, when their children marry and leave home.

Class C [15,710 persons in 3822 families, 20·7 per cent of the total population]. The margin of income in the class is a large one. There is, however, evidence that not a few of those in this class are living in a state of poverty. On the other hand, many of those whose incomes approach 30s. are living under conditions but little inferior to those obtaining in Class D.

Class C comprises all classes of labour excepting the lowest paid labour on the one hand and skilled labour on the other. The families belonging to it are distributed almost all over the working-class districts of the city. The average rent paid is 4s. 4d., which is equal to 15·6 per cent of the average income.

Class D [24,595 persons, in 6099 families, 32·4 per cent of the total population]. This class comprises all families with 30s. or over who do not keep domestic servants. These families may be divided into two sections, viz.—(1) Families in which the fathers are skilled workers, or foremen who have risen through superior ability, or men who on account of their high character have been placed in well-paid positions of trust. (2) Families in which the fathers are unskilled workers earning less than 30s., but where the total family income is raised above that figure on account of the sums contributed by children who are working.

Where the father is a skilled workman, his sons will generally be apprenticed to the same or to some other skilled trade. Frequently they become clerks, but are seldom brought up as mere labourers. From the social standpoint 'clerking' is looked upon as an advance, but the social prestige thus obtained is sometimes purchased at the cost of a diminished income. The number of girls belonging to Class D who enter domestic service, except as nurses, is small and is decreasing. They prefer to become dressmakers, shop assistants, or clerks, or find employment in the confectionery factories. Except in families where the income is high, say £3 or £4 a week, or in which the wife is either deceased or a confirmed invalid, the daughters usually earn their own living in one way or another.

The houses occupied by the families classed as D are distributed more or less all over the city, but there are some districts peopled only by this class, and chiefly by that section of it comprising skilled workers, and those holding responsible positions as foremen, etc. The houses contain, as a rule, three bedrooms, a kitchen scullery, and sitting-room. In the latter are often found a piano, and occasionally a library of thirty books or more. Some of the houses have bay windows and a small front garden. They are for the most part sanitary. The average rent paid is 5s. 4d., which is equal to 12·8 per cent of the average income.

There is, partically speaking, no poverty in Class D except such as is caused by drink, gambling, or other wasteful expenditure, the latter due in some cases to ignorance of domestic economy. There is no doubt that the average weekly expenditure upon alcoholic drink by the families in Class D is considerable. They have more money available for this purpose than those in the other classes.

In consequence of the limited education they receive, the intellectual outlook of Class D is narrow. They do not as children stay long enough at school to acquire intellectual tastes, or even the power of applied reading and study. To this broad statement there are, of course, not a few exceptions—thoughtful men and women who throughout their lives take every opportunity of extending their knowledge by reading, and in other ways. But, for the most part, the reading of Class D is confined to the evening papers, to more or less sentimental or sensational novels, or to the endless periodicals made up of short stories, scrappy paragraphic comments upon men and events, columns of jokes and riddles, and similar items of a merely trivial character. And apart from reading, when literary or historical subjects are presented in the form of popular lectures, the number of those who are interested is comparatively small. Well-delivered lectures upon scientific subjects are, how-every, appreciated.

Shut out to a great extent from the larger life and the higher interests which a more liberal and a more prolonged education opens up to the wealthier classes, it is not surprising that, to relieve the monotony of their existence, so many artisans frequent the public-house, or indulge in the excitement of betting, and that professional football matches and race meetings often exercise so undue and unhealthy an influence upon their lives. The surprise is rather that the exceptions are so numerous. It is from the thoughtful men of Class D that the Trade Unions, the Co-operative Movement, and Friendly Societies find many of their leaders. The Temperance Cause, and other efforts for social advancement, gather not a few helpers from this class.

The writer fully and regretfully recognizes the fact that the direct influences of the Christian churches over the men and women in Class D is comparatively small . . .

It is a growing practice for the families in Class D to take a few days' summer holiday out of York. During the August Bank Holiday week, working men from York crowd into Scarborough, and many of those who do not take such an extended holiday avail themselves of the cheap day and half-day excursions run by the N.E. Railway Company. Probably, however, travelling is more usual among the artisan classes in

York than elsewhere, owing to the large number of railway employees who have the advantage of cheap 'privilege' tickets.

Life of the Women in Class D. No one can fail to be struck by the monotony which characterizes the life of most married women of the working class. Probably this monotony is least marked in the slum districts, where life is lived more in common, and where the women are constantly in and out of each others' houses, or meet and gossip in the courts and streets. But with advance in the social scale, family life becomes more private, and the women, left in the house all day whilst their husbands are at work, are largely thrown upon their own resources. These, as a rule, are sadly limited, and in the deadening monotony of their lives these women too often become mere hopeless drudges. Especially does illness in the family, not infrequent with three or four growing children, tell heavily upon the mother, who has then to be nurse, cook, and housemaid all in one. The husband commonly finds his chief interests among his 'mates', and seldom rises even to the idea of mental companionship with his wife. He rarely ill-treats her; but restricted education and a narrow circle of activities hinder comradeship, and lack of mental touch tends to pass into unconscious neglect or active selfishness. It must be remembered, too, that we are dealing with a class who do not keep domestic servants. The mother of a young family is not therefore able to escape from her circumstances through the cultivation of those social amenities which are the relief of her wealthier sisters. Even when able to get away for a day's holiday, or to go out for the evening, she is often obliged to take a baby with her.

In conclusion, it is important to remember that, taken as a whole, Class D is that section of our population upon which the social and industrial development of England largely depends, and is the one which will always exercise the most important influence in bringing about the social elevation of those in the poorer classes.

B. SEEBOHM ROWNTREE, *Poverty: A Study of Town Life,* chap. 3.

CHAPTER 4
THE £.s.d. OF LIVING

Attempts to compare the living costs of the present with those of a generation or so ago are all too likely to prove frustrating. In the main this is because of the great changes in the value of money, its purchasing power, that have occurred in the period of World Wars and economic crises and successive devaluations; but there is also the scarcity of surviving material on which comparisons may be based. Few people can be bothered to keep household accounts, and shopping lists, jotted down on backs of envelopes or other scraps of paper, are thrown away as soon as their purpose has been served. All the more welcome and valuable, then, such 'documents' as are brought together in this chapter.

In the first place, we have a number of 'cases' from the small volume *Family Budgets; being the Income and Expenses of Twenty-eight British Households, 1891-94*, published in 1896 under the auspices of the Economic Club of London. This gives the results of an inquiry that was carried out by a committee under the chairmanship of Charles Booth in different parts of the country, and the amount of factual detail is matched by the human interest of the real-life stories.

Secondly, we have drawn upon a series of articles that appeared in the *Cornhill Magazine* in 1901. In an introductory note the Editor explains that they are 'an attempt to put down in £. s. d. the proportions of the yearly earnings which are devoted to rent, food, clothing, education, amusements, etc., in average families throughout the kingdom', ranging from the household of a working man in receipt of 'good weekly wages' to that of a wealthy man 'whose income reaches the magic figure of £10,000 a year'.

I

London Plumber

———⟨⟩———

The man's parents were Londoners. His home was unhappy, owing to the drinking habits of his father, and, as the eldest child, he was kept much at home to help his mother and look after the children, with the result that his education was much neglected. Nominally at school for four or five years, he was absent more than half the time. At the age of twelve he was glad to leave school, and start work as an errand boy. His mother now died, and he went to live with an aunt, and engaged himself at a low wage to a plumber.

Having a natural liking for this work, and thinking his want of education would not seriously impede him in it, he deliberately chose it as his trade, soon picked it up, was entrusted with skilled work, and stayed with the same employer nearly seven years. At this time his aunt died. Though he paid her for his lodging, he was 'not too comfortable' with her; but, when he removed to other lodgings, he found them much more uncomfortable. He was now thrown out of work, through a quarrel with his foreman, and could get nothing to do for a fortnight. Having, however, saved £10 or £11, he married during the fortnight within a few weeks of his aunt's death.

The wife was born in London. She lost her father (a cabman) when she was very young, and went to the King Edward's Schools for destitute children at Southwark, a charitable institution, whence she was drafted at the age of 15 into domestic service as a general servant. This situation was so uncomfortable, that she left it at once for another. In all, she tried five places, remaining 3 years as a nursemaid in one of them, and marrying from the last.

Since his marriage, the man's employment has been marked by extreme irregularity and uncertainty. When her first-born was 6 months old, the wife fell ill of bronchitis and required more nourishing food. To obtain this, her husband, who had no work at the time, allowed the rent to fall in arrear 11s., when their home (worth about £5 to them) was distrained upon, and broken up. Since then they have not been able to get on their legs again.

On one occasion, when he lay ill for a month in St Thomas's Hospital, his wife was forced to apply for out-door relief, having absolutely no resources. The necessary steps of appearing before the Guardians, receiving the Overseer's visit, etc., were not surmounted for nearly a fortnight, when they were 'almost starving'. They were allowed 2s. 6d. a week, and received this for two weeks. Directly the husband came home convalescent, the relief stopped. It has not been applied for except this once. The misfortune of the time, the tardiness of the relief, and the surliness of the Overseer, are looked back upon with some bitterness of recollection by the man, who is devoted to his wife and children.

Some months ago their fourth child, a boy of two months, died of inflammation of the lungs, on a cold day, when the last penny had run out, and there was no fire in the room. The loss of the child is keenly felt: they repine too, that the funeral was necessarily of the cheapest (30s.) and plainest. As the man puts it: 'We could not have the little fall-things, wot shows respect.'

Neither trials in the past nor fears for the future have, however, broken down their honesty, cheerfulness, or self-respect. The wife extorts the maximum of utility from their slender resources. Her husband has no further aspiration than the hope of permanent and regular employment. A good week, when it comes, clears off the debts and shadows of the bad, and provides for the time some satisfaction of the more urgent needs of clothing or substantial food which have been forced into abeyance. Comfort, arising from neatness of home and person is relatively high; but the standard of this precarious living is so low, that it is difficult to conceive of a lower, apart from actual starvation.

Moral circumstances. On Sunday afternoons the children are sent to a Wesleyan Sunday School. In the evening they are put to bed early, and their parents go to the Wesleyan Chapel 'to pass away an hour'. They incur no expenses in these respects. The man does not smoke, neither he nor his wife drinks. The family is orderly, truthful and honest; but offers no soil for the cultivation of foresight in the direction of saving. Earnings are spent within the week. The eldest boy is sent to the Board School at a cost of 3d. per week levied for each week during which he is at least once present.

Hygiene.—The man is of strong constitution. His only illness since marriage arose from lead poisoning, due to the inhalation of ingredients of colour on a day when he resumed work with an empty stomach after two weeks enforced idleness. This was the occasion of his transfer to the hospital. The demand for beds led, as he asserts, to his premature discharge. Having no money to pay his fare, he walked home (3 miles), and the same night had two fits—his first and last attacks—attributed to weakness and fatigue.

The wife was strong until after the birth of her first child, when, endeavouring too soon to get about her work in the house, she caught cold, which brought on a lung trouble, never since got rid of. Her mother came to nurse her; but the eviction of the family (*see above*) happening at the time, she was, through the kind offices of her doctor's sister, sent the same day to a convalescent home at Kilburn, and there kept for four weeks at 8s. 6d. a week, her husband ultimately bearing half the expense. The oldest boy is consumptive. The family often lacks the warmth and nutrition necessary for the preservation of health. In case of illness application is made to a charitable dispensary which provides medical advice, medicine, bandages, etc., to accepted patients, who must pay 1d. on each visit on application, and find their own bottles. The doctor now attending the wife, spoke to a charitable lady of her want of coal during a severe illness, and the want was supplied.

The children play in their school-yard, and sometimes in a neighbouring park, but this is restricted by the fear of their parents that they might get into bad company.

Sources of Income. The man (age 30) describes himself as a three-branch man. His main business is that of jobbing plumber. The usual wages of a London plumber are said to be 9d. an hour, and the weekly hours of labour $56\frac{1}{2}$ generally, in the suburbs, 53 in the 'City', and large suburban firms. This plumber trusts to his local connexion, and the information supplied by comrades, for his jobs.

When out of work he applies to firms, and sometimes to likely householders. Other resources failing he tries to earn a trifle as a porter at auction rooms, or wherever he can get a job for the time. He is not deft at paper-hanging, and it took him 14 hours to hang 9 pieces at 6d. a piece, with his own paste (costing $2\frac{3}{4}$d.) His tools, worth about 5s., would cost 30s. to replace. He is often unable to do a job because his tools have been pawned. There is nothing else upon which he can raise a loan. The interest charged is $\frac{1}{2}$d. in the 1s. for each month, and $\frac{1}{2}$d. for the pawn-ticket.

The wife (age 29) is too delicate to do charing, or take in work. She makes the children's stockings and all their garments, except the girl's dresses. She has a small sewing machine. But her main contribution to the economy of the family is her very skilful housekeeping, which circumvents poverty by the most ingenious expedients.

The children (boys, ages 8 and 5, and girl age 3) are not old enough to earn money. The boy of eight is, however, sent to do the small errands. He is found to receive sympathetic attention when he has a farthing, or half-penny to lay out; while his father or mother would often be told that orders of such small value could not be executed. When there is no definite measure for a 'ha'porth' his parents think he 'gets the benefit of the doubt'. He is also useful about the house, and, for his mother's health, lights the fire before she gets up; but complaint is made that he burns more wood in the process than a grown person would do.

The family has no credit, nor can it count upon the aid of relatives, except that at rare intervals it gets a cast garment, which the wife makes up. When they lost their baby, the man's brother, though actually out of work, 'made' 30s. (i.e., by pledging) and lent it to them to pay the funeral expenses. And the wife's mother, now dead, took in the man and his children when they were homeless. Last Christmas they received a 4-lb. joint of beef and a ¼-lb. of tea from a lady at the chapel, who observed that they 'used the place regular'. The pleasures of memory as to this feast are still very vivid.

The Family's Mode of Existence. Meals. Breakfast 8 a.m. Tea, bread and margarine or fat bacon. Dinner 12.45. Bread and margarine. Two or three days a week, meat and vegetables or fish. On Sunday, when possible, suet pudding is added. Tea 5 p.m. Tea, bread and margarine. There is never supper. The man takes a flask of tea with him in the morning, and warms it where he is working; he carries his bread and butter. His dinner, bread and cheese, or bread and a rasher of bacon, at an eating-house costs 2d. or 4d. When he is working within easy distance he comes home to dinner.

Dwelling, Furniture, and Clothing. The house is situated near Loughboro' Junction in the S.E. of London, in a neighbourhood thickly peopled by the lower middle class, by artisans of small regular earnings, railway servants, etc. This family occupies the top or second floor. Its two rooms are well lighted and ventilated. The front room is the living room of the family and the bedroom of the parents. The boys sleep in the back room, the girl on a bed-chair in the large room. The rent is 4s. a week.

The furniture and clothing are very scanty, but kept fairly (not perfectly) clean. The best room has a rough carpet, a few cheap prints, a chest of drawers, and a little American clock. Out of doors the man wears an overcoat, which is warm and conceals a deficiency of other clothing. Indoors, or at work, the overcoat is removed, and reveals him in shirt sleeves. The bed-clothes are a thin counterpane, and little more.

Recreation. The man plays a little upon the flute, mainly to amuse the children, in whom he finds his chief pleasure. Sitting, coatless, before the fire of an evening, a boy on one knee and a girl on the other, he sings or whistles, and as he says, ' 'as a game with 'em in my way'. A 7.30 p.m. (having arisen at 7 a.m.) the children go to bed; and the man goes to his brother's to have a game of dominoes.

Expenses are scarcely ever incurred for recreation, but last Bank Holiday they all went for a country walk towards Dulwich, and hired a mail cart for the children, three hours at 3d. an hour.

The man himself has never been in a Museum, although born in London. He is sensitive to the feeling that, in any public building, he or his children might be looked down upon as having 'no right to be there' because they are not smartly dressed. Neither he nor his wife has been to a theatre or entertainment since marriage. 'We have pantomime enough at home', they say. The children play with each other, and with the neighbour's children in the street.

Family Budgets; being the Income and Expenses of 28 British Households 1891-94.
Case No. 1.

2

Poor Law Officer in London

At the time of my birth my father was 42 years of age, and was working as a warehouseman in a large firm of house furnishers. Between the ages of 4 and 5 I was sent to school (a voluntary Church School), and I have a lively recollection of the loving care and attention I received, both in the infants' division and upper classes. At the age of 8 years, having a good treble voice, I joined the church choir, and received from 7s. to 16s. per quarter for my services, a welcome addition to the family income.

Shortly after my 12th birthday, my father was attacked by a cancer in the tongue and was compelled to give up work. He was a member of a Friendly Society which brought in 10s. per week. My mother had some time previously obtained the care of some offices, earning about 10s. per week, and my sister, four years older than myself, was apprenticed to the pianoforte silking, and was earning a few shillings and partial food. I had, beside, a brother, four years younger, going to school.

Father continuing to get worse, I was taken away from school, having passed the seventh standard examination, and put to work in his old firm, being promised a junior clerkship, a promise which was never kept; and I continued to do the work of a furniture porter, which was very distasteful to me. My wages were 6s. per week.

After one year of this, I applied for a berth in the Railway Clearing House and passed the examination, but, having no influence, I did not obtain work.

My father died after being at home, ill, for twelve months, I being 14 years of age, and then the struggle for existence began, but we never asked nor received charity of any description, and always managed to dress well and live in respectable houses. My mother, at this time, worked very hard and lived harder. This continued until I was nearly 17, when, owing to a quarrel with one of the men, a drunkard, I refused to work with him and was fined 2s. 6d. for insubordination, refused to pay it and left as an alternative.

I now applied again to the Clearing House, passed two more examinations, and, being recommended by the chairman of one of the London Railways, obtained employment at £35 per annum, rising £10 each year up to £75. About this time I became acquainted with my wife, who was the sister of a shopmate, and was a linendraper's assistant.

I had also joined the volunteers and served three years, going to the reviews at Brighton, and Portsmouth, my first real holidays, having never before been for more than the annual school excursion, and I would like to say, for the satisfaction of those who subscribe to these treats for children, that it was always the happiest day of the year to me.

The next four years were very pleasant, although the hard work and the unfamiliar nature of it tried my sight and health very much, but I liked it, and appreciated the Library and Magazine clubs, also the swimming club, of which I was a member of the committee, and then I had my sweetheart and her friends to visit; altogether I was very happy. At the end of the four years, I was a successful candidate for my present appointment at £80 per annum, and left home, having to reside in my district. At the end of six months I got married owing to the discomfort of my lodgings, and the effect of the bad living, long hours, standing in close, hot, unhealthy shops on my sweetheart's health.

Twelve months after marriage I was shifted to another district, and was provided with house accommodation, coals, and gas, in addition to my £80. One week after moving my wife was confined, the baby dying through an accident at birth; the nurse got drunk, and I had to turn her out, my wife was very ill and had to go to the seaside as soon as she was able. This same week my mother was, also, taken ill and was bedridden twelve months, and has never been able to support herself since. She has been wholly dependent upon me over twelve months.

At this time I got into debt about £20 and it has hung like a millstone round my neck ever since, with the interest of 10 to 15 per cent.

We have now three children, but they are very healthy, and so are we. My wife plays the piano and sings very well, and I the violin, a little. I am also a member of the church choir. We have a good many friends to visit, and who visit us, and we go to theatres and concerts as often as we can afford it, or get free passes; and when we are at home alone, we amuse ourselves with music and reading.

Two years ago my salary was increased to £90 per annum, and we are gradually recovering from the expenses and losses of our early married life. (Average weekly expenditure, 41s. 7¾d., of which 26s. 10d. is for food and drink.)

Statement made by an Assistant Relieving Officer (age 26, with wife age 27, three small children, and mother age 64). *Family Budgets, 1891-94*; Case 4.

3

Cornish Fisherman

The household consists of a fisherman, his wife and four children (ages 8, 7, 4, and 5 months, two of them step-children). The husband was born in St Ives, and has always lived there. He has been married five years. He has been a fisherman for twelve years. Goes out line-fishing, on all-night work, working on his own account, but owning neither net nor boat; to hire a boat he clubs with three others. He has no regular earnings, sometimes making nothing for weeks, sometimes 8s., 11s. or 14s. per week. He also does odd jobs occasionally, such as boat painting. The harbour dues, divided between the four who hire the boat, are 10s. for the season; other expenses are 3s. 6d. or 4s. each for lines, and a share of the catch for the hire of the boat, and for the use of the other men's labour.

The family lives in a three-roomed cottage, one of a small double row forming a narrow alley. They seldom eat meat, and live chiefly on bread and tea. The wife cannot read or write. She cannot get credit at the shop, but gets a little help from a sister and her neighbours.

(Average weekly income, 10s. 10d.; average weekly expenditure, 9s. 3¼d. of which 6s. 2d. is for food and drink, rent 10d., and fuel 10½d.)

Family Budgets, 1891-94; Case 13.

4

Railway Foreman

A foreman, age 54, in the S.E. Railway Company's service in a town in Kent [Ashford]. He was born near Hythe, has been in the service of the Company about 34 years. He has been married 32 years. His wife is a native of Kent and was formerly a domestic servant.

Two sons are away from home; the eldest, a driver on the S.E.R., is married and living at Deal; the second is in the Army. The two elder girls are in service near London, as parlour-maid and upper housemaid; they clothe and help to keep an invalid sister, who is apprenticed to a dressmaker. The third son is a turner in the railway factory; he gives a small contribution to the family income, which probably covers the apparent deficit.

Besides his wages, 24s. a week, the husband has uniform provided by the railway company, and has the right of privilege fares at ¼d. a mile. The hours are from 6.30 a.m. to 7.30 p.m., with intervals of half an hour for breakfast and one hour for dinner; these he has at home. The work, moving heavy goods, is very exhausting, and the warehouse is draughty.

They live in a healthy four-roomed cottage belonging to the railway company. It is fairly well furnished. There is a garden attached to the house, and they also hold a strip of land from the railway company, for growing potatoes, at the nominal rent of 3s. a year; they obtain from them all the vegetables they need. They use a good deal of meat and milk. They purchase coals, boots, and the greater part of their clothing through clubs; the wife pays 1s. a fortnight to a coal club, 1s. a week to a clothing club, and the husband pays 26s. a quarter for two shares in a shoe club. (Weekly average income, 25s. 6d.; weekly average expenditure, 28s. 6½d.)

Family Budgets, 1891-94; Case 14.

5

Scottish Artisan

————◆————

(By the head of the family—an artisan with wife and four children ages 11, 7, 4, and 2).
Family budget written for the purpose of showing how much comfort can be attained and provision made for the contingencies of life, and these are want of work when trade is dull, sickness, old age, and the needs of wife and family in the event of death overtaking the father while the family is young.

My average income for this year has been about 43s. per week, but when trade is good it will be about 47s. per week. [Average weekly expenditure, 37s., of which 22s. is for food and drink.]

* * *

Sir,—I will give you a short account of what we have done since we were married. In the first ten years we saved past £150, and that after taking all the pleasures of life. We are all well clothed; our house is comfortably furnished (the household goods are insured for £150 in case of fire); every holiday, that is at the fair and new year, during the first eight or nine years of our married life, we were always away from home, we never refrained from enjoying ourselves in a legitimate way, but we always took care to keep it within bounds.

I had not always as large an income as I now have, but I remember my wife saved 18s. of her first pay [housekeeping money], although there were many things she could have spent it on, but she has always made her ends subservient to her means. She was not many days married until she began to knit me under-clothing, and from that day to this neither my children nor myself has ever worn any under-clothing that has not been made with her own hand; the children's clothes have all been made by her own hands, she having a sewing machine. If there is anything bought at any time, made and ready, it is for the purpose of getting a pattern from for future things.

To show what can be done I will give an example: there was a sale of goods that had been lying in stock for some time; my wife bought a piece of strong cloth for 15s., out of which she has made a suit of clothes for church, one pair of trousers for school, for our eldest boy, aged ten past, a little overcoat for his brother aged 3½ years, and there is as much

154

left as will make an overcoat for some of them in the coming winter if required, that is why I am able to put 2s. 6d. per week down for the upkeep of boots, clothing, etc. She also for the first five or six years made all her own dresses, but gave it up when the children began to need her time.

I think I have said enough to show how we have saved means while taking the good of life; we are now reaping the benefits; we are able to live in our own house [bought through a building society] at a comparatively early age; we have a house of five apartments, with bath-room, closet and out-houses, with a piece of garden.

My own part in the housekeeping is not much; I give up into her hands my pay as I get it, have no purse of my own, if I need it I get the keys of the drawers; I account for all that I may spend of my own free will. I give her my opinion, if needed—I let her see that I appreciate her efforts, and have in her my only companion. I do not take any strong drink on principle; I do not smoke, but that is because I have never learned it, not that I object to it—I consider it a harmless indulgence.

We find our chief amusement in reading; I take some little part in the social affairs of the town, and the training of the children takes up our time, and we have our friends whom we visit, and who visit us in return, and then there is the garden; we have always plenty to amuse us, and the only thing is that we find the time too short for all that we have to do.

The children, two of them, are at school, and when they come home and get their homework done for the next day, play about the place; as our cottage is in the suburbs of the town they have plenty of space and freedom to play with the other children; the two youngest play about the garden all day long.

My wife is not a native of the town we are in, she came to it as a domestic servant. Had been a servant from 15 years of age, was 23 years of age when married, and I 24 years, but she had a noble example in her mother who is one of the noblest women I have ever known.

*   *   *

Table showing dinners for week beginning 31 January 1892:

Sunday.—Apple tart and tea. (No meat as a rule, partly to leave the mother leisure for church, etc.)
Monday.—Soup, meat and potatoes; ½ lb. of boiling meat.
Tuesday.—Stewed meat and vegetables and potatoes; ¾ lb. stewing meat.
Wednesday.—Soup made with bone, and remainder of apple tart left from Sunday.
Thursday.—Collops, vegetables and potatoes; ¾ lb. collops.
Friday.—Soup and semolina pudding.

Saturday.—Stewing meat and potatoes; ¾ lb. meat.

Children get no butcher's meat; they get the sauce and potatoes, and a piece of bread after, and mother and I have always a cup of coffee after dinner.

Family Budgets, 1891-94; Case 15.

(b) HOW TO LIVE ON—

I

Thirty Shillings a Week

The class we are considering is one of men earning from twenty or twenty-five to forty shillings a week, and for our instance we put the sum at thirty shillings, not as the average of a full week's wages, which would be a little higher, but as a general average, allowing for missed time, slack periods, and the like. Our particular example is of a man—a married man, of course—living in a humble though decent neighbourhood of London, at no very great distance from his work. We will suppose the children to be three, and of school age.

We will fix our man's rent at seven shillings a week. For that he will get three rooms, being the half of one of the six-roomed houses that make the bulk of the streets in East London. Thus it is seen that rather less than a quarter of the income goes in rent. It is a counsel of prudence among the middle classes, I believe, to pay no more than a tenth of the income in rent; though perhaps in practice the sum is commonly something nearer an eighth. The relatively higher rent of small houses arises from an excessive demand, and from the fact that a workman *must* live within a reasonable distance of his work. Workmen's trains are all very well, but he prefers not to begin and end a hard day's work with a long railway journey.

Now to our balance sheet. On the one side is the thirty shillings of wages, and nothing else. We will suppose that thirty shillings is duly entered by being brought home whole on Saturday, which is the general pay-day, though some men are paid on Friday. The 'missis' begins the other side of the account by going shopping on Saturday evening, taking her husband with her to wait outside shops and carry the heavier parcels.

157

She will probably visit the grocer's first, because his goods do not vary in price with the lateness of the hour, as do the fishmonger's, the butcher's, and the greengrocers'.

At the grocer's she sets herself up with grocery for the week. She buys a quarter of a pound of tea, which comes, nowadays, to 4½d. This may last the week with care, but if a friend comes to tea, or some other unexpected call be made on the supply, another ounce or so may be bought towards the week's end. Next she has a quarter of a pound of coffee, ready ground—3d. A pound of loaf sugar and two pounds of moist will be enough for the week, the former costing 2d., and the latter, at three-halfpence a pound, 3d. Then she will buy a jar of jam, containing three pounds, for 7½d. The next purchase will be half a pound of butter, which will cost 6d. Eight eggs for 6d., a pound of bacon rashers at 8d., and half a pound of Cheddar cheese—probably American —which will cost 3d.

The great purchase of the evening will be that of the joint for Sunday's dinner. It will consist of six or seven pounds of beef or mutton, bought with a sharp eye to price, quality and freedom from bone, and it will cost from two to three shillings—let us say half a crown. This will provide meat for the best part of the week—hot on Sunday, cold two, or more probably three, days afterwards, and made into stew for still another day. With this we will put down a penny for suet.

So much for the butcher. At the fishmonger's the housewife's buying will be regulated by the prices and qualities of the day, to say nothing of her own and her husband's fancies. There will be cod, hake (a good and very cheap fish, often sold for cod, and here costing 2d. and 2½d. a pound), eels, mackerel, haddocks, skate, herrings, all at varying but low prices; and for 10d. she will buy enough to make a little supper to celebrate Saturday evening, a little for Sunday's breakfast, and some more to use for breakfast or tea on Monday or Tuesday. In the hot weather she will cook it soon, so that it may keep the better.

The greengrocery will depend much on the purchases already made. Three pence for potatoes and three pence more for greens will about represent the expenditure. If my arithmetic serves me, it will be found that the evening's payments have been exactly 7s. 6d. To this we must add the price of three loaves of bread bought early in the afternoon and costing 7½d., and half a quartern of flour bought at the same time for 3d. This will bring the whole Saturday marketing expenditure to 8s. 4½d. So that when the landlord takes his 7s. on Monday morning, more than half the week's money will be knocked down. But let us put the landlord aside for a moment and go on to estimate the remaining household expenses.

As to food, there will be bread to get for the rest of the week, and this will cost 1s. 3d. This, with the three loaves already bought, allows one loaf a day. The joint of meat will probably hold out, in one shape or another, over Thursday's dinner, and then something else—fish, sausages, or what not—will be bought for Friday and Saturday. This, with what is called a 'relish' for tea or breakfast—it may be fish, or an egg, or a rasher of bacon—on an occasion or two in the latter part of the week—will cost 2s. Extra vegetables will be needed, some of them for Thursday's stew, and the cost of these may be put at 9d.

In the matter of fuel, expense will vary, of course, with the season. Almost always the workman is afflicted with a sad lack of storage room, and this means that he cannot avail himself of low summer prices to lay in a stock. It must be remembered, however, that except on washing days only one fire will be used in the winter, for the cooking is done in the living-room. In the summer a fire is only used when heavy cooking is to be done, a small oil stove sufficing for the occasional boiling of a kettle or the frying of a rasher of bacon. Taking one thing with another the year round, fuel—coal and wood—will cost our workman 2s. a week.

Paraffin oil, for lamp and stove, will cost 6d. for the week, and perhaps one packet of Swedish boxes of matches will be used—especially if the workman smoke, as he usually does—and these matches will cost 1½d. Soap, starch, blue, and soda will cost 6d. a week, and blacking and blacklead 1½d. The washing and ironing will be done at home, of course, but clothes will be put out to mangle at a cost of 3d. Pepper, salt, and mustard, and so forth will average 1½d. a week.

In the matter of clothes, I am brought to a stand. Particular clothes are needed in particular trades, and some trades are more destructive of clothes than others. Some workmen buy cheaper clothes than other workmen, and while some are careful of their garments others are not. Some children's clothes are bought at the slop-shop, but more are made at home from father's and mother's cast-offs. If all the family are boys or all girls, clothes descend in the same way from the biggest to the smallest, being shortened and 'taken in' for each successive wearer; but if boys and girls are mixed the old clothes will not go so far. Again, some women are very neat with joins and patches, while others cobble miserably, or not at all. A practice is sometimes followed of setting aside a sum of about 2s. a week for clothes, boots, and repairs. The 2s. alone would, perhaps, scarcely do it, but the thrifty housewife has ways of saving a penny now and a penny again; of selling bottles and rags; of 'making shift' without some small thing at a time when a lack will not be serious; and, by hook and crook, of scraping up little sums which can be hoarded secretly and brought out on occasion.

Two shillings a week, then, for clothes, and a shilling for clubs and insurances. This is a very necessary shilling, for the benefit club represents medical attendance, which otherwise might be a considerable item. The club may cost 6d., or it may be a trifle more. If 6d., the rest of the shilling will provide a penny a week insurance for the wife and each of the children, and one at 2d. for the bread-winner.

Four shillings is the sum left, and plenty there is to do with it. If the children go to a voluntary school, there may be a few coppers in school pence to pay, but the average child goes to the Board school, and nowadays pays nothing. Shall we allow half a crown for beer and tobacco? I think that would be very moderate indeed. If we give the workman and his wife but a single pint of beer each a day, the cost will be 2s. 4d. for the seven days. This allows each half a pint at dinner and half a pint at supper at 4d. a quart, the usual price of the ale or 'half-and-half' which they drink. But that would leave only 2d. for tobacco, so I really think we must increase the half-crown to 2s. 9d., to give the man an ounce and a half of shag—a very modest allowance.

And now 1s. 3d. is left for savings, postage, literature, amusements, and all the rest of it. We will not give the shilling to fares, because distance from work would probably mean a smaller rent, and the one thing would balance the other. Moreover, we began with the stipulation that the man lived near his work. But without train-fare there are a hundred ways in which the one-and-threepence may be swallowed up in a moment, and truly it is a small sum for contingencies. Indeed, an occasional extra half-pint of beer would wipe it away. Yet there are many families who save it, and even add to it, thanks to the patient expendients of the 'missis'. The income and expenditure account of the week, then, will stand thus:

	£	s.	d.		£	s.	d.
Wages	1	10	0	Rent		7	0
				Meat and fish		5	5
				Bread and flour		2	1½
				Grocery		1	8
				Cheese, butter, bacon, and eggs		1	11
				Greengrocery		1	3
				Firing		2	0
				Oil and sundries		1	7½
				Allowance for clothes		2	0
				Club and insurance		1	0
				Beer and tobacco		2	9
				Balance in hand for contingencies, petty cash, etc.		1	3
	£1	10	0		£1	10	0

ARTHUR MORRISON, *Cornhill Magazine*, April 1901.

Illustrated London News (1891). British Museum Photo

Hop-pickers starting from
ndon Bridge Station at midnight
r the Kentish hop-fields

ne feathers for an East-End 'belle'

'The Poor in Great Cities' (1894)

10. Sketches in Messrs Bryant & May's match manufactories in Bow. Top, a girl making braided lights, and (right) a man dipping safety matches. Centre: girls cutting down and boxing 'Ruby' and 'Runaway' matches. Bottom left, wrapping patent safety matches, and (right) boxing wax vestas

2

A Hundred-and-fifty a Year

The lower middle class is the backbone of the commonwealth. Let us consider some of the elements of which this great class is composed.

Amongst the earners of a yearly wage of from £150 to £200 we find certain skilled mechanics; bank clerks; managing clerks to solicitors; teachers in the London Board Schools; the younger reporters on the best metropolitan papers; the senior reporters on the best local papers; second division clerks in the Colonial, Home, and India Offices; senior telegraphists; sanitary inspectors; relieving officers; clerks under the County Councils; many vestry officials; police inspectors; barristers' clerks; organists, and curates in priest's orders.

I have thought it best to take a typical example of this financial section of society and show how life can be, and is, lived in many hundreds of homes on a minimum income of £150 a year, from which it will follow that a somewhat easier life can be lived on any sum between that and a maximum of £200. The case I take is that of a cashier in a solicitor's office—a man of high character, good education, and high ideals, who, from his fourteenth to his fortieth year, has earned his living in his chosen profession. For ten years he has been married to the daughter of a once well-to-do farmer, who for some time before her marriage had found it necessary, in consequence of agricultural depression, to go out into the world and earn her own living in a house of business. In her father's house she had learned the domestic arts. In her independent life she learned the value of money. And here we must remember that a wife may be the very best investment that a man ever made, or she may be the worst.

Our typical couple are fortunate in having but two children— fortunate not merely because there will be fewer mouths to feed but because the wage-earner's mobility will not be unduly checked. The question at once arises, how that family shall be housed.

To the worker in the City of London or in Westminster one of three courses is practically open. Either he must live within easy distance in lodgings in some such locality as Trinity Square, S.E., and Vincent Square, S.W., or in one of those huge clocks of flats to be found in such districts as Finsbury, Lambeth, or Southwark; or he must go further afield and find an inexpensive house in one of the cheaper suburbs, Clapham, Forest Grate, Wandsworth, Walthamstow, Kilburn, Peck-

F   161

ham, or Finsbury Park. That he will be well advised to adopt the latter course there can be no possible doubt, and this although he will have to add to his rent the cost of travelling to and fro.

In the first place he will be able to house himself at a lower rental; in the second place his surroundings will be far more healthy; in the third place his neighbours will be of his own class, a matter of chiefest importance to his wife and children, the greater part of whose lives will be spent in these surroundings. There are thousands of snug little suburban six-roomed houses which can be had for a rental of from 10s. to 12s. 6d. a week, and it is in these that the vast majority of those who earn from £150 to £200 a year are to be run to earth. When we get into what we may call essentially the clerks' suburbs—Leytonstone, Forest Gate, Walthamstow, and such like—it is astonishing what a difference an extra shilling or two a week will make in the general character of our surroundings.

Our specimen couple were fortunate in being enabled to live in a twelve-and-sixpenny house, in a very different road from the road of ten-shilling houses, by the fact that a relative rented one of their rooms. In the budget at the end of this article, however, I have put down 10s. as the weekly rent, as a lodger's accounts would in various ways complicate matters. The result is that we have, with rates and taxes at £5 3s. 5d., the sum of £31 3s. 5d. gone in housing our family, a terribly large but necessary slice out of an income of £150 a year. Just compare this with the proportion of one-tenth of income generally set aside for that purpose amongst the so-called 'upper middles'.

Having then decided upon a home in the suburbs, the next expenditure is the wage-earner's railway fare to and from his work. In all probability the distance will be from four to six miles. This would mean at least sixpence a day spent in travelling, were it not that all the railway companies issue season tickets at reduced rates. Some of them, however, do not offer these facilities to third-class passengers. We must, therefore, in a typical case put down at least £7 a year for a second-class 'season'.

Now to face the very considerable expenditure on Dress. And in this particular, the unit of the class with which we are concerning ourselves is in a very different position from the skilled mechanic who may be earning a like income. It is more and more recognized as an axiom in those businesses and professions which are in immediate touch with the client, that the employees, whether they be salesmen in shops or clerks in banks or offices, must be habited in what may be called a decent professional garb. The bank clerk who looks needy, or the solicitor's clerk who is out-at-elbows, will find that he has little chance of retaining his position. Here he is clearly at a disadvantage compared with the man who works with his hands and who only has to keep a black coat for high days and holidays. Thus the 'lower middle' bread-winner is forced into an extravagance in the matter of clothes out of all proportion to his income.

Nor is it his own clothes alone that will be a matter of anxiety, for whatever may be said of false pride and suchlike, a man is most properly not content to see his wife and children dressed in a manner unbecoming their station. The wife must of course be her own and her children's dressmaker, for it hardly needs stating that 'making up' is out of all proportion to the cost of material. This applies more particularly to the children's clothing. A clever mother will cut down and alter her old skirts into serviceable frocks for the girls; and the father's discarded waistcoats and trousers will be metamorphosed by her deft fingers into second-best suits for the boys. She will take care in buying dress materials for herself to wait for the drapery sales at the end of the summer and winter seasons and obtain them at half the price paid by her less thoughtful neighbour.

Boots are an expensive and important item which will run away with at least four per cent of our income. The far-seeing housewife will take care that each of her family has at least two, and more wisely three, good strong pairs in use at the same time. She will thus not only materially reduce the doctor's bill, for the children will be able to be out and about in all weathers and so rarely take cold, but she will also effect a final saving in the boots themselves, which will last half as long again if the leather is given proper time to dry.

Plain living will be a matter of course on an income of £150 a year, but this does not necessarily connote cheap food. Not only is good food more palatable and nourishing but it is cheaper in the upshot because there is less waste. Take, for example, half a leg of mutton at 10d. a pound (quoting for the moment the local butcher's price). The first day it will be served hot with vegetables, the second day cold with salad, the third day tastily hashed, and there will be no appreciable waste. Compare this with a neck of mutton of the same weight costing something less per pound. Not only will a large proportion of its weight be made up of fat and bone, but it will make a far less appetizing and far less nourishing dish.

There is another question for the housewife to consider besides 'What shall I buy?', and that is, 'Where shall I buy it?' The local butcher will charge about 10d. a pound for a prime leg, but the thoughtful housekeeper will instruct her husband to call in before leaving town at some such market as Leadenhall, where he will get the very best 'New Zealand' at 6d.—a saving of nearly 3s. on an eight-pound joint! The same in the matter of groceries. Here the wise woman will get her husband to do her marketing for her at one of the great central stores where he will pay cash.

This is, of course, calculating on the complaisancy of the husband. If he is too proud to carry the fish-basket or parcel of tea home with him she must do the best she can near at home. In some districts she will find large local stores only second to those to be found in the City.

Here, then, is the sum of £47 9s. which will be found set down in our annual budget for food, reduced to weekly terms:—Meat and fish, 7s.; greengrocery, 1s. 3d.; milk, 2s. 6d.; bread, 1s. 6d.; grocery, 6s.

It will be noticed that the budget makes no mention of beer or other strong drinks. This is because my typical couple happen to be tee-totallers, and what they can do without others can too. Tobacco, on the other hand, is included, because the wage-earner happens to be a smoker—though a very moderate one at that.

The item 'house expenses' covers the necessary renewals of crockery, kitchen utensils, carpentering requisites, etc., besides the occasional employment of a charwoman, and such little washing as has to go to the laundry—the bulk, of course, being done at home.

The item 'Insurance and Benefit Club' represents an annual premium of £2 1s. 3d. for a life policy of the value of £100, effected at the age of twenty-five; 4s. for another £100 in the case of death being by accident; 3s. for insurance of furniture against fire; and £2 paid to a Friendly Society as provision against sickness.

The item '£5 for a Summer Holiday' will seem to many ridiculously small, but when we add to it what would have been the cost of living at

Budget	£	s.	d.
Rent (£26), rates and taxes (£5 3s. 5d.)	31	3	5
Railway travelling	7	0	0
Life insurance and benefit club	4	8	3
Newspapers, books, etc.	4	10	0
Gas, coal, coke, oil, wood, matches	9	17	0
Summer Holiday	5	0	0
Tobacco	2	5	0
Birthday and Christmas presents	1	10	0
Stamps and stationery		12	0
Food	47	9	0
House expenses	5	4	0
Boots	6	0	0
Tailor	6	0	0
Dress for wife and children	13	0	0
Balance to cover doctor, chemist, charities, &c.	6	1	4
	£150	0	0

home, it will be found enough to cover the necessary travelling, lodging, and extra board for a fortnight's holiday.

'Newspapers, books, etc.—£4 10s.' should not represent all the reading done in the family, for the man of intellectual tastes and high aims will have provided himself in his days of bachelorhood with something in the shape of a library; besides which he will, unless his neighbourhood is scandalously behind the times, live within easy distance of a Free Library.

Education for the children, it will be noticed, has no place in our budget. This is because our typical pair are wise enough to know that the teaching to be got under the Elementary Education Acts is incomparably better than any private teaching within their means.

G. S. LAYARD, Cornhill Magazine, May 1901.

3

Eight Hundred a Year

Eight hundred a year! To the toiling clerk it seems unbounded wealth; to the woman of fashion a poor thing in pin-money; to those who usually start marriage on such an income, the professional man, or the younger son with a narrow berth in the Civil Service, it is a sum upon which the two ends can be made to meet with comfortable success or inconvenient uncertainty, according to the requirements and habits of the people who have the spending of it.

First of all comes the house-rent. I know that the accepted rule is to spend a tenth of income upon rent. But I would advise a rent of over £80—say, £90, or even a little more—holding that two people with an income of £800 would be justified in spending at least £130 of it on rent, rates and taxes.

Choose your house with some regard to the street in which it stands, not on account of the social repute of that street, but of the practical advantages of its position. But position is not everything or nearly everything; the two things most important to health, and consequently to spirits, are light and air. So care should be taken to secure a house in not too narrow a street, and not too closely built up at the back, so that any sun that is going may have a chance of entering the rooms and cheering the inmates.

Having taken your house and put down £130 out of your £800 for rent, the next question is the question of servants. Two is the right number, a cook at £20 a year, and house-parlourmaid at £18. With two such servants, if they are well-meaning and fairly intelligent, a woman can have her household conducted with order and daintiness, *if she chooses*, which means that she must be willing to supervise and interest herself in the details of the establishment.

If a woman marries on £800 a year, she ought not to be too proud or too indolent to lend a constant head and an occasional hand to the conduct of the house—nor her husband either for the matter of that. Thus he should be his own butler, and, besides taking charge of the cellar, should decant, if not the everyday claret or whisky, certainly any wine which he offers to his friends. The wife should dust the china and ornaments; it prevents breakages, and gives the servant more time to get through her morning's task of scrubbing, sweeping, silver cleaning, and the like. She will, of course, take the entire charge of her store and linen cupboards, will inspect every article when it comes back from the wash, and may well assist in the mending.

We come now to the sum necessary for housekeeping expenses. In this I include food; household necessaries, such as lamp-oil, candles, soap, and the like; washing and window-cleaning. These expenses ought to be, and with careful management can be, covered by £4 a week, and I would divide the items as follows:

	£	s.	d.
Washing (including household linen and servants' washing)		12	0
Window-cleaning		1	4
Meat	1	0	0
Groceries	1	0	0
Bread		4	0
Vegetables		3	6
Milk		3	6
Eggs		2	6
Butter		4	6
Fish		4	0
Bacon		3	0
	£3	18	4

The allowance for the tradesmen's books is not extravagant, especially the sum set down for groceries, as so much is included under this heading—matches, blacklead, polishing paste, firewood, and many other insignificant but money-costing articles, besides the items mentioned above and the more prominent necessaries of tea and coffee, sugar, jam, and cheese. Still, a household of four people, and more than four people, can be adequately provided for on £4 a week, so I set down the housekeeping expenses at £200 a year.

The rates and taxes, housekeeping and servants being accounted for, we will pass on to the husband's side of the household, which means wine and tobacco. If he drinks claret, his wine bill cannot well come to less than £30 in the year; but many of my men friends maintain that he ought to drink, not claret, but whisky, in the ordinary way, and one of them has furnished me with a list which I subjoin, and which reduces the sum by £10:

	£	s.	d.
Whisky, 4½ doz. at 36s.	8	2	0
Claret, 9 doz. at 15s.	6	15	0
Port, 1½ doz. at 42s.	3	3	0
Sherry, 1 doz. at 32s.	1	12	0
Brandy, 2 bottles at 5s.		10	0
	£20	2	0

As for smoking, a man who marries on £800 a year must like a pipe or learn to like it. If he is but a moderate smoker, smokes tobacco at 6s. 6d. a pound, and allows himself 100 cigars and 200 or 300 cigarettes in the year, he will cover his expenses in this direction with £10.

And now comes the question of clothes and pocket-money. The husband needs more pocket-money than the wife, and the wife needs more clothes than the husband. The latter, what with his omnibus or tube fare, his lunch, his cup of tea in the afternoon, and his 'Westminster' or 'Pall Mall', will spend 2s. or nearly 2s. a day. The amount cannot be calculated at less, for even though he should save 2d. or 3d. a day, there is Sunday to be considered, and it will not be a blank day in expenditure if he goes to church and contributes to the collection or to his club and has tea or a brandy and soda. He must certainly have his 12s. a week, and that means £30 a year, or a little more. Then he will spend £40 on clothes, so that his personal allowances cannot be less than £70.

The wife will require less pocket-money; she must content herself with £20 a year, and out of that she must pay her club subscription, if she belongs to a club, her expenses of locomotion, and the cab fares to and from the dinner parties. Her dress, on the other hand, will cost more than her husband's, and we must allow her £50, so that the sum employed by each in personal expenses is the same, that is to say, £70 a year.

Then there is the doctor, and as under this heading we will include the dentist and the chemist's bill, we cannot set apart less than £30. Coal will come to £12 in the year, and gas, or its equivalent, to £9.

Repairs are always a formidable item. You always hope that there will not be much to do next year—a fond delusion, for next year invariably exacts as much as its predecessor, and occasionally more; for the kitchen boiler may burst, or snow comes through the roof, or the range goes wrong, and the recurring necessity of painting the house outside seems to arise so much oftener than it ought to. You must set aside, I think, taking one year with another, £50 for repairs, and think yourself lucky if you are able to keep within that limit. In repairs I include cleaning, the cleaning of chintzes, curtains, and carpets; and the keeping up of the supply of all that is needed in the house, such as linen, brooms and brushes, china, glass, etc. For once let the supply go down, and you will find it almost impossible to get it up again, unless somebody leaves you a legacy. So it does not pay to let your sheets and dusters pass into the rag-bag without putting others in their place, and £50 a year will not be too much to make good the general wear and tear.

There remains now postage and stationery to be paid for. Five pounds we must put down for stationery proper, that is to say, paper, envelopes, and blotting-paper. Then 5s. a week, which is £13 a year, should be allowed for little extra expenses, such as the despatching of parcels, the purchase of a few flowers and the like, and out of this fund stamps, postcards, and telegrams must be paid for.

There remain only savings, holidays, amusements, and charity. Our couple must put by £50 a year. They must allow another £50 for holiday expenses, the cost of lodgings or hotels, travelling, and tips. A long stay with friends is a saving in holiday expenses, but Saturday to Monday visits, or holidays spent in going from house to house, are most costly, the constant railway journeys and tips running away with more money than would be spent in modest seaside or country lodgings, or at a Swiss hotel *en pension*. That leaves £35 for entertaining, amusements, and charity—not a large sum.

Playgoing must be strictly limited, for theatre and music-hall tickets run away with a lot of money, and there is always the expense of the journey hither and thither. The real lovers of music can indulge their taste at very little cost. On the whole it comes to this, that a pretty home, comfortably kept, and an easy mind, unshaken by the thought of the Christmas bills, are better worth having than a large acquaintance, much entertaining, and many amusements; and that for most people who live on eight hundred a year these things are not compatible.

Now we will make a list of the figures as I have drawn them up:

	£
Rent, rates and taxes	130
Housekeeping	208
Servants' wages	38
Husband's allowance	70
Wife's allowance	70
Repairs	50
Holidays	50
Doctor	30
Wine	20
Tobacco	10
Coal	12
Gas	9
Stationery	5
Postage, &c.	13
Entertaining, &c.	35
	£750

The list as given admits of an increase in the numbers of the household, as the addition of a child, or even two children would necessitate but little alteration in the figures, and it is drawn up on the assumption that the couple who have the spending of it are an average couple with no special gift of management.

G. COLMORE, *Cornhill Magazine*, June 1901.

4

Eighteen Hundred a Year

The expenditure of an income of £1800 a year will vary a great deal in detail according to whether it is spent in London or the country. Taking London first—the old idea was that house-rent should absorb only one tenth of the income; but this in London is practically impossible. The house rent which, on an income of £1800, in most cases had better not exceed £200, including rates and taxes, may very easily mount up to £340.

There seems to be a very general impression that living in a better locality and a more central part of the West End is an actual economy; and this may be the case if cabs are much used, but if the Underground or 'buses be the usual mode of locomotion, very little is saved except time.

For the sake of argument I will say that the young couple decide on the more fashionable locality, and weight their income with a disproportionately high rent. Under these circumstances I think the disposition of their income and general expenditure would work out into something like the following table:

	£
Rent, rates, and taxes	360
Housekeeping, including living, washing, lighting	550
Repairs, insurance, cleaning, painting, etc.	100
Coal	60
Dress (man and woman)	200
Wages, including beer, and 4 servants	130
Wine	60
Stamps, newspapers, stationery, etc.	30
Doctors, dentists, accidents, journeys	100
New house linen	20
Charities	40
	£1650

Cabs, amusements, and presents will have to be saved out of clothes or journeys; with so heavy a rent putting by money some years will be very difficult. Any bill that cannot be paid weekly should be paid quarterly. One bill I fear often postponed is that of the doctor. I think it would be immensely to the advantage of both doctor and patient if it were a more received custom that the general practitioner should be given his half-guinea, like the M.D. his guinea, at the close of each visit.

Servants. Speaking in a general way, every maid represents an additional £60 or £70 a year, and every man servant another £70 or £80. These sums cover all the expenses connected with a servant, including wages.

In the eighth volume of Mr Charles Booth's wonderful book, *The Life and Labour of the People in London,* there is a chapter on domestic indoor servants which all young householders would do well to read. It is with no small surprise one realizes how very limited in number, as compare d with the population, are the people who can afford to keep any servants at all. Mr Booth says, 'With three servants—a cook, parlourmaid and housemaid—a household is complete in all its functions; all else is only a development of this theme.' Most of my young women friends will be surprised to hear that he gives the lady's-maid no place at all, and of course she is the easiest to suppress without altering the style of living or inconveniencing the husband in any way. A large class of people who keep three servants, even if they increase them to four, add a kitchen-maid, or an up-and-down girl, rather than a lady's-maid. I am inclined to think that in early years of married life a lady's-maid, besides being a great comfort, partly pays herself by the saving of dressmakers' bills, and turning old things into new. It is fancy things made at home that really pay, not petticoats and underlinen. The lady's-maid, too, must undertake the mending of house linen, an important duty, as very few housemaids can be trusted to do fine needlework at all.

There is no economy in stinting the daily food, either for the dining-room or the servants. Servants who come to a certain class of master and mistress look upon good feeding as their due as much as sheets to sleep in or the wages which are handed out to them quarterly.

It is both economical and clean to make an arrangement with the laundress to do the maids' washing at so much a week, instead of giving 'washing money' to the servants themselves. I also think it of great importance that the beer money, instead of being paid weekly, should be added to the wages and paid quarterly. If masters and mistresses only realized the number of young servants who have been taught to drink by being tempted to take the spirits on the cold grey morning when they come to their work, masters and mistresses would be more careful to lock away the whisky and brandy before they go to bed.

Living in the country on an income of £1800 a year changes the expenditure in many ways; in some more expensive and in others cheaper. The most important reductions will be in the house rent:

	£
Rent, rates, and taxes	180
Housekeeping (living, washing, lighting)	450
Repairs, insurance, cleaning, painting	100
Coal	80
Dress (man and woman)	180
Wages, including beer (4 servants)	130
Wine	50
Stamps, stationery, newspapers	30
Doctors, dentists, accidents, journeys	100
New house linen	20
Charities	40
	£1360

The table shows a considerable reduction, and, if saving is not very necessary, a pony carriage and groom can be added (£130), besides the obligatory garden, which, well done, including wages and all expenses, must be counted at £150 a year. So the table now stands at £1640.

With these luxuries the margin is as narrow as the London one. Any careful housekeeper will find it easier to make reductions in the country, though it will probably be at the expense of having friends to stay, which is one of the pleasures of living in the country.

Furnishing can be done even more simply and sensibly than in London. If washing house linen is more, cleaning of curtains, chintzes, etc. is infinitely less; three months of London making things much dirtier than a year in the country.

Poultry-keeping in the country is a pleasure and an interest. If the garden is carefully and knowingly stocked, to supply the wants of every month in the year, the saving in the weekly books is considerable. Everyone who has space should keep pigs; nothing so prevents waste or pays better.

MRS EARLE, *Cornhill Magazine*, July 1901.

5

Ten Thousand a Year

As the subject of this article is to be £10,000 a year to spend, I have chosen for an exemplary budget the expenditure of an ordinary well-favoured couple, who have been left £10,000 a year, with a solid capital behind it and no inherited burdens.

What is wanted is to gain full satisfaction for your money, to hold up your head and enjoy life, you who have been born unfettered by fluctuating rent-rolls and inherited debts. And the only way I can see for you to reap the full advantage of your prosperity is to make a firm resolve that you will have a margin; that, notwithstanding all temptations, you will keep that margin. Half the minor problems of domestic life are swept away with a margin. . . .

Having demonstrated the great importance of having a margin, it follows that all the items of your expenditure should be fixed with a view to keeping it. First and foremost,—don't overhouse yourself. Don't go and see an enchanting house in Grosvenor Square, and think, because you can afford to pay the rent, you can afford to live in it. Where would your margin be if you did? Don't go and buy a large landed estate in the country because it is going cheap, and fondly imagine that you are going to live there and keep your margin. The moment you lose sight of this margin you will be a poor man.

Suppose that a London house will be wanted. With £10,000 a year you will neither be able to take a very large house nor, on the other hand, can you take a very small one, as unless you have an unusually strong individuality, you cannot elect to live with three maids in a small house in Kensington Square when you are known to have £10,000 a year. 'What do you *do* with your money ? . . . If only I had the spending of it!' And so on.

In consequence of all this you will content yourself with the medium-sized 'mansion', either in London or the country—or both. One of moderate size in an accessible part of London would represent from £450 to £500 a year, its rates and taxes about £150, and the upkeep, painting, and repairs, an average of £200 a year. A good London house of this sort of rental, and kept in good condition, can easily be let every season for £600 or £700.

As far as the country part of your life is concerned, it is impossible to do more than generalize. One man will want to hunt, another to shoot; fishing will be the elixir of life to a third, politics the dry bread which nourishes a fourth. But whatever his country pursuits or his intellectual interests, the man must content himself with about one-fifth of the income with which to satisfy them—that is, between £2000 and £2500 a year; this sum should provide him with a very fair amount of interest and variety in whatever lies his particular fancy. . . .

Next in importance to the housing question is the housekeeping. As the size of the house was more or less decided by the size of your income, so the scale of your housekeeping will be practically decided by the size of your house.

Given, we will say, a house on the south side of Eaton Square, with perhaps ten or twelve servants and a really good cook, I defy any woman, unless she attaches undue importance to economy (and even economy can be carried too far, to the detriment of all *joie de vivre*) to keep her books as low in proportion as in the small house in Kensington Square with three maids. There, it is easy; everything encourages economy. Economy is the spirit of the house, and the three maids pride themselves on saving the scraps, or, if you are exceptionally blessed, they might even be persuaded to help you eat them.

You give a dinner with a bowl of roses, a roast chicken, and an ice from Gunter, in a little white-panelled room. It is all charming, and costs the proverbial twopence-halfpenny. But this is not the case in the larger house, where spending is the spirit of the household. There, your dinner-party will be a very different affair. The moderately good dinner, which is excusable in the small house with a limited household, is not admissible in a large house with plenty of servants, where the dinner must be perfectly cooked, the waiting must be perfect, and the flowers and et-ceteras must all be in keeping. Servants who are capable of thus shining at dinner-parties will not be the class of servants that help to keep the books very low in everyday life. The only practical way of contending with the difficulty is to fix a sum over which the books shall not go and to leave the minute details alone.

A fair average for the housekeeping books, if flowers and vegetables are provided by the country house, would be from £20 to £22 a week. The wages of twelve or fourteen servants would average between £350 and £400, and the upkeep of a London and a country house in linen, etc. would be close upon £200. There would then be £200 yearly for wine, £130 for coal, £70 for lighting, £130 for the butler's book, which includes all telegrams, postage of letters and parcels, hampers, cabs, etc.; £70 indoor liveries; £150 stationery and little bills.

Set aside £150 to cover the railway expenses of moving your household twice yearly, and all small journeys for visits, etc., £600 yearly would provide the upkeep of a good working stable for London or country—two pairs of horses, and two ponies or hacks.

Both the man and the woman would require £450 for clothes, private expenses, and subscriptions; and then another bugbear arises, in the shape of education.

For the sake of argument, suppose there to be three children, two boys and a girl. As babies, £200 would easily cover their expenses; but hanging over you would be the training of their youthful minds. Having £10,000 a year, you would not have the shadow of an excuse not to give them the best of everything. So, if you are a wise man, from the time their baby lips spread melodies, or the reverse, over the house, you would lay by £300 a year against the evil day when Eton claimed them for her own. You would have accumulated in this manner, in the first ten years of their existence, £3600 towards carrying them through their private and public school life. Another ten years' saving would be a small drop in the ocean towards starting them in the world. Thus you would have provided for twenty years of their existence without having to alter your own way of life. And after that I draw a veil, as it will simply be putting your hand in your pocket at every turn. Meanwhile the girl can be kept through those twenty years for rather over £100 a year.

Public rates and taxes are the final twist of the torture screw, and they will grind out of you close upon £500. This would be taking the income tax at 8d. or 9d. in the pound; anything over that, like the present 1s. 2s., would be an 'adverse circumstance' to be met by the margin.

Budget	£
Country property expenses	2200
London house, inclusive of rates and taxes, decorative and other repairs	800

House books, inclusive of beer and washing and household washing	1200
Wages	400
Coal	130
Lighting	70
Liveries (indoor)	70
Butler's book, for all postage of letters, parcels, hampers, cabs, etc.	130
Stationery and small bills	150
Wine	200
Entertaining and amusements	350
Upkeep of two houses in linen, chintzes, general wear and tear, etc.	200
Dress and private expenses (£450 each)	900
Education and children's clothes	500
Stables	600
Small journeys and visits	150
Illness	100
Taxes (income and other)	450
Charities	400
	£9000

This will leave you with a balance of £1000 for margin.

LADY AGNEW: *Cornhill Magazine*, August 1901.

EAST LONDON WATER SUPPLY!

Company's Turncock. "NOW, LOOK 'ERE, DON'T YOU GO A WASTIN' ALL THIS 'ERE VALUABLE WATER IN WASHIN' AND WATERIN' YOUR GARDENS, OR ANY NONSENSE O' THAT SORT, OR YOU 'LL GET YOURSELVES INTO TROUBLE!"

CHAPTER 5

HOUSING THE WORKERS

(Royal Commission on the Housing of the Working Classes, 1884-85)

Ever since the Industrial Revolution towards the end of the 18th century 'housing the workers' has been one of the most pressing of problems, and (as present-day experience continues to prove) one of the most difficult to solve.

The first attempt to deal with the matter by Act of Parliament was the Labouring Classes' Lodging House Act of 1851, which enabled town councils and local boards of health to erect (if they felt so disposed) 'lodging houses for artisans'. In the next quarter of a century several other Housing measures were passed, but by the 1880s the situation seemed as bad as ever. The public conscience was aroused, and in the spring of 1884 Gladstone appointed a Royal Commission to inquire into the Housing of the Working Classes.

The list of royal commissioners was headed by the name of the Prince of Wales (Edward VII), and among the rest were Cardinal Manning and Lord Salisbury, soon to be Prime Minister. The chairman was Sir Charles Dilke, President of the Local Governnent Board, one of the most promising of the younger Liberals.

The Royal Commission issued its first report in May 1885; this dealt with housing conditions, both urban and rural, in England. It was shortly followed by reports on housing conditions in Scotland and in Ireland. Chief among the Commission's recommendations was a wide extension of the housing powers of local authorities, and as a result the Housing of the Working Classes Act was passed in 1890, which empowered local authorities to provide dwelling-houses for the working-classes—thus opening the way for the 'council houses' that are so prominent in our social landscape.

I

Moral and Material Effects of Overcrowding

In considering what are the effects moral and material of the present conditions of the housing of the working classes, especially in the Metropolis, it will be convenient to deal with overcrowding as a centre around which most of the others group themselves.

The first witness to be examined, Lord Shaftesbury, expressed the opinion more than once, as the result of nearly sixty years' experience, that however great the improvement of the condition of the poor in London has been in other respects, the 'overcrowding had become more serious than it ever was'. This opinion was corroborated by witnesses who spoke from their own knowledge of its increase in various part of the town.

The facts and figures which have been quoted in known instances where persons of all ages occupy the same room at all hours would be sufficient to establish the moral evil of the single room system, even if specific corroborative evidence were not forthcoming both as to the prevalence of this evil and also as to the widespread existence of the system which is the cause of it.

Lord Shaftesbury said, 'The effect of the one room system is physically and morally beyond description. In the first place, the one room system always leads as far as I have seen to the one bed system. If you go into these single rooms you may sometimes find two beds, but you will generally find one bed occupied by the whole family, in many of these cases consisting of father, mother, and son; or of father and daughters; or brothers and sisters. It is impossible to say how fatal the result of that is. It is totally destructive of all benefit from education. It is a benefit to the children to be absent during the day at school, but when they return to their homes, in one hour they unlearn everything they have acquired during the day.'

In some cases where grown up sons and daughters sleep in the same rooms, lodgers are taken in addition to the regular inmates, a fact which greatly increases the tendency to immorality.

* * *

The Rev J. W. Horsley, chaplain of the Clerkenwell prison, has made a study of the sources of crime which comes under his personal notice, and he not only says that he entertains 'the very strongest opinion' that overcrowding is a great cause of immorality, but he goes on to declare that every case of incest he has ever come across, with one exception, has been traceable to the one-room system. The rector of Christ Church, Spitalfields, is equally positive from his own personal observation that there is a 'great deal of incest' which is attributable to overcrowding, as are cases of juvenile prostitution which he has himself had knowledge of.

These two clergymen are not alone in their opinion, but it is right to mention that there are other witnesses who either do not acknowledge the existence of the worst phases of immorality, or attribute instances of it to other causes. The curate of St Philip's, Clerkenwell, thinks that the statements about incest and overcrowding are exaggerated, but says that he has known of cases which he would attribute rather to drunkenness than to the one-room system; he, however, allows that this system increases the liability to such occurrences. The vicar of St Paul's, Bunhill Row, does not think that the bringing up of a large family in one room conduces to immorality provided no lodgers are taken in. .... The subject is not one which calls for speculative opinions, and there cannot be any question that every effort should be made to put an end to a state of things which familiarizes children of tender years with scenes they ought never to witness.

Mr Marchant Williams [Inspector of Schools for the London School Board] says in connexion with this question, 'I speak from knowledge of the facts: I have not the least doubt about the overcrowding I have witnessed being productive of immorality. I visit a house and ask the woman how many rooms she occupies, and she tells me two. Then I ask her, "How many in the family?" Her answer is "We are 10 or 11". "How many beds?" "Two beds." "I suppose you and your husband occupy one?" "Yes, and two or three of the younger children." Then there are an eldest son and an eldest daughter, aged perhaps 20 or 18 or 19, as the case may be, and when I shrug my shoulders, the reply very often is, "You must bear in mind that my daughter does not, or that that my daughters do not, always come home at night, they do not always sleep here". They are prostitutes, and they are encouraged as prostitutes by their parents.'

Before leaving this painful subject, Your Majesty's Commissioners feel bound to put it on record that while the evidence before them reveals an undoubtedly bad state of things, they find that the standard of morality among the inhabitants of these crowded quarters is higher than might have been expected looking at the surroundings amid which their lives are passed.

★　　★　　★

If there has been some attempt to throw doubt on overcrowding and the single-room system being the immediate cause of immorality, no one has ventured to express an opinion that they are not most destructive of bodily health.

It probably is not necessary to go into the question of the amount of air per head in sleeping rooms necessary for the maintenance of health; the amount which the vestries were said in evidence to recognize as sufficient, 300 feet for each adult, is not excessive, being one half of the minimum allowed in prisons and police barracks, and greatly less than the amount allowed in workhouses, but the amount found in tenement houses often falls far short of that moderate allowance. Even if it did not fall short cubic space is not the only point to consider. There must be a relation between cubic space and conveniences for ventilation. What is needed is unused air.

Although the poor cannot observe the laws of sanitation in such dwellings as have been described, yet it is probably an instinctive knowledge of this want which makes many of them recognize that if they are to keep their children well they must keep them in the streets; if they attempt to make them stay indoors the result is sickness of various kinds. Infants cannot have this attention paid to their needs, and infantile mortality among the poor is enormous. Carelessness on the part of mothers is an accompaniment of overcrowding, and to these causes was ascribed the high death rate among infants under five years of age in certain areas which were the subject of special investigation.

But there is a great deal of suffering among little children in overcrowded districts that does not appear in the death-rate at all. In St Luke's ophthalmia, locally known as the blight, among the young is very prevalent, and can be traced to the dark, ill-ventilated, crowded rooms in which they live; there are also found scrofula and congenital diseases, very detrimental to the health of the children as they grow up.

Among adults, too, overcrowding causes a vast amount of suffering which could be calculated by no bills of mortality, however accurate. Even statistics of actual disease consequent on overcrowding would not convey the whole truth as to the loss to health caused by it to the labouring classes. Some years ago the Board of Health instituted inquiries in the low neighbourhoods to see what was the amount of labour lost in the year, not by illness, but by sheer exhaustion and inability to do work. It was found that upon the lowest average every workman or workwoman lost about 20 days in the year from simple exhaustion, and the wages thus lost would go towards paying an increased rent for a better house.

There can be little doubt but that the same thing is going on now, perhaps even to a greater extent. That overcrowding lowers the general standard, that the people get depressed and weary, is the testimony of those who are daily witnesses of the lives of the poor. The general deterioration in the health of the people is a worse feature of overcrowding even than the encouragement by it of infectious disease. It has the effect of reducing their stamina and thus producing consumption and diseases arising from general debility of the system whereby life is shortened.

Nothing stronger could be said in describing the effect of overcrowding than that it is even more destructive to general health than conducive to the spread of epidemic and contagious diseases. Unquestionably a large amount of the infection which ravages certain of the great cities is due to the close packing of the population. Typhus is particularly a disease which is associated with overcrowding, and when once an epidemic has broken out its spread in overcrowded districts is almost inevitable. In Liverpool nearly one fifth of the squalid houses where the poor live in the closest quarters are reported as always infected, that is to say, the seat of infectious disease.

Housing of the Working Classes, 1st Report, pp. 14-16; P.P. 1884-5, vol. 30.

2

'Is it the pig that makes the stye . . . ?'

Before leaving the effects upon the people of the evil conditions in which they live, and before entering upon the causes which have produced these evils, it will be well to consider in which of the two categories certain facts should be placed. The question, to quote the title of a pamphlet mentioned in evidence, is, 'Is it the pig that makes the stye or the stye that makes the pig?' That is to say, are the dirty and drinking habits of a portion of the very poor who live in overcrowded dwellings the cause or the consequence of the miserable circumstances in which they are found?

It will be seen that the temperance question is involved in this examination, and the strictest caution is necessary not to let regret and disapproval of the ravages of intemperance divert attention from other evils which make the homes of the working classes wretched, evils over which they have never had any control.

Lord Shaftesbury's testimony is worth quoting. 'I have both heard and read remarks that are very injurious to the masses of the people, and likely to prevent any reforms being made on their behalf, to the effect that they are so sunken, so lost, so enamoured of their filth, that nothing on earth can ever rescue them from it. Now I am certain that a great number of the people who are in that condition have been made so by the condition of the houses in which they live. I have no doubt that if we were to improve the condition of the dwellings, there would be a vast number of very bad cases who would continue in the filth in which they began; but I am sure that no small number might be rescued from it by being placed in better circumstances, might have greater enjoyment of health, and might thus be much improved in their general condition.

'This is the operation of it: At the time that these alleys I speak of existed, we have known, from observation and evidence, a number of young people come up to London in search of work. A young artisan in the prime of life, an intelligent active young man, capable of making his 40s. or 50s. a week, comes up to London; he must have lodgings near his work; he is obliged to take, he and his wife, the first house that he can find, perhaps even in an alley such as I have described. In a very short time, of course, his health is broken down; he himself succumbs, and he either dies or becomes perfectly useless. The wife falls into despair; in vain she tries to keep her house clean; her children increase upon her, and at last they become reckless, and with recklessness comes drinking, immorality, and all the consequences of utter despair.

'Again, with regard to these tenement-houses, I should tell you that many of the immediate occupants in these tenement-houses are not exclusively to blame. You go up the rickety staircase, and you see the filth, but it is not their filth; it is the filth of the family that has just preceded them. I should suppose that there would be from 60,000 to 70,000 people in London who seldom remain three months in any one place. I remember that the rector of Regent Street, Gordon Square, told me that in the whole of his district he did not believe there was a single family that had been there more than three months,—they were always on the move. Look what happens. They go into these tenement-houses; they remain there a couple of months or three months; they go out again, and are succeeded by another family; they leave all their filth, and nothing is cleared away. The other family come in, stay three months, and deposit their filth, and off they go. It is perfectly impossible for those poor people, with the best intentions, to keep their houses clean. Their hearts are broken, and they have not the means of doing it. They do not know how soon they shall go; they are merely wanderers on the face of the earth. That migratory class is the most difficult one that we have to deal with.'

Lord Shaftesbury's view is not shared by all the witnesses who were subsequently examined on the point. The Rev J. W. Horsley considers that intemperance is both the cause and consequence of overcrowding, but chiefly the cause, and he points to the rare instances of a teetotaller being found living in a slum with his family in one room. There is a large consensus of evidence, from both the clergy and from other observers, that drink causes people to drift into the slums and to increase the overcrowding. It is shown that the continual drinking, not necessarily drunkenness, not only produces many of the evil habits but causes too large a proportion of the slender wages of the poor to be spent thereby, and that if drinking were given up greater comfort would in many cases follow.

Apart from the temperance question, it appears that in other respects the poorer classes often manage their incomes with imperfect economy. A case was mentioned where a family in receipt amongst them of large wages have crowded into a single room in order to have more money to spend in amusement; in the evenings they would all go to the music-hall, and on Sunday to Brighton and other places. This was, no doubt, an exceptional instance, but the overcrowding in such a case would not be compulsory, and the evidence points to the fact that there are many who could get into better lodgings if they would be more judicious and economical in their expenditure. It has been pointed out that men do not always take better rooms when their wages are better, and the poor cling to their miserable lodgings, and return to them in preference to living in better quarters.

Precarious Incomes of the Poor

But apart from the demoralizing influence of the surroundings in which their lives are passed, it must be borne in mind that the work and wages of a large proportion of the dwellers in the poorest quarters are most precarious, and the uncertainty of their incomes is sufficient cause to discourage them from struggling after better homes. It has been said of them that 'they are never a shilling ahead of the world'; they have just enough to get through the week, and in the best times are sure to be a week in arrear in purchasing power. Deeply involved in debt, they cannot move to a strange district where they are unknown and where they could not obtain credit.

Dirty Homes

Dirt is an evil almost as conducive to social misery as drinking and other self-indulgence. Dirty homes are said to be due to the habits of the people. Some of them seem to be quite indifferent to the dirt; but there is excuse for their indifference. There are houses inhabited by the poor the floors of which a woman could not scrub, because they are absolutely rotten, and the more that is done to them the worse they become, so under these conditions the most cleanly women could not be clean, even if the supply of water were at all times sufficient, and this has been shown not to be the case.

The warmest apologist for the poorest classes would not assert the general prevalence of cleanly habits amongst them. On the contrary, there is the most lamentable ignorance on all sanitary matters, which explains their objection to the circulation of air, and why they block up ventilators, and from choice keep the corpses of their dead for many days in their living rooms before burial.

Education is necessary to counteract the results of habits which, uninterrupted by outside influences, have become second nature. In criticizing the tendency of the very poor to overcrowd, and their objection to ventilation, it must never be forgotten, however, that the human body has a natural desire and need for warmth, and that the circulation of fresh air, which is necessary to the health of a well-nurtured body, chills the half-starved ill-clad frames of the men and women whose homes have been described. It is common to find an absence of bed-clothes among the scanty appointments of the wretched dwellings, and there is little wonder than the inhabitants huddle together and aggravate the danger of their overcrowding by blocking out the draughts of air that have no virtue for them.

Destructive Habits

Before quitting the subject of the habits of the dwellers in the poor districts, mention should be made of the destructive faculty which often results in wanton damage to fittings and to the structure of the houses. It is sometimes said, that if a certain class of the poor were put into decent dwellings they would forthwith wreck them and reduce them to the condition of the most miserable. It must be remembered that struggling industrious workers and the semi-criminal class often live side by side—sometimes under the same roof. The latter are the destructive class, and there is no doubt that in certain quarters, inhabited both by honest and by disreputable persons, taps are wrenched off and sold for old metal, wooden dustbins are broken up and burned for fuel, and property of every kind is destroyed in the most ruthless manner.

Drink

To return, however, to the question whether drink and evil habits are the cause or consequence of the condition in which the poor live, the answer is probably the unsatisfactory one that drink and poverty act and re-act upon one another. Discomfort of the most abject kind is caused by drink, but indulgence in drink is caused by overcrowding and its cognate evils, and the poor who live under the conditions described have the greatest difficulty in leading decent lives and of maintaining decent habitations.

Housing of the Working Classes, 1st Report, pp. 14–16; P.P. 1884–5, Vol. 30.

3

Low Wages and High Rents

Turning to the unquestioned causes which produce overcrowding and the generally lamentable condition of the homes of the labouring classes, the first which demands attention is the poverty of the inhabitants of the poorest quarters, or, in other words, the relation borne by the wages they receive to the rents they have to pay.

In considering the rates of wages, whether high or low, sight must never be lost of the precarious condition of the earnings of many of the working classes. Evidence has been given to show how uncertain is the employment of the majority, how a period of comparative prosperity may be followed by a period of enforced idleness, and how consequently their existence and subsistence can only be described as from hand to mouth. But even if employment were regular, the wages are so low that existence must be a struggle at the best of times.

A large class of persons whose earnings are at the lowest point are the costermongers and hawkers, whose average appears to be not more than 10s. or 12s. a week. This represents continuous toil, and although the income is a most precarious one, yet it is not rendered so by days and season of idleness as is the case in occupations about to be mentioned, but it is dependent upon the state of the market. The large class of dock labourers follow such an uncertain employment that their average wage is said by some witnesses to be not more than 8s. or 9s. a week, and at the highest is put down as from 12s. to 18s. a week. 5d. an hour is about the rate paid, but unfortunately the supply of unskilled labour is so much in excess of the demand that these people are not employed upon the average more than two days a week. The average of labourers' wages among the residents in Clerkenwell is said to be about 16s. a week, and this of course means that there are many who earn less. This also is about the figure at which labour is said to be obtainable at Bristol.

Sack-making and slop-tailoring are two occupations carried on to a great extent in the homes of the poor, and they are both remunerated at starvation wages. Artizans of course command a higher wage, and 25s.

a week seems to be an ordinary rate for many of that class who inhabit tenement houses. There is, however, a great fluctuation in wages, and it is very difficult to strike an average. A small area investigated will present features which do not exist in another district, perhaps within a stone's throw, and if 20s. a week be taken as a general average it does not follow that the same average will be true of other parts of the metropolis.

Rent

The facts now to be ascertained are what are the working classes, who are unaided by any charitable or philanthropic housing-enterprises, called upon to pay as rent in the open market for their dwellings, and what relation does that payment bear to their average earnings.

Mr Marchant Williams has given valuable evidence on this point. From personal investigation of parts of the parishes of St Luke's, St Giles's, Marylebone, and other poor quarters of London, he finds that 88 per cent of the poor pay more than one fifth of their income in rent; 46 per cent pay from one fourth to one half; 42 per cent pay from one fourth to one fifth; and only 12 per cent pay less than one fifth of their weekly wages in rent. These figures are gathered from an inquiry extending over nearly 1,000 dwellings, taken at random in different poor parts of the metropolis. Among them 3s. $10\frac{3}{4}$d. is the average rent of one room let as a separate tenement, 6s. of two-roomed tenements, and 7s. $5\frac{1}{4}$d. of three-roomed tenements. Rents in the congested districts of London are getting gradually higher, and wages are not rising, and there is a prospect, therefore, of the disproportion beween rent and wages growing still greater.

In the provinces the rents of houses and of tenements are much lower than in London. Three shillings a week was quoted as being paid in one instance for a single cellar in Newcastle, and 2s. 6d. was said to be the usual price of a single room in that city, but rents, as a rule, for obvious reasons, such as the comparative cheapness of land and building, run much lower in provncial towns than in London.

Causes of high rents

High rents are due to competition for houses and to the scarcity of accommodation in proportion to the population. It might be asked why cannot the pressure be relieved by a distribution of the now crowded masses over the area of the metropolis, inasmuch as it is a well known fact that for various causes certain districts contain a large number of uninhabited houses, many of which are suitable for the working classes. The answer to this query is that an enormous proportion of the dwellers in the overcrowded quarters are necessarily compelled to live close to their work, no matter what the price charged or what the condition of the property they inhabit.

It has been seen how crowded the poor central districts of London are, and one reason is that for a large class of labourers it is necessary to live as nearly as possible in the middle of the town, because they then command the labour market of the whole metropolis from a convenient centre. Sometimes they hear of casual work to be had at a certain place provided they are there by 6 o'clock the next morning, so they must choose a central position from which no part of the town is inaccessible. The dock labourers are a class that must be on the spot, because they have always to wait for calls that may arise at any moment. When ships are going out or coming in the labourers may be seen by hundreds standing in single file at the dock gates waiting for their turns, as those who get in first are first employed. The Mint in Southwark on the south of the Thames and the central district on the north are the furthest distances from their work where these people can live.

Then there is the extensive and hard-working population of coster-mongers. They are found in large numbers in the dense thoroughfares of St Luke's, Clerkenwell, and St Pancras, and in the low districts of Southwark. There are strong reasons for their living on the spot where their wares find a ready sale. The poor form their own markets, and there is the same difficulty of moving a market that there is of moving an industry, and both of these facts increase the pressure of over-crowding. The only choice a costermonger seems to have in settling his residence is either to live near the locality where he obtains a market for his goods or else near the place where he lays in his stock; hence, on the latter account, their dwellings are also found in the crowded courts round about Drury Lane, within reach of Covent Garden.

Nor are there wanting instances of skilled artizans who likewise must live close to their work: for instance, there are the watchmakers of Clerkenwell, because the apparatus required in their trade is so costly that no man can afford to have the whole of it; he therefore borrows from his friends, and may have to borrow three or four times in the course of the day.

Then there are the women who must take their work home, such as those who work for the city tailors; and the girls who are employed in small factories, such as those for artificial flowers; these also have to be in attendance morning after morning (like the dock labourers) whether there is work for them or not, for if they are not within calling distance they lose it. This precarious element in the struggle for employment is thus a most powerful cause of the pressure upon habitable space.

The mention of the women and girls suggests another reason why certain localities are overcrowded. The subsidiary employment of wife and children has to be taken into consideration when the poor choose a place of residence. Whatever the contributions of these members of a family may be to the maintenance of the household, there is no doubt that the work of charwomen and seamstresses, and the labour in which children are employed, attract great numbers to the densely populated districts which provide such employment, and away from the suburbs where such work would be out of reach.

There is moreover to be considered the difficulty many of the poor have in moving from a neighbourhood on account of the credit which they have built up with the little shopkeepers of the district. Again there is the question of cheap markets. In the remoter suburbs food is much dearer than in the centre of the town, where the costermongers who themselves help to increase the pressure on space compete with the small shopkeepers as purveyors of provisions at a lower rate than they can be obtained in remoter districts: to these causes must be added the natural reluctance that is found among the poor to leave their old neighbours and form new associations. . . .

Migratory habits

The migratory habits of the poor, so far from relieving the overcrowded districts, add considerably to the competition for houses and consequantly send up the rents. There are first of all the migrations from one part of London to another, caused by the shifting of the town population. Then there are cases of sudden pressure, as, for instance, the influx into Whitechapel and Spitalfields of foreign Jews, whose religious observances, apart from their habits of life, require them to live together. Again, there are the labourers from other large towns, and also the immigrants from villages, who come up with the idea that in London they cannot fail to get work; that 'in the country one may get it but in London one must get it'.

Demolitions.

The pressure, with all its evil consequences, caused by immigration is small compared tothat produced by demolition. When the demolitions are so extensive that the people have to depart, then the consequence is that new slums are created elsewhere.

There are demolitions for clearance purposes undertaken by owners for the improvement of their property, or by the local authority under certain Acts, viz. for the purpose of erecting artizans' dwellings in the place of the buildings removed. There are demolitions for the widening and improvement of public streets; there are those which take place in consequence of the erection of public buildings, such as board schools;

and there are those carried out by railway companies in the construction and enlargement of their lines and stations.

Demolitions have taken place for all these purposes, and although the health and appearance of London have vastly improved in consequence of some of them, and though others have been a great boon to the better class of the poor, yet they have been accompanied with the severest hardship to the very poor, increasing overcrowding and the difficulty of obtaining accommodation, and sending up rents accordingly.

Housing of the Working Classes, 1st Report, pp. 16-19; P.P. 1884-5, vol. 30.

4

Tenement Houses

Tenement houses may be roughly said to be houses which are occupied at weekly rents by members of more than one family, but in which members of more than one family do not occupy a 'common room'.

The great majority of these houses were originally built for single families, and have since been broken up into tenements, with a family in each room or several families in each house. Although this is a highly lucrative arrangement for the persons in receipt of the rents, the sanitary condition of these houses is rendered worse by reason of their having been utilized for a purpose for which they were not constructed, there being, as a rule, not more than one water supply and only one closet for each house.

There are many streets in certain parts of London, where the worst mischief is going on, which have an outside look of respectability, the houses having the appearance of decent dwellings for single middle-class families. A large number of them have no wash-houses, no backyards, and some no back ventilation whatever, a good many having been built upon what were formerly the courts or gardens of larger houses.

The street doors, where they exist, are rarely at any time shut in houses of this description in the poorest quarters. The consequence is that the staircases and passages at night are always liable to be crowded by persons who, presumably having no other place of shelter, come there to sleep. The custom is so usual in the worst parts of London that in the Mint, Southwark, there is a well-known expression for persons so taking shelter who are called ' 'appy dossers'.

Housing of the Working Classes, 1st Report, pp. 8-9; P.P. 1884-5, vol. 30.

5

Housing Defects and Deficiencies

As regards the drainage of London, the improvement that has taken place in the present generation is enormous; the system of universal house drainage has taken the place of the cesspool system with remarkable effect both on the death rate and the habits of the people.

Notwithstanding the great change for the better, the evidence proves conclusively that there is much disease and misery still produced by bad drainage. The work of house-drainage is imperfectly done, frequently in consequence of there being little supervision on the part of the local authorities. The connexion with the sewers is faulty, and in addition to the ordinary consequences of defective drainage the bad work and bad fittings make the houses cold and draughty. There has been much building, moreover, on bad land covered with refuse heaps and decaying matter. Since 1879 builders have been compelled to cover the refuse with concrete, so far as the house extends, but sufficient control not being exercised over the quality of the concrete it frequently cracks, and the noxious gases escape into the houses.

In the provinces there are great complaints of the ill effects of bad sanitary arrangements. In Bristol the fact of many of the poorer houses being built upon land which is subject to periodical floods is a great source of sickness. At Exeter the high death rate is considered to be mainly due to the defective sewerage system and deficient house drainage. There is much room for improvement in the matter of ashpits and dustbins: in Half Moon Court there was a case given in evidence of five houses having only one between them. Vegetable substance, the refuse of costermongers, is frequently thrown into open dustholes, and was described by a witness as lying for weeks decomposing and poisoning the atmosphere of the close courts. In Liverpool it was stated that in houses, in which all the rooms were not occupied, cellars, and even parlours, are frequently used as receptacles for decaying refuse, and where the dustbins were outside the house they were placed just under the windows. A member of a building firm who has had large experience in the erection of dwellings for the working classes said that he had no doubt that the neglect of dustbins was the means of communicating scarlet fever to whole rows of houses. . . .

Water Supply

The water supply of London and the great towns is better than it was, but its inadequacy is still the cause of much unhealthiness and misery. The single water supply for an entire tenement house, often many storeys high, has already been mentioned. The supply, it has been stated by witnesses, is in some parts of London very uncertain, and when it is drawn it is kept by the poor in tubs, sometimes in sleeping rooms, there being no storage accommodation in most of the small dwellings. Even where there is a supply in the houses a large number of them are supplied from one and the same cistern for the purposes of flushing the closet and for drinking. The cistern is sometimes uncovered, and is often close to the closet-pan and to the dust heap.

The cutting off of the water supply by companies on account of nonpayment of the rate also leads to much evil. . . .

Water-Closets

The closet accommodation is itself most defective in spite of the extensive power confided to local authorities by the law in this respect. In Clerkenwell there are cases, as described, where there is not more than one closet for 16 houses. In a street in Westminster, a witness stated that there was only one for all the houses in the street, 30 or 40 people inhabiting each house; and that it was open and used by all passers by. In other parts of London a similar state of things was said to exist, compared with which the one closet accommodation to each tenement house of many families is a satisfactory arrangement. In St Luke's closets were found in the cellars in a most disgraceful state of filth and stench, and close to the water supply. In the same parish it seems to be no uncommon thing for the closets to be stopped and overflowing for months. In some parts of London they are used as sleeping places by the houseless poor of the class who haunt the staircases. In Bristol privies actually exist in living rooms: and elsewhere in the provinces there are instances where no closet accommodation at all is attached to the dwellings of the labouring classes.

Noxious trades

Noxious trades are a grave source of insanitary conditions especially when carried on in already unhealthy dwellings. Rag-picking is a powerful means of conveying disease owing to its filth. Sackmakers and matchbox makers often do all their business in the room in which their families live and sleep. The latter have to keep their paste warm, and the smell of it is most offensive. The most pernicious of the trades, however, is rabbit pulling, in which the fur is pulled from the skins, making the atmosphere most offensive, owing to the process adopted in the trade, and the fluff-laden atmosphere has the most harmful effect upon the lungs. Haddock curing and smoking are perhaps more disagreeable than dangerous, but the practice of costermongers sorting in their rooms and under their beds their unsold stock, watering it in the morning to give it the appearance of freshness, must be the means of bringing into the houses large quantities of decomposing matter.

Structural Defects

The sanitary evils last mentioned are independent of the condition of the buildings in which they are found, but there are also evils directly connected with the structural defects of the houses apart from the absence of sanitary appliances [e.g. houses with no back yards and no back ventilation, houses built back to back with air and light blocked out, the existence of cellar dwellings contrary to law].

'Jerry building'

It is perhaps needless to give a detailed description of the way in which many modern houses are run up for the working classes. What is called 'jerry building' is too well known to need evidence to prove its characteristics. There can be no doubt that the houses are often built of the commonest materials, and with the worst workmanship, and are altogether unfit for the people to live in, especially if they are a little rough in their ways. The old houses are rotten from age and neglect. The new houses often commence where the old ones leave off, and are rotten from the first. It is quite certain that the working classes are largely housed in dwellings which would be unsuitable even if they were not overcrowded.

Housing of the Working Classes, 1st Report, pp. 9-12; P.P. 1884-5, vol. 30.

6

'ware Cholera!

In July of the year, as cholera was very prevalent in Egypt, and considering the great traffic between that country and England, alarm arose lest the disease should be brought to our shores, and so be spread among us. Our vestry, as I believe were all others in the metropolis, was at once supplied with a set of rules or orders by the Local Government Board,

Illustrated London News (1893): British Museum Photo

11. A Collier's Cottage in Co. Durham

Photograph, London Borough of Tower Hamlets

12. The London Dock Strike of 1889: one of the great propaganda processions photographed as it leaves the East India Dock gates

The 'race for the chain' as the dock gates are opened to admit casual labour

The Graphic (188

as has always been done in former visitations of that epidemic. The vestry immediately took up the matter, and I drew up a handbill as follows:

Parish of St James and St John, Clerkenwell

SANITARY PRECAUTIONS

The inhabitants of the parish are earnestly advised to take the following precautions during the present season of the year:

1. *Drainage, Refuse, etc.*—To give notice at the vestry hall of defective drainage, choked drains, or offensive water-closets; of accumulations of house refuse or other decaying animal or vegetable matters. It is also most important to burn all vegetable refuse.
2. *Ventilation.*—To keep the houses clean and well ventilated, especially the sleeping rooms.
3. *Water-supply.*—To clean out the water butts frequently; to give notice at the vestry hall of defective supply, and especially of any communication between the waste-water pipe and the water-closet.
4. *Improper food.*—To avoid eating unripe or stale fruit, stale fish, or tainted meat; also to be temperate in the use of ale, beer, or other fermented liquors.
5. *Diarrhoea.*—To obtain medicine or seek medical advice immediately diarrhoea comes on.
6. *Sinks.*—To pour water daily down the sinks, and keep on the covers of the sinks.
7. *Disinfectants.*—To throw disinfectants, especially carbolic acid, into water-closets, sinks, and offensive yards. (As carbolic acid is poisonous, particular care should be taken to place the word 'poison' upon every bottle or package containing same.)
8. *Dustbins.*—To give notice immediately of any accumulation in the dustbin.
9. As cholera is prevailing abroad, and may possibly be brought here, it may be well pointed out that in former visitations, when attention has been paid to the above precautions, its advent has been harmless, but when they have been neglected severe mortality has ensued.

By order of the Sanitary Committee, J. W. GRIFFITH, M.D.,
Medical Officer of Health to the Vestry.
Vestry Hall, Clerkenwell, July 30th, 1883.

Carbolic acid may be obtained free by the poor on application at the vestry hall.

Housing of the Working Classes, 1st Report, p. 718; P.P. 1884-5, vol. 30.

The Farm Labourer's Cottage

At the conclusion of their inquiry into working class dwellings in urban centres of population Your Majesty's Commissioners commenced their rural investigation by first calling a number of persons who represented the interests of the agricultural labourers in different counties. . . .

Mr Selby, an agent of the Agricultural Labourers' Union, and formerly a labourer himself, testified to the condition of certain parts of Wiltshire, to which he had paid special attention. In one village he described several cottages in which the structural defects were considerable. The bedrooms in one case were not high enough to stand up in, and in another case two small bedrooms, each of which was entirely filled by the bed, were occupied by a man and his wife and seven children, from 16 years of age downwards. In another there was a case of a widow and her family of six, the eldest son being 25, sleeping in one bedroom. At a third, a labourer and his daughter, with her husband and six children, all slept in one bedroom, not more than 14 feet square, the sloping roof at the highest point being about 7 feet from the ground; but in that case there appeared to be a downstairs room not used for sleeping purposes.

In the rural districts there is less plea for absolute necessity for overcrowding in sleeping rooms than in the metropolis, that is to say, the single room system, as it is found in the metropolis, has no existence in agricultural villages. Single room cottages—those containing only one room for all purposes—are found in rare cases; as a rule, the most miserably housed families in the rural districts have another room in addition to the sleeping chamber, and it is from habit or from the nature of the room that they do not utilize the living apartment for the purposes of sleeping. Two roomed houses in some localities in this and in other counties are very common, and it is in them that the worst overcrowding exists. The structural and sanitary condition of some of the cottages of Wiltshire was described to be very bad. At another village they were found to be falling to pieces from neglect; in some cases the bare thatch being visible upstairs and letting in the rain.

Mr Samuel Pike, another agent of the Union, gave evidence as to Dorset and parts of the adjacent counties. He described the sanitary condition of cottages as very defective; some have no stairs but a ladder by which to walk up to the upper rooms, and no stone or board on the floors, only the earth, or perhaps worn-away concrete. In this district

Mr Pike said that the cottages of the labourers chiefly contained one small room downstairs and two upstairs, and that there was under these conditions overcrowding of the kind described. There was a case of 11 persons, two parents and nine children, including a boy of 19 and a girl of 15, occupying two small rooms. Similar evidence was given from the neighbouring county of Somerset.

Mr Alfred Simmons, the secretary of the Kent and Sussex Labourers' Union, spoke of the improvement that had taken place in some portions of his district in the cottage accommodation, but described the sanitary conditions as very bad indeed.

Mr George Ball, the agent of the Labourers' Union in Essex, said that generally speaking the cottage accommodation in the rural districts of that county was, to quote his words, 'very sad indeed', at one village visited by him one bedroom was the rule. In another, which he described as the worst village in Essex [Steeple Brompstead], he found the cottages both badly constructed and in bad repair, few of them having rooms more than 6 or 7 feet high, and there were numerous instances of overcrowding.

The Rev C. W. Stubbs described the condition of the labourers' cottages in certain 'open' [i.e. not all owned by one landlord] villages in Buckinghamshire. His late parish of Granborough contained about 50 cottages; of these only one had more than two bedrooms, and 17 had only one bedroom, and he described the 'wattle and dab' huts in which the poor are most frequently housed in that county. These have usually a lean-to at the end of the cottage in which the people store their things, and in one corner of which there is an open privy draining into the nearest ditch.

In contrast to the foregoing may be cited instances in which great improvements have been carried out, with the result of the cottagers being housed in comfort and under sanitary conditions . . . but while many landowners have shown considerable interest in the work of the better housing of their poorest tenants, it cannot be denied that there are cases in which the condition described can be traced to the neglect of the freeholder.

In Wiltshire a very common rent seems to be about 1s. a week, while the averages of wages are put at from 9s. to 13s. a week. The wages of a shepherd in the same county, who earns 16s. a week all the year round, and has besides a cottage and garden, may be considered an exceptional instance. Shepherds, moreover, like carters and certain other servants, have to work for very long hours and also on Sundays. In Dorsetshire there was said to be no uniform rate. In on district where the wages are about 11s. the rent of small cottages was said to be about 7s. a month, that is to say, 1s. 9d. a week. In Essex the agent to the Labourers'

Union stated that the wages of ordinary farm labourers average 11s. a week, while the rent of cottages he computes at about 1s. 8d. a week ... The occupation of a cottage is sometimes considered as part of a man's weekly wages. This is the case where cottages are let with the farms and sublet by the farmers. This, in the opinion of the men themselves, is said to be one of the greatest grievances that they have to suffer from. They are engaged at so much a week and the cottage, and the hardship is stated to be that as it is reckoned part of their wages they are liable to be, and sometimes are, turned out at a week's notice. There is evidence from different parts of England that there is more dissatisfaction among the labourers with regard to this part of the cottage question than about anything else; the insecurity of the tenure is felt more severely even than the misery of the accommodation.

Housing of the Working Classes, 1st Report, pp. 24-26; P.P. 1884-5, vol. 39.

8

A Country Parson's Plea for the Decencies

What I want to state respecting the condition of the cottages [in the village of Olveston, Gloucestershire, about 10 miles from Bristol] is this: that first of all, they do not admit of sanitary habits; and in the next place they very much tend to immorality. For instance, not many weeks ago I came across a cottage in my parish, which I was not aware of before, in which there was only one bedroom. There were two beds in that bedroom, and when I say that the vacant space left after subtracting that which was occupied by the two beds was three square yards, I am giving you a large measurement. In that room on those two beds there slept the widowed mother, a young man, the eldest son, about 21, a girl of 17, very handsome, a young boy, and a young girl, that is to say, five living persons. This has been so far improved that an additional bedroom has been fitted up; but that is the state of a great number of cottages. I do not mean to say that they have one bedroom only, but even with two bedrooms, if there is a large family, the decencies of life cannot possibly be maintained.

We all know, in the first place, that modesty is the great safeguard to a woman; and when young girls are brought into contact with men by overcrowding in that sort of way, and by going to offices [latrines] which are exposed to public view, the fine edge of modesty must of course be very much blunted; and there is no doubt that that does lead to a want of that high moral feeling for which the sex ought to be distinguished, and in the end to immorality, to communication with each other before marriage, and such like.

Then as regards the men themselves, when a man finds his house in a wretched state, with bad dirty floors, water coming in at the roof, and offensive drainage, he naturally, if he has the opportunity, turns to more comfortable quarters in a public-house; and so drunkenness begins, and then all kinds of evil follow, want of attention to wife and children, and, in the end, pauperism. I have not myself a doubt that if the working classes in the rural districts were well housed, we should have a great deal less immorality, far fewer illegitimate births, and a great deal less drunkenness.

I should recommend some such standard as this. (1) Houses with good roofs and floors. Roofs are better attended to than floors. If I could take you into some of the bad cottages in my own parish and in the neighbourhood, you would be horrified at the state of the floors, and you would at once say that no decent woman could keep those floors tidy, or even sanitary, having regard to all the wet and mud and everything else that collects on them.

Then (2) there should always be a back kitchen, a sort of place where they could do all their washing, and that sort of thing; and (3) there should be a back exit, that is to say, there should be a draught through the house. There should be (4) an oven in the house. The absence of a proper oven for baking causes the people to buy their bread off bakers, and bakers' bread is not only dearer but much less nutritious than the bread baked in their own ovens. Then (5) there should be a boiler in the house; and (6) where practicable a well and pump. Then it is very important that there should be (7) a cistern to catch rain water from the roof. A cistern is an immense advantage to a house. Those cottages that have a good cistern for catching the rain water are in much better condition: the washing is done better, and the houses are kept considerably cleaner. Then there is another point which is very important, and that is (8) that all the windows should be made capable of being opened. There are many bedrooms in the cottages of the working classes in rural districts where the windows cannot be opened at all. Then there should be (9) not less than three good bedrooms.

By a good bedroom I mean one (10) with a fireplace in it. A fireplace is not only necessary for warmth in the winter, but it is quite as necessary for ventilation in the summer. I will give you an instance in my own parish, which occurred last February. In a house in which a young man was very ill with inflammation of the lungs, there was not a single bedroom with a fireplace in it. By supplying a mineral oil stove, which I have in my house, I gave every assistance I could to raise the temperature to what the medical man wished it to be; but it happened to be during the few cold days that we had this year, and it was impossible to raise the temperature. The young man died, and the medical man considered that this was almost entirely in consequence of the impossibility of getting the temperature raised.

Then (11) I think each cottage should have a garden, sufficiently large at any rate to supply vegetables for the people. I should be satisfied with a quarter of an acre, but I think that something more than a quarter of an acre would be better. Then (12) the outside offices should be removed to a distance from the house. (13) The pigsty should be as far as possible from the house. That is necessary for sanitary reasons. The smell of the pigsty close to the house is one of the most insanitary conditions connected with the houses of the rural population.

Then another most important point is (14) that the closet, or outer offices, whether near the house or not, ought to be of decent construction. You never saw such ruinous places in your life as they are, the wet coming in at the roof, dirtying the seat, and often there being no door at all, so that there can be no privacy; and in a great number of instances they are so placed that even if there was a door you could have little or no privacy. For instance, they ought to be placed in such a way that a young girl can go to the closet without being observed by the men who are the inhabitants of the cottage and all the passers by.

I am a great advocate for earth closets; and if you have earth closets there should be no cesspools, of which there are a great many near the cottages, filthy places. I believe that the people wherever earth closets are placed, work them well. It is to their advantage to do so, because they get the manure for their gardens. If there are not earth closets there should be a proper system of drainage to carry all the bad matter away to a distance; but drainage is a very difficult matter.

The next thing when you have got all these things (if you could ever suppose that we should get them) when we have got the cottages in repair there is a great need of intelligent inspectors to keep them so. It is the most difficult thing in the world to get people to keep their cottages in repair. Several of my worst cottages are not fit for human habitation. I would not put a pig in them; I would certainly not put a horse on any consideration to live in some of the cottages in my parish.

REV EDWARD GIRDLESTONE, MA, Canon of Bristol and Vicar of Olveston, Glos.; Housing of the Working Classes, 1st Report, pp. 636-9; P.P. 1884-5, vol. 30.

9

When the Londoners Go 'Hopping'

There is another section of the population, who cannot be classed as either urban or rural, whose housing requires consideration. These are the hop-pickers and the fruit-pickers, who annually settle in Kent and in one district (Farnham) of Surrey for about three weeks during the autumn for the harvest of the hop grounds, and in the fruit-picking season for shorter periods. It is calculated that in an average year there are at least 70,000 persons, men, women, and children, employed in this labour, of whom the great majority are immigrants, and of whom about 25,000 come from London. The latter are, for the most part, the roughest and neediest of the London poor. . . .

The lodgings provided for these immigrants are principally hopper-houses, barns, cowsheds, stables, and tents. The hopper-house is generally a long, low, brick and tile building, divided into 10 or 12 compartments, and accommodating from eight to a dozen persons in each compartment. Sometimes cooking sheds are provided, which are necessary for the people, not only for cooking their food, but for drying their clothes. Tents, which are purchased second-hand from Government, are often used; as they are usually supplied without cooking sheds, the condition of the women and children, who rarely have a change of clothes, is in wet weather most pitiable. Overcrowding is frequent unless great supervision is exercised, and there is great difficulty in separating the sexes, and the married people from the single.

Housing of the Working Classes, 1st Report, pp. 57-8; P.P. 1884-5, vol. 30.

10

Workers' Housing in Scotland

The single-room system appears to be an institution co-existent with urban life among the working classes in Scotland. What in England is known as the tenement system is so firmly established that even in modern legislation the word 'house' is used for any separately occupied portion of a building, while the word 'tenement' represents the whole edifice, the English use of the terms being reversed.

The size and height of ancient Scotch houses, in the old town of Edinburgh for instance, would be sufficient to show that they were always intended for the habitation of many families, even if this were not a well known historical fact, though of course there are a good many houses which a century ago were occupied by persons in good circumstances now converted into tenement houses (in the English sense).

The system is so firmly established in Scotland that the Scotch law provides for the difficulties which may arise out of the joint ownership of a house in portions. It is set forth in the title that necessary repairs of the roof, the drains, or the water pipes must be borne by all the owners in certain proportions, and it is said that no practical difficulties ever arise out of the arrangement. . . .

It is not in Edinburgh alone that are found these large tenement houses (the English expression is used for convenience), nor are they always ancient buildings. At Paisley they are said to be on the increase, and it seems in Scotch towns to be as usual to run up an edifice of great height containing a number of separate dwellings as it is in England to build a row of two-storied cottages.

At Glasgow it is acknowledged that an extraordinarily high proportion of its people live in single rooms, but it is said that the single rooms are much larger than elsewhere. Some confusion may arise from the use of the word 'house' in the Scottish sense and it must be borne in mind that the references in evidence to the frequent existence of 'single-room houses' are not to hovels containing only one apartment, but to single rooms separately occupied in edifices of considerable size. In Edinburgh there are said to be 14,000 single-room tenements; in Glasgow 25 per cent of the whole population live in single rooms; and in Dundee there are 8,221 houses of one room, containing 22,870 inhabitants.

The chief reason for this seems to be that the occupants of the single-room tenements cannot afford to pay for more accommodation. The custom of the poorer classes in Scotch towns may have something to do with their mode of life, but it is probably for the most part a question of rent. It must be borne in mind that mill-girls in parties of two or three, widows, married couples with no children, and others who form a sensible proportion of those who live in single rooms may inhabit them without harm. . . .

Much evidence was given by witnesses from large towns to the effect that a considerable proportion of the labouring classes in Scotland would be able to house themselves in far greater comfort if it were not for the large sums they spend on drink. The evidence of Glasgow witnesses is virtually repeated in other words by many other witnesses who were questioned on this point. 'There are some of them in great distress living on very little money, and there are others again that could afford perfectly well, if they chose to do it, to spend a larger proportion of their earnings on house accommodation, but they prefer to spend it on drinking or something else.'

The dilapidated condition of many of the habitations of the poor is another great evil. At Glasgow, the custom of building houses in hollow squares was said to be a great evil, and the back-to-back system in the crowded courts was described as 'the curse of Glasgow'.

Complaints are made of the insufficiency of waterclosets; there is the greatest difficulty in giving each family separate watercloset accommodation owing to the method in which houses are divided into separate dwellings. The water supply is not as good as it should be, that is to say, the supply is not carried up the long flights of stairs in the lofty houses; but an improvement is taking place in this respect. . . .

Housing of the Working Classes (Scotland); C 4409 (1885), pp. 4-5; P.P. 1884-5, vol. 31.

THE SWEATER'S FURNACE: OR, THE REAL "CURSE" OF LABOUR.

SAMBOURNE

"All the circumstances of the trade, the hours of labour, the rate of remuneration, and the sanitary conditions under which the work is done are disgraceful . . . In the 'dens' of the Sweaters, as they are called, there is not the slightest attempt at decency. . . . In the vast majority of cases work is carried on under conditions in the highest degree filthy and unsanitary. In small rooms, not more than nine or ten feet square, heated by a coke fire for the presser's irons, and at night lighted by flaring gas-jets, six, eight, ten, and even a dozen workers may be crowded . . . The stench and foul vapours about the place are very bad . . . As regards hours of labour, earnings, and sanitary surroundings, the condition of these people is more deplorable than that of any body of working men in any portion of the civilised or uncivilised world."—See Lord Dunraven's Speech on the Sweating System.

" *In the sweat of thy brow shalt thou eat thy bread!* "
What hideous echo from mock-
    ing lips
Rings through this den of despair
    and dread,
Where the hot fume mounts and
    the dank steam drips?
What devilish echo of words di-
    vine?
Oh, gold hath glitter and gauds are
    fine,
And Mammon swaggers and Mode
    sits high,
And their thrones are based on *this*
    human stye!

"That hole of sorrow," the last
    dark deep
Of DANTE's dream, may no longer
    keep

Its horrible eminence. Singers
    sweet
Of buds that burgeon and brooks
    that fleet   [Spring;
Beneath the touch of the coming
Come here, cast eyes on this scene
    —and sing !
Sing, if the horror that grips your
    throat
Will leave you breath for one
    golden note ;
Rave of March in a rhythmic rap-
    ture;
Rhapsodise of the coming of May,
Seek from the carolling lark to
    capture   [lay
A lilt of joy that shall fire your
With a rural jubilance strong to
    drown
The maddened moan of these
    thralls of Town.

CHAPTER 6

SWEATED LABOUR

(Select Committee of the House of Lords on the Sweating System, 1888-90)

What came to be known as the 'sweating system' first attracted public notice in the middle of the last century when, following a series of revealing articles in the *Morning Chronicle*, a London newspaper, Charles Kingsley exposed its iniquities in his pamphlet *Cheap Clothes and Nasty* and his novel *Alton Locke*.

Kingsley's accounts of 'sweaters' dens' in the East End of London, in which so much of the cheap tailoring of the time was produced, deeply shocked his readers. Those who knew the district, however, were not in the least surprised. At any time in the previous half-century it might have been possible to stumble into some such 'fetid, choking den' as Kingsley described, in which 'seven or eight sallow, starved beings, coatless, shoeless, and ragged, sat stitching, each on his truckle-bed'.

Nothing much happened as a result of the exposures. The alternative to the squalid and overcrowded 'dens' that Kingsley and his fellow Christian Socialists proposed was the self-governing workshop or producers' co-operation, but whenever this was tried it proved a flop. So the agitation died down, and the 'system' continued.

From time to time there was a revival of interest and public concern. Thus in 1876 there was a scare about the possible risk of infection from clothing that had been produced in insanitary workshops, but the hubbub soon subsided. Then about ten years later there was a fresh outcry. And now the menace was supposed to consist of an influx of poor foreigners, chiefly Russian and Polish Jews fleeing from persecution and oppression in their own country, who were threatening the livelihood of English workers in the East End.

In those days there was no ban or check on alien immigration. The immigrants were received at the London docks by their friends and co-religionists, given temporary accommodation, and then found jobs in one or other of the local industries—tailoring, boot and shoe making, and cabinet-making in particular—which were already desperately overcrowded.

The agitation reached the newspapers, and in the spring of 1887 Lord Salisbury's Conservative government instructed John Burnett (1842-1914), a former secretary of the Amalgamated Society of

Engineers who had been recently appointed to the newly created post of Labour Correspondent of the Board of Trade, to make a personal investigation of the most notorious of the allegedly sweated trades. Burnett at once got down to work, and before many months had passed had submitted reports on labour conditions in the tailoring industries in the East End of London and in Leeds, and also in the chain and nail-manufactures at Cradley Heath.

Burnett's report on the first-mentioned was published early in 1888, and on February 28, Lord Kenry (Earl Dunraven and Mount-Earl) moved in the House of Lords for the appointment of a Select Committee 'to inquire into the Sweating System at the East End of London, and to report thereon to this House'. A Select Committee was thereupon appointed, with Lord Kenry as its chairman and including among its members the Archbishop of Canterbury, Lord Derby, and Lord Rothschild.

The Select Committee published five reports: Nos. 1 and 2 in 1888, Nos. 3 and 4 in 1889, and the fifth and final one in 1890. Lord Kenry was chairman until February 1890, when the draft report he had prepared was rejected by his fellow-members and he resigned. His place was taken by Lord Derby, and the report that was at length adopted had been drawn up by Lord Thring.

All the 'documents' in this chapter are taken from one or other of these five reports. First, under (a) we have a large part of John Burnett's report to the Board of Trade on the 'Sweating System in the East End of London', together with some selections from the evidence submitted.

Particular interest attaches to the evidence of Miss Beatrice Potter (No. 3), who four years later became Mrs Sidney Webb, under which name she is so generally known. As will be seen, she disagreed with Burnett's emphasis on the importance of the contract system and the effects of pauper immigration, and supported her views with a reference to her own experience as a 'plain trouser hand' in several tailoring workshops in the East End. (For her account of this experience see Chapter 7).

Next, under (b), we move on to the labour conditions in the London docks. The evidence taken under this head was included in the Select Committee's second report, and on the basis of this a general statement of the industry was prepared, that was published in the 5th report. In between the publication of these two reports took place the 'great dock strike' of 1889, which resulted in such great changes in the conditions of the dockers that the Committee decided that any recommendations they might make would not be worth while.

The story of the Dock Strike of 1889 has been often told; the most authoritative account is that written by Hubert (later Sir Hubert)

Llewellyn Smith and Vaughan Nash and published in 1890. But it may be remarked here that outstanding among the men's leaders was Benjamin Tillett (1860-1943), who gave evidence before the Select Committee on the Sweating System (No. 3). At this time he was working as a labourer in tea warehouses at the Docks and making desperate efforts to keep going the insignificant little trade union that he had started the year before. Even among the dockers he was little known, but within a year or two his name, with those of Tom Mann and John Burns, was ringing round the globe. After the strike he played a large part in the formation of the Dockers' Union, and later of the Transport & General Workers' Union.

In their 5th Report the Select Committee published a detailed account of the chain and nail-manufactures that were carried on in the Cradley Heath district, in the 'Black Country' where Staffordshire and Worcestershire meet. This is largely reproduced in (c), and then in (d) we have the Committe's conclusions and recommendations.

On the whole, the results of the Select Committee's labours were found to be disappointing. The 'sweating system' continued much as before until in 1909 the Trade Board Act was passed, which provided for the setting up of Boards, composed of equal numbers of employers and workpeople, in four of the 'sweated' trades, viz. ready-made and wholesale bespoke tailoring, paper box-making, machine-made lace and net finishing, and chain-making. The Boards were required to fix minimum rates of wages, which were enforceable at law. The Trade Boards procedure was subsequently extended to many more trades.

I

John Burnett's Report to the Board of Trade

In conformity with your directions I have made inquiries into what is known as the 'Sweating System' at the East-end of London, especially in the tailoring trade.

The system may be defined as one under which sub-contractors undertake to do work in their own houses or small workshops, and employ others to do it, making a profit for themselves by the difference between the contract prices and the wages they pay their assistants. The scale of business of such sub-contractors varies greatly, many who are called sweaters employing one or two assistants only, while workshops in which 10, 20, or even 30 to 40 are employed are also numerous. The mass of those employed under the system labour in workshops where much fewer than twenty are engaged, or in the houses, which may be single rooms, of the 'small sweaters'.

Except for the best kinds of clothing, the old-fashioned tailor is being crushed out, and the great bulk of the cheap clothing trade is in the hands of a class who are not tailors at all in the old sense of the term. The demand for cheap clothes, irrespective of quality, has continually tended to bring down the rates of remuneration of the least skilled among the workers, and has caused the introduction of the most minute systems of subdivided labour. Instead of the complete tailor, we have now men who only make coats, or waistcoats, or trousers. We have cutters, basters, machinists, pressers, fellers, button-hole workers, and general workers, all brought to bear upon the construction of a coat.

The learning of any one of these branches is, naturally, so much easier than the acquisition of the whole trade that immense numbers of people of both sexes and of all ages have rushed into the cheap tailoring trade as the readiest means of finding employment. The result of this easy entry into the trade has been an enormously overcrowded labour market, and consequently fierce competition among the workers themselves, with all the attendant evils of such a state of things.

Matters have been made infinitely worse during the last few years by an enormous influx of pauper foreigners from other European nations, chiefly German and Russian Jews. The previous conditions of life of the unhappy foreigners who are thus driven, or come here of their own accord, are such that they can live on much less than our English workers. They arrive here in a state of utter destitution, and are compelled to accept the work most easily obtained at the lowest rate of wages. In this way has grown up in our midst a system so bad in itself, and so surrounded by adherent evils, as to have caused, not only among the workers themselves, great suffering and misery, but in the minds of others grave apprehensions of public danger.

Perhaps the practical working of the system can be best illustrated by taking the case of a small sweater newly commencing business on his own account, he in all probability having been previously employed in a sweater's shop.

In the first place, he must have a workroom. This he finds by using the room or one of the rooms in which he and his family resides. He then obtains a sewing machine for which he pays 2s. 6d. per week under the hire purchase system. He is then ready to take work either from a chief contractor or from an intermediate agent as he may be able.

The work is already cut out for him by the head clothier or contractor. If he is able to 'baste' the parts of the garment together he probably does so himself. If not, he must employ a 'baster'. As a rule, the 'basters' are men, but are sometimes females. Next he requires a machinist. Again in the vast majority of cases men are employed as the work is heavy. A presser is also required. This is the heaviest kind of work in the trade and men are invariably employed to do it. The sweater will also require the services of two or three female workers, one to work button-holes, one to do felling, and one as a learner to make herself generally useful and to carry work between the warehouse and the workshop.

The ease with which men can become sweaters greatly intensifies the evils of the trade. It is the desire of every man who works under the system to become as soon as possible a sweater of other people and to get into the business on his own account. The number of sweating dens therefore increase with startling rapidity. There are, in fact, some streets in Whitechapel and St George's-in-the-East in which almost every house contains one or more sweating establishments.

The smaller sweaters use part of their dwelling accommodation, and in the vast majority of cases work is carried on under conditions in the highest degree filthy and unsanitary. In small rooms not more than nine or ten feet square, heated by a coke fire for the pressers' irons, and at night lighted by flaring gas jets, six, eight, ten, and even a dozen workers may be crowded. The conditions of the Public Health Acts, and of the Factory and Workshop Regulation Acts, are utterly disregarded, and existing systems of inspection are entirely inadequate to enforce their provisions. At a moderate computation there must be at least 2,000 sweaters in the East-end of London, and of these not more than one-third can be known to the factory inspectors, hidden, as their shops are, in the garrets and back rooms of the worst kinds of East-end tenements.

After the small-house workshops come those built over the back yards of the houses, which, if not clean and comfortable, are more spacious and better ventilated, but even some of these are miserable places where men and women are huddled together without regard to either health or decency.

In the sweating shops the women are in the proportion to men of about two to one, but the tendency is for this proportion to become greater. Very few children are employed, child labour being too slow and requiring too much supervision to be found profitable by the sweaters.

In a trade carried on under such conditions, and composed of such materials, it is only to be expected that as to wages and hours of labour the position of these workers must be miserable in the extreme. Now, both as to the duration of their toil and their remuneration, it is found that there is no approach to uniformity whatever.

First, as to hours of labour. Females and 'young persons' are supposed to be protected by the Factory Acts, which limit the duration of their toil to 12 hours per day with an allowance from that of one hour for dinner and half an hour for tea. Saturday is, of course, a shorter day, but it is important to observe that as Saturday is the Jewish Sabbath, persons of that persuasion are allowed to work on Sundays up to four o'clock. It is quite certain, however, that the Factory and Workshop Acts are continually, if not, indeed, systematically, being violated in this particular. The usual hours of the women are supposed to be from 8 to 8 with the meal intervals allowed. As a rule, the hour for dinner is always taken, but the tea half-hour is in very many cases not allowed at all. If a female worker were to insist upon a regular half-hour for tea she would be sent about her business. Tea or coffee is prepared for the workers if they require it, or they may prepare it themselves with the appliances which the workroom furnishes, but they must bite and sup as best they can between the stitches of their work.

It is in regulating the hours of the women that the factory inspectors should be of most service; but how can two or three inspectors keep in check the multitude of sweating dens of East London? Basements, garrets, backyards, wash-houses, and all sorts of unlooked for and unsuspected places are the abodes of the sweater. Workrooms and dwelling apartments are so arranged that when women are kept after hours, and the inspector is expected, or pays a sudden visit, the women are shut up in a bedroom where the inspector has no right to go. Among the sweaters the inspector is regarded as the common enemy, and as soon as he is seen in any locality where sweaters abound, the signal of his presence is flashed on from house to house with almost electric speed, so that one or at most two unexpected visits are all he can make in any one locality.

As to the men, they are for the most part a patient submissive race, working often as much as 16 hours per day with the usual hour for dinner and the imaginary half-hour for tea deducted. The average of the trade is not less than 14 hours of actual work per day, and this even in shops where good work is done. These are the hours during the busy season of the trade. But this season lasts for only three months of the twelve, and during the other nine months the workers do not average more than half-time.

The fact that there are two Sabbaths in the week, the English and the Jewish, is found very convenient by some of the sweaters, who avail themselves of this circumstance by observing neither, if it suits their convenience to work on both. In such cases as this with mixed male and female labour, all of which must be employed on parts of the same garments, and which must proceed step by step together, it stands to reason that women are employed during the night as well as the men.

As to the sweaters themselves, their earnings and profits differ widely according to the work they do, and the number of people they employ. The range of prices for different classes of coats is very wide; during my inquiries I found it from 15s. down to 9d. It may, however, be even wider than this. Out of a coat at 9d. little profit can be expected; and it is only by low wages and resolute slave-driving that the sweater can make his money. A fair class of coat to take for a practical tailor's estimate of a sweater's profit, however, is that for which 1s. 2d. is paid, and this is a kind of coat very extensively made, going with suits sold at from 21s. to 25s. On one of these coats the outlay of the sweater is estimated at:—machining, 5d.; button-holes, 1½d.; pressing, 1½d.; felling and basting, 1½d.; trimmings, 1d.; total, 10½d.; leaving a margin to the sweater of 3½d. for rent, machines, firing, etc.

The lower-class sweaters who do the commonest work, have the lowest prices, pay the least wages, and exact the maximum of toil from their workers, make little more than a bare subsistence, and earn little, if any, more than the best of their own workpeople. . . .

This, then, is the system as it exists, described in moderate language and without exaggeration. Its supporters claim for it:

1. That in no other way can the large quantity of cheap clothing now in demand be produced at the price; because (a) there must be the most minute subdivisions of labour, and, consequently, complete organization with a view to adapt means to ends. (b). Because as the workers in the trade are now largely, if not chiefly, recruited from people not speaking the language of the country, means of communication between them and the great clothiers or contractors are necessary.

2. That the middlemen who form this means of communication, and who find workshops, machinery, and security for work, therefore supply an acknowledged want, and are not overpaid for the functions they discharge.

3. That but for this supply of cheap foreign labour England would not be able to keep up the export trade in clothing, which under this system has gradually been developed.

4. That labour in this trade is worked and paid in accordance with the law of supply and demand.

On the other hand, those who object to the sweating system allege:—

1. That by the attraction which the sweating system offers to cheap foreign labour, the labour market is overcrowded, and the native workpeople are being forced out of their trade by foreigners, who, arriving here in destitute and comparatively unskilled condition, are forced by their necessities to accept any terms that may be offered to them; the liability of their present or future support being thrown upon the ratepayers, or upon charitable organizations.

2. That the system is wrong in principle, because by introducing several middlemen, each making a profit upon labour, between the consumer and producer, a cruel and needless tax is imposed upon the workers, while, at the same time, the desire to profit by their exertions causes the middlemen in many cases to grind down and oppress their workpeople.

3. That the conditions under which the trade is carried on, the low rates of remuneration, the excessive hours of toil, the semi-starvation of many of the workers, the unsanitary condition of the work-places, and the overcrowding of tenements, render it alike destructive to the physical, social, and moral well-being of its victims, and therefore an element of physical, social, and moral danger to the entire community.

4. That if not restricted by legislation or otherwise, the continuance

of the influx of these foreigners, resulting almost entirely from this system, and rendering useless the sacrifice of thousands of our own emigrants who go or who are sent abroad, will not only cause the further disorganization and demoralization of native labour, but may also lead up to the development of race hatreds and their natural results.

S.C. on the Sweating System, 2nd Report, pp. 569-83; P.P. 1888, vol. 31.

2

Miss Potter among the 'Sweaters'

Miss Beatrice Potter is called in, and having been sworn, is examined, as follows (May 11, 1888):
Chairman: You have had some considerable experience, have you not, in the East-end of London? And from your personal experience you know a good deal about what is commonly called the sweating system?
—In the tailoring trade, but only in the tailoring trade.

How would you define the sweating system?—I should say that an inquiry into the sweating system was practically an inquiry into all labour employed in manufacture which had escaped the regulation of the Factory Act and trade unions.

You have worked yourself in some of these workshops, I believe?—Yes ... The only class I could not get at was the top class; it was too skilled. So that I have had the worst though not the best.

What the Committee would be glad to have, would be a description from you, if you would give it, of the shops and the nature of the work?—Practically the coat trade is in the hands of the Jews, Jewish contractors employing Jew men and, principally, Jewesses, but there are a certain number of Christians who are employed. The Jewesses are the most skilful workers, and if they cannot get Jewesses they get Christian women. The first class, the bespoke work, pays very good wages indeed; the machinists run from about 7s. to 9s. 6d., and the pressers run from about 5s. 6d. to 8s. 6d., and the women are rarely under 2s. 6d. a day, sometimes they go up to 5s. a day for twelve hours' work. Then the second class, the stock work, is also fairly paid; it is more regular than the bespoke work, but the pay is not quite so high; the machinists run from 3s. to 6s.; pressers will run from 5s. to 8s., and the women are as low as 1s. 6d.; but there are no women employed in the coat trade lower than 1s. 6d., except as apprentices, and then, of course, they are employed for what they are worth. Practically, in the coat trade, there is nothing to be complained of in the wages. You have irregular hours, and you have bad sanitation of shops.

What are the hours?—The hours for women are of course the factory hours; but then in the very lowest class, the slop trade, the employers do not pay very much attention to that, and they work from eight or half-past in the morning till 10 or 11 at night.

When you speak of the coat trade, what kind of goods are those?—The bespoke trade for the West-end and City shops. It must be distinguished from what is properly called the West-end trade, which is done by English mechanics. The coat made by an English mechanic differs entirely from the coat made by a Jewish contractor.

Could you tell the difference?—Yes; if you gave me a coat I could tell you directly whether it was made by a Jewish contractor or an English mechanic. The Jewish contractor makes his coat on the principle of making the coat first, and the lining separately, and then sewing the two together by machine right round, so that it is like a balloon, it is bagged in; but in the work of the English mechanic some seams of the lining are tacked to the seams of the coat, and then they are felled over. In the case of the Jewish contractor's coat it is all loose, so that you can pull it part, and it is like a balloon.

Then you mean to say that the clothes made in the fashionable West-end tailors' shops are really made by Englishmen?—They are principally done by the English mechanic. The best work is done in the workshop of a retail house, and the second-class work is done in the house of the English mechanic where he employs his own wife. But a good many West-end firms are beginning to employ Jewish contractors. For instance, a man like Miles, in Brook-street, and the Civil Service Stores, get some of their work done by the Jewis sweaters; but they pay very good prices for it, and the wages of labour are very good; it is only a matter of very long hours; that is the only grievance of those engaged in the best kind of work.

What is the reason that the Jewish women are preferable to the Christian women in the tailoring trade?—They are much more skilful; they can manage machines, whereas very few Gentiles can manage machines; and then they are much more regular in their attendance. In The Free Registry for Jews last winter there were no tailoresses out of employment, though there were a great many tailors, which shows that the Jewish tailoresses are in great request, even in the slack season. Then there is the very lowest layer of the coat trade; that work is done by women and men at their homes; it really does not pay the contractor to take it out. That is the sort of coat that is done for 7d. or 8d.; it hardly pays the Jewish contractor to take that coat out; so that it is done to a great extent by Gentile women. That is the very lowest work; and that is what I mean by saying that sweating, in its most intense form, has nothing whatever to do with the contract system. In fact, the contract system is the top stratum, as it were, of the trade.

How is it that the Jews are so much confined to coat-making?—Because it pays so much better. The Jews will not take up badly paid work as a rule; they cannot get their own people to work for them.

Have you any opinion as to the effects of the pauper immigration?—The actual raw greener cannot be used in the tailoring trade; he must, at least, have done tailoring at home to be of any use. Then he comes into the workshop and he serves for about three months, perhaps, for a very small wage; at the end of three months he can command as good a wage as anybody.

But how long would it take a man who had no knowledge at all of tailoring to do that?—I do not think he would go into the tailoring trade; he would go into the boot finishing. The tailoring trade is too skilled. You see, if you spoil a coat, you have to pay for it.

Then you do not think that the pauper immigration has much effect upon the tailoring trade, or any effect upon it?—I do not think it has, for this reason: that in the busy time of the year the machinists and pressers can make their own terms; there are not too many machinists and pressers; in fact, there are fewer than could be absorbed by the labour market, and it is rather amusing to see how, in the busy season, they will treat their employers. In the busy season they swear at the employers; in the slack season the employers swear at them.

I gather from you that, so far as the coat-making is concerned, you think that the people engaged in that trade are able to take care of themselves?—Yes, except as regards sanitation. In the lowest class of domestic workshop the standard of sanitation and overcrowding is very low; no doubt about it; but that is their particular taste.

You think they do not feel it?—I do not think they feel it very much.

What is the general behaviour of the sweaters towards those whom they employ; is it of a merciful or a brutal character?—They seem very much like other men; there is a good deal of geniality and kindness, I think, in the East End workshop; that is my experience of it.

How long have you been at work in the tailoring trade?—Three weeks, inclusive of the training I got.

The whole time in one shop?—No, I worked in five shops, but I could not keep my place in the coat shops, for the reason that the work is so very much more skilled than other work.

You worked the usual twelve hours a day?—Yes. Besides that, you have had a large personal experience of the way work is carried on in people's houses?—Yes, as a rent collector.

S.C. on the Sweating System, 1st Report, pp. 319-33; P.P. 1888, vol. 20.

3

Sweaters' Dens

The dwellings or shops in which the sweated class live and work are too often places in which all the conditions of health, comfort, and decency are violated or ignored. This is rarely the fault of the poor and helpless persons who are driven to them. They are obliged to live where they can. Their rents are, as a rule, extravagantly high, considering the accommodation afforded. The Factory and Workshop Act is not, and cannot be, properly enforced under existing conditions. Sanitary inspection is totally inadequate, and the local bodies have seldom done their duty effectually.

At the East End of London generally the sanitary state of homes and shops could not possibly be much worse than it is. The secretary of the Jewish Board of Guardians was in favour of taking the control of these matters from the local sanitary authority, and placing it in the hands of the factory inspectors. The object chiefly aimed at by the local authority is to keep down the rates, and this is not always compatible with a vigilant system of inspection, followed by prompt remedial measures.

There is generally but one water-closet for a large workshop or an entire house. In some of the sweaters' workshops the men or the family are obliged to sleep huddled together in any way they can. One witness states that in a room, perhaps nine feet one way and fifteen feet the other, eighteen persons slept. Sometimes sleeping places are found in cellars. 'I have seen the workmen sit at their benches, and when they ceased work they would simply lay their clothes down upon the benches and get into the bed in the corner.'

Mr Lyons described a sweater's den with which he was acquainted. 'There is one water-closet for all the workers; there are about fourteen. Besides that, the sweater lets out two rooms to families, consisting of eight to ten persons. Altogether it might be twenty-two. There is only one water-closet for males and females of the workshops, also for the tenants.' The room in which Mr Lyons was working at this time was about nine feet square, with fourteen or fifteen persons in it, a coke fire in the fireplace, and eight or nine gas lights burning. Light and ventilation are both insufficient. 'I should like to mention', said Mr Lyons, 'that for my work', as a tailor with a sewing machine, 'you require plenty of light, especially for the needle. I have had two of my fingers off on account of insufficient light.'

Mr Lakeman [factory and workshops inspector] more than confirmed these and similar statements. His general description of the sweaters' shops gives a fair idea of them, so far as we are able to judge from the great mass of evidence laid before us. 'Going into some workshops', he said, 'you find a filthy bed on which the garments which are made are laid; little children, perfectly naked little things lying about the floor; and on the beds, frying pans and all sorts of dirty utensils, with food of various descriptions on the bed, under the bed, over the bed, everywhere; clothes hanging on a line, with nothing more than a large gas stove, with the ashes all flying about, and the atmosphere so dense that you get ill after a night's work there; that is the reason I am deaf now. I get into such a bath of perspiration. I have tested the atmosphere of these rooms many times and found it 95 degrees.'

Mr Arthur Goodwyn, the sanitary inspector of the Jewish Board of Guardians, found the workshops generally in a deplorable state. They are often run up in the cheapest manner, on the site of a yard of a dwelling-house, without drainage, and with the roof leaking. The walls, as a matter of course, are reeking with damp. There was no water supply to the privies, which were inside the workshops. Overcrowding is the rule rather than the exception; filth accumulates under the floors; rag sorting is carried on in dwelling rooms; choked drains cause sewage to overflow into the rooms; and weeks pass before the regular sanitary authorities take any steps to afford any relief to the inhabitants. The tenants themselves seldom complain, probably because they know from experience the uselessness of doing so.

The medical officer of health for the greater part of this district, Dr Bate, confirmed most of these statements. Dr Bate had seen cases within his own experience of the spread of disease by clothing made up in rooms where children are lying ill with smallpox or other maladies. He had visited patients suffering from smallpox or scarlet fever who were in rooms where half-finished garments were thrown over the beds to keep them warm. Unless a medical man had been called in nothing would have been heard of these cases. There is nothing to prevent their recurrence.

How the poor live in these overcrowded regions of London was further described by Dr Squire in an account of one of his visits. 'There was a room about twelve or fourteen feet by ten, and eight feet high, as near as I could judge it by my eye. In this room there was a large bed, the only bed in the room, on which the mother of the family was dying of consumption. Although it was summer there was a large fire in the room, before which the husband was at his work as a tailor, pressing cloth, and so, of course, filling the air with steam; besides him there was his son, also at work; then there was a daughter with her sewing-machine, also at work; and playing on the floor were two or three small children, all crowded into a room which would properly contain two or three people at the most, with due regard for health.

Glasgow's sweaters

Other cities are little, if any, better off in this respect. In Glasgow Mr McLaughlin mentioned the case of a contractor employing one hundred men. He had five rooms with twenty men in each of them. 'There was a charcoal fire for heating the irons in each of the rooms; and they were making public contracts, policemen's clothing, and commissionaires' tunics, and postmen's clothing. . . . When you opened the door of the place you could not stand there unless you had marvellous strong lungs.' Most of the Glasgow sweaters carry on their work in their dwelling-houses. In one place the witness D. McLaughlin, a journeyman tailor, stated that he found 'forty or fifty women employed in an old boiler shed, or something like it, a disused part of an engineer's shop; you had to get up to it by three wooden ladders; you had to go through a joiner's shop to get to it; and there was no sanitary accommodation for the women anywhere. Another sweater's den was described by the same witness: 'We had to walk through filth to get into the workshop; it was a garret, and there were two turkeys accommodated between the workshop and the dwelling part of the house, and you had to pass through a little place nearly on your hands and knees to get into the workshop, and after you got into the workshop you could only stand straight up in the centre of the floor; in the middle it was only about six feet high.'

S.C. on the Sweating System, 5th Report, pp. xcv-xcvi: P.P. 1890, vol. 17.

4

'Foetid and abominable'

The fur trade is an extremely dirty one; the unsanitary condition of the workshop is very striking; the process is such as to make it so. A common skin is dyed, rabbit skins, and skins of animals of no great value in themselves are dyed, and made into several portions of women's attire, muffs, and other things; these skins when dyed are taken to the fur cape maker, or fur hat maker, or trimming maker; he stretches the skin, which is wet, on a board, which he places before a large fire to dry and the exhalations from that are really and truly very bad.

There are women sitting in this workshop, in which there would be no ventilation. The heat from this fire-place is very great, the large gas burners overhead adding to the intense heat of the place. The cutting of the different skins by the cutters to form something sends off fluff from the portions cut off; the workers in their cuttings do the same; the floor is strewn with shreds and dust, and heaps of skins, and there are heaps of skins in the corner which ought to be removed, and are not. The place is foetid and abominable.

There is 5s. a week paid to a woman to work in that trade for 12 hours a day, and if she does not feel disposed to take that money she gets none. I have asked: 'Why do you work here for such little money as that?' She has replied, 'Because I have not the time to seek employment elsewhere; if I go elsewhere to seek employment I lose one day or two days' work, and then I should lose the means of getting a few shillings a week.' 'But how do you live?' 'It is semi-starvation.'

MR LAKEMAN, Factory inspector, in evidence to S.C. on the Sweating System, 2nd Report, p. 456; P.P. 1888, vol. 21.

5

Girls under the Beds

In a great number of these sweaters' houses we knock and we cannot get in at all. The sweater will put his head out of window and say, 'Who is that?' 'The inspector wants to come and see your workshop', and we get an answer, and there we stay and may stay, and we may knock again, but he will not open the door until everything is put right up there, all removed from the workshop where they are; then he will say, 'Come in now', and then nothing is to be seen.

We know that the women and girls are stowed away in bedrooms and under beds and in kitchens, and so on, where we cannot follow them. My colleague and I had an instance in the case of night visiting. The door was not opened, and he peeped through the keyhole, which was a very big one, and by the light of the passage we saw girls coming upstairs as quickly as they could; and when they had got out of sight a girl opened the door, and we saw the master. 'What is it you want here at this time of night?' he said. 'We come to see your workshop.' 'Here it is.' There we saw the clothes lying on the chairs, with the needles and thread in them, evidently thrown down at the moment. 'When did your girls go away?' 'Eight o'clock.' 'Are you quite sure of that?' And we had in our pockets the evidence of one girl who had complained to us that she had been working so long that she could not endure it any more. We could not go upstairs and follow the girls.

MR LAKEMAN; S.C. on the Sweating System, 2nd Report, p. 463; P.P. 1888, vol. 21

6

Making Shirts at 7d. a Dozen

Mrs Lavinia Casey is called in and examined.

The Chairman. You are a shirt machinist? Will you describe to the Committee what the nature of your work is?—I make shirts at 7d. and 8d. a dozen; I have to pay for my own cotton out of it, and I have to pay 2s. 6d. a week for the machine; I have to pay half-a-crown a week on the hiring system.

How many shirts can you make in a day?—Two dozen; and I have little children to attend to.

You can make two dozen a day at 7d. a dozen? That is 1s. 2d. a day? What have you to find?—A reel of cotton and oil for my machine out of that.

Two shillings and sixpence a week for your sewing-machine, you say. What do your materials come to, the cotton and so on you have to find? —About 1s. to 1s. 3d. a week.

Who do you get your machine from?—Messrs Singer & Company. Does it become your property after a time?—Yes; £7 3s. I have to pay.

What happens if you get into arrears?—They will take it away from me; I am in arrears now with my machine.

If you are a certain time in arrears you lose all that you have paid upon it?—Yes.

Has that ever happened to you?—Yes.

Lord Monkswell. How many hours a day do you work?—I begin between 7 and 8 in the morning, and I have to work sometimes till 11 at night; I have to attend to the children.

But how many hours do you suppose after deducting those iterruptions?—Twelve hours.

S.C. on the Sweating System pp. 155-6; P.P. 1888, vol. 20.

7

A Halfpenny a Buttonhole

Miss Rachel Gashion is called in, and examined.

The Chairman. Are you in the employ of Mr Moses [a master tailor] as a button-holer, and are paid by the button-hole?—Yes.

How much a button-hole do you receive?—A halfpenny.

How much can you earn a-week?—I have taken as much as 26s.

You have heard it stated to the Committee that Mr Burnett in his report says that 4s. a-day is the most that a button-holer can earn; do you agree with that?—I can earn more.

Have you been making button-holes in this room?—Yes. How many have you made?—Four. And in what time did you make them?—Thirteen and a-half minutes.

And did the Committee Clerk check your time?—Yes.

Will you read out what the time was for each button-hole?—Four minutes the first, three and a quarter the second, three and a quarter the third, and three minutes the last.

You made four button-holes in 13½ minutes?—Yes.

Therefore you would have earned 2d. in thirteen and a half minutes. That would be at the rate of 9d. an hour. And would you consider 9d. an hour a good wage for a female hand to earn?—Yes.

Lord Clinton. Is that your ordinary rate of work when you are working?—Yes, I can work like that. I felt a little nervous when I was doing it here. All through the day?—Yes.

Chairman. How many hours do you work in the day?—From 8 to 8. With an hour for meal times?—Yes. And any time for tea?—Half an hour.

Are there any quicker working in the same place with you?—Not quicker than I am at Mr Moses' workshop. There are quicker. I know some who can work four button-holes more in an hour.

S.C. on the Sweating System; 1st Report, pp. 875-7; P.P. 1888, vol. 20.

8

My Life as a Trouser-finisher

Mrs Isabella Killick is called in, and examined.
Chairman.—What business are you engaged in?—On the trouser finishing. I have worked at it now about 22 years altogether; it is paid for so terribly bad now.

How many can you finish in a day now?—I cannot do more than four. . . . I have got an afflicted husband; he is dying; I do not know whether he will be dead when I get back or not; he is in an infirmary; I was there at 8 o'clock this morning to see him; he is paralysed all on one side; he has been there nine weeks.

What do you get?—I get 4½d., 3¾d., and 5d., up to 6d.; it is in my book. I have to find my own materials; I cannot earn more than 1s. 2d. a day; and I have to find my own materials and fire and lighting out of it.

What materials do you have to find?—For the twist holes, 4½d. work, you have your twist to buy; there is gimp and soap, black cotton and red cotton, and black thread; or white thread if they are white buttons.

You mean you are paid 1s. 2d., including all those articles?—I have trimmings to find out of that 1s. 2d. . . . if they are twist holes the twist will cost you 1½d. for the four sets of holes. Altogether I do not clear 1s. a day, not after finding my own trimmings, firing and all, and then I have to work many hours for that. I am up at six o'clock every morning, and never done till eight at night.

What do you pay out of that for rent?—Two shillings, and I have to support three children out of it.

Do you get about the same amount of work all the year round?—No, because it falls off slack at a certain time of the year; about two months before Christmas it falls off, then it does not start again till a month after Christmas; about three months of the year is slack.

What do you do then?—I am glad to get anything to do, a bit of cleaning or washing; I cannot be without work, as I have three little ones to support.

Has the money which you have earned been sufficient to provide food?—No, it has not; but I have had to make it do. Chiefly, I get a herring and a cup of tea; that is the chief of my living, with the rent to pay, and three children eating very hearty. As for meat, I do not expect; I get meat once in six months.

S.C. on the Seating System, 1st Report, pp. 149-51; P.P. 1888, vol. 20.

9

'How can the poor girl live?'

———————

Having ascertained that the wage [of shirt-makers] is at what might be termed below living point, I made some further visits to find out how the women live. I called on an intelligent woman who worked at Poplar for a sweater, and I said to her, 'Now you seem a very respectable woman, and your children are well clothed, and you live in a decent house; but you cannot do all this on the 5s. or 6s. a week that you can knock out through doing this weary shirt work'.

'No,' she said, 'I cannot; you see my husband brings in the rest; I merely do this as an extra.'

I said, 'Exactly; to you it is something like a lady embroidering slippers; it is a pastime, more or less, in between attending to the children or meals; it is not the serious business of your life; you have not, in other words, to live off it'.

'No,' she said. 'I have not.'

'Now, I said, will you tell me what becomes of your next-door neighbour. There is a poor girl working in this way, and who has to meet every expense in her life from the wage that she gets; will you tell me what becomes of her; she has no husband to bring in something to supplement her income; then what becomes of her? What is the result, can she live?'

'No, sir, she cannot live.'

'Can she get some other kind of work?' 'No.' I said, 'You know the result'. 'I can guess', she said.

Then I leave Your Lordships to guess what would be the result; she sells the only other thing she has to sell.

W. J. WALKER, Ceylon and South African merchant and director of the Working Women's Co-operative Association; S.C. on the Sweating System, 4th Report, p. 444; P.P. 1889, vol. 14.

10

'*You* sat *on those chairs ?*'

[In furniture making] there are all things done which make the article cheap, using Alga marina instead of hair, and using this cotton wool instead of hair, and using leather which is called Russian leather when it is not, and all those things that make up so that the eye is deceived and you cannot tell what the goods are. People buy them, and after a time find it out.

Let me give you an instance of this; a man told me he was a chair-maker; a lady came to him and bought some chairs. His price was 10s. 6d. each chair; so after a time the woman comes back to him and said, 'Did I not buy half-a-dozen chairs from you for 10s. 6d. each?' 'Yes, you did.' 'But do you know that they are all in pieces?' 'What, all in pieces; how is that?' 'Well, a short time after I had them home, and we began to sit upon them, and they all fell abroad.' 'But', he said, 'do you mean to tell me that you sat upon them?' 'Of course I sat upon them; what else?' He said, 'These ten-and-sixpenny chairs were made to be looked at, not to sit upon. If you had told me that you wanted chairs to sit upon I should have charged you 5s. a chair more for them.'

MR LAKEMAN, S.C. on the Sweating System, 2nd Report, pp. 471-2; P.P. 1888, vol. 21.

(b) LONDON DOCKERS

I

What It Means to Be a Docker

Of all the overcrowded, laborious, and uncertain callings in England, that of the casual dock labourer is one of the most miserable. It is open to everybody without apprenticeship or training, and all who are reduced to extremities fly at once to it. It is the last refuge of the destitute, the only halting place which intervenes between the friendless outcast and the workhouse.

There is regular employment for the picked hands at the docks, and the companies have a large proportion of their men who remain permanently in their service. But the 'casual' is in a most helpless and wretched condition. Artisans out of work, agricultural labourers who have come to London in the old belief that its streets are paved with gold, engineers, tailors, shoemakers, bakers, painters, costermongers, all flock to the docks when their own employment fails them. Thus, surplus labour in any trade, from whatever cause produced, instantly makes itself felt at the dock gates, and the men who were brought up to that occupation, as many were, find it more and more difficult to get a living by it.

Colonel Birt, the Manager of the Millwall Docks, described the general mass of labourers in these words: 'Speaking broadly, they are men who from some misfortune or other have been failures in their own walk of life, and have therefore turned to dock labour; and the great majority of them, absolutely from want of food, are incapable of doing any very heavy work; with every disposition, are incapable of doing it.' The dock labourer, he added, 'is ruined by the introduction of outside

223

labour, men who desert their own trade, and enter into competition with the trained dock labourer'.

The pressure is, no doubt, greatest at the London Docks, on account of their proximity to a densely crowded and very poor region of the Metropolis. Some thousands of unemployed are, it is to be feared, always to be found in that quarter, and they try the docks first. At the lower docks, the Albert, the Victoria, and others, this great and severe pressure, which obliges men to fight furiously among each other for the mere chance of employment, does not exist. There, in times of great increase of work, it is sometimes difficult to find a sufficient number of men. The men, however, would soon adjust the balance if this were a permanent, or even a frequent, condition of affairs. They are willing to go any distance for employment. Lloyd's list soon spreads the news of the arrival of a steamer, and crowds pour down to the dock gates for work. The strongest looking men are picked first; the weaker go to the wall.

Various estimates are given of the number of dock labourers who endeavour to obtain employment in and around the docks and wharves in London. Mr Tillett, the Secretary of the Dock Labourers' Union, estimated it at 100,000, of whom only 2,400 belong to any union. Colonel Birt thought that a 'monstrous exaggeration', and put it 75,000 at the very outside, and probably not more than 30,000, but he admitted that 100,000 might for more or less days in the year have worked at the docks. It is obviously very difficult for anyone to form an exact estimate, because the numbers vary greatly from day to day, and no accurate statistics appear attainable. Men are always arriving from the rural districts in search of employment, and until they find something else to do they go to the docks or wharves. They may remain there weeks or months, or only a few days, and it is almost impossible that their going and coming can be closely registered.

The meaning of 'plus'

The method of work and the scale of payment vary in different docks. The method of work may be divided into the 'task' and 'contract' systems. It is in connection with both these systems that many grievous complaints, and some serious abuses, have been brought to our notice.

What is called 'task' or 'piece-work' is really time payment, calculated upon an estimate of the proper amount of work to be done in a given time. The men are paid at the rate of 5d. per hour, and a certain amount of work has to be done in a certain number of hours. If a ship is worked out in less than the estimated time, a proportion of the money so saved was handed over to the men, and is styled 'plus'.

13. Saturday night in
Whitechapel Road

Cassells' 'Living London'

ooking supper in the kitchen of a London lodging-house

The Graphic (1886)

14. Rahn's Court, Shadwell, in London's East End

The Graphic (1886)

A woman sack-maker at work in the East-End court illustrated above

The Graphic (18

This 'plus' is the source of much complaint on the part of the men. 'Plus' acted as a premium on exertion. The harder the men worked the more 'plus', and consequently the more wages they earned. What they complain of is that the dock companies increased their estimate of the quantity of cargo to be handled in a given number of hours for 5d. an hour in proportion as the men dealt with more and more cargo in a given number of hours under the stimulus of 'plus'; and that consequently they are now required to work much harder than formerly for the same hourly pay, and that their 'plus' has dwindled down to such an extent as to be no longer divisible among all hands employed on a job. Formerly every man had a share in it, whereas at present it suffices only to give something extra to the 'royals' or 'permanent' hands, who act as gangers.

It is further alleged that 'plus' is unfairly calculated; that in two ships working out the same the 'plus' is often different, and in two ships working out very differently the 'plus' frequently is the same . . . Whether the men's suspicions on this point are well founded or not, it is certain that they are in complete ignorance of the basis, facts, and figures upon which the 'plus', which is a portion of their wages, is calculated, a state of things certain to give rise to misunderstandings and discontent. They ask to be allowed to have access to the calculations on which the 'plus' is fixed, a demand that appears most reasonable to us . . .

In the East and West India Docks and Tilbury Docks, some of the work is done by contract, but by far the greater part is carried on under the task system, which, under certain circumstances, admits of a bonus being divided among a favoured few. The men's earnings, without the 'plus', are 5d. per hour, paid by the company in any event. At the London and St Katherine Docks, which include the Royal Victoria and Albert Docks, the greater part of the work is done by contract, while at Millwall the contract system is almost entirely in force. It is only at the East and West India and Tilbury Docks, that the custom of 'plus' prevails. . . .

The dock company where the contract system is in force lets out the loading and unloading of vessels, the storage of goods in the warehouses, and other divisions of the labour, to sub-contractors. A sub-contractor may employ only half-a-dozen hands, or he may have a score or more, paying them at a rate which will leave him a profit on their labour. The men are paid so much an hour, but the tonnage is calculated also, and if it is found that the men have earned more than the price per hour, usually 5d., the balance is supposed to be divided among the upper grade of labourers at the end of the week. This balance is, as has already been described, called 'plus', or as one of the labourers described it, 'sweating money', and it is practically the abuse of the contract system and the manipulation of this 'plus' which brings the dock labourers within the scope of the inquiry conducted by your Committee.

'Tickets' in the 'pub'

The arrangement of dock labour is further complicated by the fact that a sub-contractor may let out his contract to other persons; it may go through as many as seven different hands, though the ordinary number appears not to exceed three. The complaint made on behalf of the dock labourers is that an undue proportion of the profit of their work is absorbed by the different contractors who stand between them and the chief employer, and they contend that the intervention of these sub-contractors or middlemen is unnecessary. The sub-contractor knows that numbers of labourers are always waiting for employment, and as there is no settled basis of prices, he can usually manage to get a gang under him on his own terms. In many cases they devise a system of tickets, which give the possessors a claim to priority of claim to employment. These tickets are often distributed in a public-house, and out of them the sub-contractor or his friends, as it is alleged, contrive to exact an advantage for themselves. The necessitous man who is driven to seek work at the docks as a casual finds himself 'sweated' at every step that he takes. The remedy asked for by the labourers is that the dock companies should themselves appoint foremen to give out the work, thus dispensing altogether with the sub-contractor.

Even when a man has succeeded in getting a job, he never knows whether he will be kept on all day, or dismissed after two or three hours. The men assert that, in order to avoid paying them for the dinner hour, they are sometimes taken on till dinner time, and then discharged and taken on again after dinner; and that in other cases they are made to go in to work at half-past seven in the morning, although their pay does not begin till eight, so that the contractor gains considerably out of the men under him.

When a man is injured

If the labourer employed under the contract system is injured while at work, he has no legal remedy against the dock company, and, practically, no remedy against the contractor, for the latter is poor, or is supposed to be, and it is considered useless to bring an action against him. It was stated that one of the reasons for the adoption of the contract system, and one of the motives for refusing to abolish it, is that the dock companies are shielded by it from claims for compensation in case of injuries to their labourers.

The dock companies denied these statements, and some considerable doubt rests upon this part of the case. It is certain that compensation for injury is sometimes made, and it is not probable that dock companies desire to evade responsibility; yet it is clear that the contract system tends to relieve them of it. The contractors are the responsible persons; they support each other, and a labourer knows very well that if he brings an action against a contractor, or makes a complaint to the company, his chances of future employment are exceedingly small. He prefers therefore to suffer in silence, unless the injury be exceptionally severe. . . .

The ranks of the applicants for work at the docks are more crowded than ever, and at the same time the amount of wages to be earned is less. On this point the labourers themselves, and those who are entitled to speak for them, gave testimony of a very positive character. Mr Tillett informed us that 'a docker sixteen or eighteen years ago could average right through the year about 24s. or 25s. a week; now the same man does not average more than 7s. right through'. Formerly, however, the pressure of men seeking work was nothing like so great as it is now. Most of the companies, Mr Tillett stated, 'have built sheds, and the men get under these sheds in the wet or bad weather, which saves them from going home; and so the dock companies can always rely upon finding a good number of men in the sheds'. Thus it is that they need no longer engage men for one moment longer than they have actual need for them; in fact, if the evidence be correct, it is not necessary to pay them in full for the work actually done. The supply is greater than the demand, and that fact interferes even with the course of fair play and justice.

An average day's work for an ordinary 'docker' is not more than three hours, taking the year round; but there are times when a gang may be called upon to work twenty-two hours at a stretch, in the unloading of a mail steamer, and so far from looking upon this as a hardship, they welcome so long a spell of work as a stroke of good fortune. To be out of employment is the greatest evil they have to face; to be in it on any terms is a relief.

The 'docker' never knows when his turn may come, or whether it will come at all. He is not sure how long it will last when it does come, and he cannot calculate how much he will be paid. If a strike is going on in any trade, or business is depressed, the crowd round the dock gates, always pushing and struggling for work, becomes greater every hour. Amid this crowd, the holder of a ticket, which has been given out beforehand by the contractor, stands the first chance. The casual, without a ticket, may stand for many hours or days together without getting work, until, as one of their number told us, they are reduced to a 'perfect abject state which is indescribable. They lose all spirit of manhood and independence.' Sisters of Mercy, the Salvation Army, and local societies sometimes distribute soup tickets among them; but it is not charity they plead for, but work at a fair rate of wages. A stronger trades union such as the stevedores appear to have established, would do more for them, in their own opinion, than any form of charity that could be devised.

The labourers who came before us gave their evidence in a remarkably intelligent, straightforward, and manly way, and were evidently smarting under a deep sense of injustice.

'Preference men'

Besides the common dock labourer, or casual, there is the 'preference man', or 'royal', who receives 5d. an hour, and is generally called upon to take charge of a gang; he is, in fact, what is called in other trades 'a ganger'. One of these men stated that he had been at the work for 20 years, and that the rate of pay had been continually going down. His complaint was also keen with regard to the 'plus', and it may be briefly stated, once for all, that there is a universal feeling among the dock hands on this subject.

The testimony of the dock hands is also quite unanimous with regard to the increased difficulty of obtaining a livelihood at their occupation. This difficulty is partly attributed to the introduction of machinery, which has enabled the docks to unload a ship in as many days as it used to take weeks. A steamer will now arrive, clear her cargo, and be ready for loading again in a very few hours. Machinery has made the work of unloading ships both cheaper and quicker. The men do not object to the employment of machinery, but insist that they ought to share and that they do not share in the benefits derived from it. They think that the dock companies derive an undue advantage by charging the captains or owners the same prices as they did in 1869, while they have lowered the wages all round. But the men would not complain if they could get their work directly from the companies. They ascribe most of their wrongs to the contractor. It is alleged by some of them that a system of favouritism, or even of bribery, is adopted to swell the contractor's gains. The men are compelled to give the sub-contractor beer before he will give them the ticket which secures them a priority in obtaining work.

All these statements are denied in the most emphatic terms by the contractors and by the dock authorities, but here is this distinction to be drawn, that whereas the men speak of what they see and know, the chief authorities at the docks can only report what they are told or have reason to believe.

S.C. on the Sweating System; 5th Report, pp. lxxiii-lxxvii; P.P. 1890, vol. 17.

2

Ben Tillett on 'the profession'

Mr Benjamin Tillett called in and examined (November 20, 1888).
Chairman: You are the Secretary of the Dock Labourers' Union?—Yes.
Can you tell us how many members there are in the society?—About
2400.

Does that comprise men working at all the docks in London?—At
all the docks and most of the wharves.

Are you a dock labourer yourself?—Yes.

How long have you been in the trade?—Twelve years. I have spent the
best part of the twelve years in wharf work, which is identical with dock
work, with the exception of the unloading of vessels; all the warehousing
is done on the same lines as is done in the docks.

How long have you been Secretary of the Dock Labourers' Union?—
Fifteen months.

Is that the only society existing among the dock labourers?—The
only bona fide society.

How many dock labourers do you estimate are at the docks and
wharves in the port of London?—About 100,000.

And out of that 100,000 only 2400 belong to your union?—That is all
at present.

★   ★   ★

Can you tell me what the numbers of the dock labourers were twelve
years ago?—The number then would not be more than a third of what
they are at present; it was a profession at that time.

How do you mean 'a profession'?—At that time a man who followed
up dock labour did nothing else, and if he was a man that really wanted
work he could always be sure of ten months work out of twelve; at the
rate of nine and ten hours a day.

There are a great many more men in the trade now?—They come
from all quarters now.

Do you mean that men work as dock labourers and then go away and
work at some other trade?—Yes; there are plenty of painters who get
work in the summer, and who have to follow the docks when their work
as painters falls off; then there are bricklayers' labourers; then there
are the costers. I may say that the costers are coming to us now more
than ever they were, because of the number of foreigners really that take

229

up their particular trade. Then we have more coming from the skilled trades now than ever we had . . . engineering work, tailoring work, shoemaking, baking, and the ropemaking work.

How do you account for all these tailors, shoemakers and bootmakers, and others being out of work; do you account for it by anything besides what you have mentioned, namely, the introduction of machines?—In the ropemaking it has only been the machines; but with the tailoring and shoemaking and the baking trade, it is chiefly on account of the foreigners who are ousting our men. . . .

S.C. on the Sweating System, 2nd Report, pp. 111, 121-2; P.P. 1888, vol. 21.

3

Domestic Arrangements

The majority of the dock labourers are forced to live in either one or two rooms. I should say that about 70 per cent of them are married men; the others are frequently to be found in what we call 'doss-houses'; they pay there for a bed at the rate of twopence or threepence a night. But the reason of their being able to live at all is that there is some kind of communism among them, for they help each other; and it is the practice among them to pay for each other's beds or 'dosses' when the man has not had a turn of work.

But the majority of the labourers live in back rooms, the more respectable living in two or three rooms. What we call the more respectable would be the 'Royals', or permanent hands working at the docks, but the ordinary man who has come down from a trade or profession, and is forced to go to work at the docks is unable to pay more than 3s. or 3s. 6d. a week rent, and that, of course, has to be contributed to by the wife and his children. In most cases the wife of a docker taking her earnings right through the year can earn more than he can himself . . . washing, matchmaking, charing, all kinds of rough work.

BENJAMIN TILLETT, S.C. on the Sweating System, 2nd Report, page 135; P.P. 1888, vol. 21.

4

Dock Labourers as the General Manager Sees Them

These deal porters and corn porters are fine powerful men: they can do almost any kind of work; if there is no work in the grain they trust to the wood, and if there is not work in the wood trade they will look to guano. Taking them altogether, these high priced men earn good wages all the year round.

Perhaps their greatest enemy is the weather; their work, or the great bulk of it, is open air work. If we have a day like this, when it rains very heavily, their occupation is gone; they have lost a day. These fine fellows have a capital in their strength; they are not dependent like these other poor fellows upon other people; they can command work, and they get it fairly well throughout the year.

There is one important thing, though; I have known these corn men earn over a sovereign a day; they have made a very long day of it, and have worked uncommonly well, and were entitled to, and worthy of, every shilling they got; but they have got the sovereign. If a man does by luck earn a sovereign by a very hard day's work, he can afford to lie by. In the case of these men their money is irregular; sometimes the sum is very big that they earn, and at other times they may be lying by for one or two days; but they earn very fair wages all the year round; and what satisfies me of that is this, that they have got the physical strength to do the work; no man in a starving state could do the work these men do; they live well, and they work well . . .; they are the aristocracy of the dock labourers.

A casual labourer, if he has strength and is steady, soon picks up more or less skill as a casual, and he will by degrees work into the higher class, but the physical strength is the first condition; a physically strong man is tolerably sure of work. It is these unfortunate fellows, most of whom are without physical strength; the very costume in which they present themselves to the work prevents them doing work. The poor fellows are miserably clad, scarcely with a boot on their foot, in a most miserable state, and they cannot run; their boots would not permit them. They are the most miserable specimens; there are men who are reduced to the direst poverty, men with every disposition to work well, but without the strength to do it. There are men who come on to work in our docks (and if with us to a much greater extent elsewhere), who come on without having a bit of food in their stomachs, perhaps since the previous day;

they have worked for an hour, and have earned 5d.; their hunger will not allow them to continue; they take the 5d. in order that they may get food, perhaps the first food they have had for 24 hours.

Many people complain of dock labourers that they will not work after four o'clock. It is the fact that the great bulk of these poor men will not work after four o'clock. Of course by working from eight to four they would get 3s. 4d.; they might have the opportunity of earning two or three hours more work, and make 10 or 11 hours work, but most of them will not do it. It is a great source of complaint with some people; but really if you only consider it, it is natural. These poor men come on work without a farthing in their pockets; they have not anything to eat in the middle of the day; some of them will raise or have a penny, and buy a little fried fish, and by four o'clock their strength is utterly gone; they pay themselves off; it is absolute necessity which compels them to pay themselves off; their strength will not allow them to go on; they want food and they want money, and are anxious to invest it in food. Many people complain of them for not working after four, but they do not know the real reason.

If there was no large class of casual dock labourers we could rub on, because we employ very few of them; our work is of a heavy and rough character, and can only be done by the physically strong. At this season of the year we employ a fair number of the poor men. This is what they call the fruit season: these little boxes of figs and raisins you see in the shops came over from Smyrna, and from ports in Greece; a poor weak man can handle those, and the poor dock labourers are employed to do that. We may have 100 or 150 at that sort of work day by day, but that is the only time when we employ them.

COL. G. R. BIRT, general manager of the Millwall Docks; S.C. on the Sweating System, 2nd Report, pp. 279-80; P.P. 1888, vol. 21.

5

'Men struggle like wild beasts'

As a rule I have to struggle for employment. Yesterday I earned 2s. 3d.; this is the first work I have done since last Friday . . . I have been down at the London Docks, No. 5 gate, every morning since last Friday, at the usual hour for calling on, that is, half-past eight, and I have been unsuccessful in obtaining employment until yesterday; yesterday I was there from half-past eight till half-past eleven. At half-past eleven I should say that there was something like 350 men waiting for employment at this special gate. A contractor by the name of Clemence came to the gate for, I think it was, 14 men; it was either 14 or 16 men, and of course there was a struggle. As I said before, they have a certain number of tickets to give out; and there was a struggle between us men at the gate who should be lucky enough, as it were, to gain one of these tickets.

It is a common occurrence for men to get seriously injured in a struggle like that. Your Lordships may imagine a kind of cage, as it were, where men struggle like the wild beasts; we stand upon one another's shoulders. I myself have had 8 or 10 men on my shoulders and my head, and I have been hurt several times in a struggle for employment like that, though I have been at the docks every morning at the usual time for calling on. The first is half-past eight, and in the great majority of cases the usual time that I am fortunate enough to get employment is between eleven and one o'clock; that is to say, I have the privilege, it may be called, of earning from 1s. 9d. to 2s. 6d. . . .

JAMES GRAY, dock labourer (Thursday, Nov. 22, 1888); S.C. on the Sweating System, 2nd Report, page 207; P.P. 1888, vol. 21.

6

After the Strike

Dock Labourers. As many of our recommendations under this heading have become superfluous, it is necessary to point out that after we had ceased to take evidence and after this Report was in type, a strike took place resulting in important modifications of the system under which work is carried on in the Docks. The principal effect of such modifications may be summarised as follows:—The contract system has been abolished, and a system of piecework, subject to certain conditions, has been substituted for it. Payments are made by the Dock Companies direct; all hands employed upon a job, including foremen, share equally in 'plus'; the minimum rate of pay is 6d. an hour ordinary time and 8d. an hour overtime; overtime is from 6 p.m. to 6 a.m. Outsiders, if discharged by the Company, cannot receive less than 2s. pay. The new terms came into operation on the 4th of November, 1889, and it will thus be seen that, without going into minor causes of dissatisfaction, the grievances and which the suggestions of your Committee are intended to meet have already been satisfied to a large extent.

S.C. on the Sweating System, 5th Report, p. lxxiii; P.P. 1890, vol. 71.

(c) CHAIN AND NAIL-MAKERS OF CRADLEY HEATH

Chain and nail-making do not give employment to a great number of persons, but in scarcely any of the industries that have come under our notice is so much poverty to be found, combined with such severe work and so many hardships . . .

Chain-making is carried on chiefly at Cradley Heath, and in villages comprised within an area of three or four miles. It is a small industry, not more than from two to three thousand persons being engaged in it. The larger descriptions of chains, known as cable chains, are made in factories; block chains, cart-horse back-bands, dog chains, and other smaller kinds, are made in the district, in small shops attached to the homes of the workers. In most cases there is a workshop at the back of the house, fitted up with an anvil, a stone block, and other appliances. The occupier of the shop may let it out, wholly or in part, to four or five other persons. A shop of the kind described, with a dwelling-house attached to it, lets for from 3s. to 3s. 6d. a week.

The business is carried on in this way: the worker receives a certain weight of iron, and he has to return a corresponding weight of chain, less an allowance, which is, or ought to be, four pounds in the bundle weighing half a hundredweight, for waste in working. It is stated that workmen can occasionally save some iron out of the allowance for waste, which they work up on their own account, and sell to 'foggers' at low rates, to the general detriment of the trade. One of the most common charges, however, brought by the workers is, that the necessary weight for waste is not allowed them, and consequently they are unable to return the requisite weight of chain.

Function of the Fogger

The sweater in these trades is known as the 'fogger'. He goes to the master, takes out the work, and distributes it among the men and

234

women. When it is done he takes it back to the master. Sometimes the fogger works himself, but more frequently he acts merely as a go-between. It is also stated in evidence that the workpeople are compelled in many cases to buy the provisions and other things they require at the fogger's shop, or at a shop kept by his relations or friends; in fact, that he manages to get the workers into his power, and obliges them to deal at his shop, under penalty of refusing to give them work. When the fogger has a shop, the prices he charges for his wares are said to be of an exorbitant character. For American bacon, which an ordinary tradesman sells for 5½d. a pound, they charge 8d.; for sugar they make their customers pay a half-penny per pound above the usual price; for tea they charge more by 50 per cent. than other shops. It is also stated that the fogger does not always wait for orders, but sends in articles to the men, which they are obliged to take, for fear of losing their work.

Various other charges have been made against the 'fogger'. To understand them it is necessary to explain the system of working, which is this: Chains are paid for by the cwt. Less work is required for a cwt. of the larger than of the smaller chains, and consequently the smaller the size of the rods used in making the chain the larger is the payment per cwt. The sizes of iron run downwards from No. 1, which is the largest. The harder and better the iron the more difficult it is to work. The fogger is often accused of giving out iron of the wrong size or quality. This complaint was put before us, among others, by a woman in the trade. The large masters, she said, would not be bothered to give her the small quantity of work she was able to do. She therefore has to take it from a fogger. He gave a certain sized iron, which he called No. 5 but which was really No. 6, and the woman only received 13s. per cwt. for making it, instead of 17s., which is the regulation price.

Another charge made against the fogger is that he exacts an excessive price for repairing tools. It is also stated that occasionally material in an unsuitable condition, that is, bent or crooked iron rods, is served out, and that the workers have to straighten it at their own expense, no allowance being made to them for so doing. It is a subject of complaint also that an excessive allowance is charged for the weight of the bags in which the nails are weighed.

'We don't live very well'

The witnesses show that a hard week's work on common chain, averaging twelve hours a day for five days out of the week, provides no more than a bare subsistence for the man or woman engaged in it. The Rev H. Rylett, a minister at Dudley, acquainted with the district, stated that the women get from 4s. 6d. to 6s. 6d. a week. A man can make about

3 cwt. of chain in a week, for which he receives 5s. per cwt., so that he would receive about 15s. One of the workwomen said that she could usually earn 5s. a week, or something like that, out of which she had to pay 1s. for firing. Another stated that, working from seven in the morning till seven at night, she could make about a cwt. of chain in a week, which she was paid from 4s. to 6s. 6d., the price varying. 'We do not live very well,' she said; 'our most living is bacon; we get a bit of butter sometimes.'

Jane Smith, aged 14 years and 9 months, who points and helps to cut nails, began to work when she was about 13, works from 7 to 7, and is not strong enough for the work. A girl of eighteen stated that she worked twelve hours a day, and that her net earnings would be about 7s. 1d. Sometimes she had bacon for her dinner; never fresh meat. She gave the weight of the heavier of the hammers she used at from 7 to 8 lbs., but Mr Hoare who weighed them found they weighed 1 lb. and 2½ lb. respectively. It may be here mentioned that the price of a dog chain which is made by these women for three farthings is, in London, from 1s. to 1s. 3d. The value of the materials would be about 2d.

A nailmaker said that out of his week's work only about 8s. 6d. remained for himself, after deducting firing and other charges; 'and I have worked for that amount of money', he added, 'till I did not know where to put myself'. In another case a husband and wife work together, and there are three children, two at school and none at work. The man does the 'heading', the woman the 'pointing' of the nails. Their united work brings in from 18s. to £1 a week; out of that about 2s. 3d. for 'breeze', about 5s. for carriage, 2s. 6d. for rent of house and shop, schooling of the children 6d., 6d. to 9d. deductions on account of underweight, and the man has to devote from half a day to a day to repairing his tools. Eighteen shillings or £1 does not represent their average weekly earnings over a year, as some weeks they do not get any work at all. Their general hours of work were from seven in the morning till nine at night, with half-an-hour for breakfast, an hour for dinner, and half-an-hour for tea for the man. The witness herself had no regular time for meals, 'on account of there being no one in the house to do the work besides myself'.

The hands employed in factories are better paid, the cases which we have cited being taken from persons who worked in their own homes. Mr George Green, a member of a firm of nail and chain makers carrying on business near Dudley, stated that the average wages per week, taken from the books of his firm, were, 'for women, 8s. 2d., young women 9s. 4d., youths 12s. 7d., less 12½ per cent, which would be about the cost of their breeze and the rent of their workshop'. Referring to men's wages, Mr Green said that they were getting 'on an average, 26s. 11d.

net'; but in 1888 he thought they would only have been earning 'about 22s.'

We have stated that twelve hours appear to make an ordinary full day's work, but the Rev H. Rylett said 'it is quite a common thing for these people to work ten to twelve hours a day, and even thirteen or fourteen hours a day. 'I have frequently gone through this district, and it is as common as possible to find these people working up to 8 and 9 o'clock at night. In fact, you may go through the district when it is pitch dark, and there are no lamps in some parts, and you will hear these little forges going and people working in them, and you wonder when they are going to stop.'

Mr Homer said that the Union had failed to shorten hours, as the men would break away from the rule restricting the hours of work. He added that the race had deteriorated in the last ten years.

A woman told us that she carried a quarter of a mile, on her neck, chain weighing, it would seem, on an average, half a hundredweight. Another woman carried a hundredweight of chain 20 or 30 yards, and Mr Hoare said that women carried a 60 lb. bundle of nails a mile.

'Immoral', 'Indecent'

Before, and for some time after, the appointment of your Committee, startling statements appeared in various public journals with regard to the employment of women in these trades, and the immorality which was alleged to be one of the consequences. We found nothing whatever to justify these imputations on the character of the people. As a rule, they are well conducted, and although it may be objected that some of the work is unfit for women to do, there is no warrant for the assertion that it is indecent. We may give a brief summary of the evidence on this question.

Mr Homer stated that 'in shops, where they have big young women blowing for them, very often there are doings that will not bear the daylight; they are immoral'. The Rev H. Rylett thought that the arrangement of many of the shops, together with the absence of control facilitated immorality. Several of the witnesses considered that it was 'unbecoming' and 'improper' for women to work a machine known as the 'Oliver', subsequently described. One witness said that in hot weather he had seen the female workers 'stripped, with only a skirt or two on, and no body on their frock or gown'. Mr Bassano, who had lived in the neighbourhood nearly all his life, stated that prostitution is wholly unknown in the district; out of five hundred births in the preceding half year, twenty-six were illegitimate, but nine of the mothers were domestic servants; three only were chainmakers. Mr Morris stated that during three years' experience, he had 'never seen any woman dressed in such a way as to be indecent'. He had 'seen women dressed with their clothes thrown back in hot weather'.

The girls who blow the bellows are said to be employed in a way that is not always decent. 'I have seen', said one witness, 'a girl, to my astonishment, stuck up in the roof blowing bellows with her feet; a veritable treadmill, a treadmill under the worst possible conditions.' One of the inspectors discredited this statement. He said that he had never seen anything immodest or indecent in the way the work was carried on, and he added, 'You may certainly see far more indecency in the stalls of a London theatre than you may see in a chain and nail shop in the way of clothing'.

Using the 'oliver'

The work of cutting cold iron by means of the 'oliver' falls with great severity on the women who are employed at it. The oliver is a heavy sledge hammer, worked with a treadle by means of a spring, and when used for cutting cold iron it is totally unsuited for women. Mr Ker said: 'I have found among women, especially those that have been working at heavy work, that they are very liable to misplacements of the womb, and to rupture, and also among married women I find that they are liable to miscarriages, as they frequently go on working when they are in the family-way.' He believed that women ought not to be allowed to use it at all, and we fully agree with him.

The homes in which these poor people live are generally of the most squalid and deplorable kind. The drains are at the best defective; sometimes there are no drains whatever. Mr Ker, certifying surgeon for the district, testified that heaps of manure are often to be found opposite the workshops and dwellings. In some cases, there is only one privy provided for three houses, and that is in a detestable condition. Typhoid is 'much more common than it ought to be'. Mr A. Smith, Sanitary Commissioner of the 'Lancet', said that the people at Cradley threw all their slops into the main street, whence some of it flows into surface wells, the water of which is used for drinking purposes. There is water supplied by a company, but the people prefer the well water, but this preference may be accounted for by the fact that they can get the well water for nothing, whereas they have to pay for the other.

The mortality among children under five is great; more than half the total deaths. This is ascribed in part to early marriages and unhealthy parentage. It is 'a common thing' for girls and boys to marry at fifteen or sixteen, and to bring on themselves the charge of a family when in a state not far removed from starvation.

S.C. on the Sweating System; 5th Report, pp. xxv-xxxi; P.P. 1890, vol. 17.

(d) THE 'SWEATING' COMMITTEE'S REPORT

The Committee have sat to receive evidence on 71 occasions, and have examined 291 witnesses. . . . We have endeavoured to extract from the principal witnesses a clear idea of what they understood by the term 'sweating'. The replies received were neither clear nor consistent. It was urged by some that sweating is an abuse of the sub-contract system, and consequently that there can be no sweating where there is no sub-contracting. Others, on the contrary, maintained that sub-contracting is by no means a necessary element of sweating, which consists, according to them, in taking advantage of the necessities of the poorer and more helpless class of workers, either by forcing them to work too hard or too long, or under insanitary conditions, or for 'starvation wages', or by exacting what some witnesses call 'an undue profit' out of their labour.

We do not propose to enter upon any discussion of the various definitions placed before us. It is enough to say that we considered our inquiry should embrace—(1) The means employed to take advantage of the necessities of the poorer and more helpless class of workers. (2) The conditions under which such workers live. (3) The causes that have conduced to the state of things disclosed. (4) The remedies proposed.

Such having been the scope of our inquiry, and ample evidence having been brought before us on every matter comprised within its scope, we are of opinion that, although we cannot assign an exact meaning to 'sweating', the evils known by that name are shown to be—1, A rate of wages inadequate to the necessities of the workers or disproportionate to the work done. 2, Excessive hours of labour. 3, The insanitary state of the houses in which the work is carried on.

These evils can hardly be exaggerated. The earnings of the lowest classes of workers are barely sufficient to sustain existence. The hours of labour are such as to make the lives of the workers periods of almost ceaseless toil, hard and often unhealthy. The sanitary conditions under which the work is conducted are not only injurious to the health of the persons employed, but are dangerous to the public, especially in the case of the trades concerned in making clothes, as infectious diseases are spread by the sale of garments made in rooms inhabited by persons suffering from small-pox and other diseases.

We make the above statements on evidence of the truth of which we are fully satisfied, and we feel bound to express our admiration of the courage with which the sufferers endure their lot, of the absence of any desire to excite pity by exaggeration, and of the almost unbounded charity they display towards each other in endeavouring by gifts of food and other kindnesses to alleviate any distress for the time being greater than their own.

As a rule, however, it must be remembered that the observations made with respect to sweating apply, in the main, to unskilled or only partially skilled workers, as the thoroughly skilled workers can almost always obtain adequate wages.

When we come to consider the causes of and the remedies for the evils attending the conditions of labour which go under the name of sweating, we are immediately involved in a labyrinth of difficulties.

First, we are told that the introduction of sub-contractors, or middle-men, is the cause of the misery. Undoubtedly, it appears to us that employers are regardless of the moral obligations which attach to capital when they take contracts to supply articles and know nothing of the condition of the workers by whom such articles are made, leaving to a sub-contractor the duty of selecting the workers and giving him by way of compensation a portion of the profit. But it seems to us that the middleman is the consequence, not the cause of the evil; the instrument, not the hand which gives motion to the instrument, which does the mischief. Moreover, the middleman is found to be absent in many cases in which the evils complained of abound.

Further, we think that undue stress has been laid on the injurious effect on wages caused by foreign immigration, inasmuch as we find that the evils complained of obtain in trades, which do not appear to be affected by foreign immigration.

We are of opinion, however, that certain trades are, to some extent, affected by the presence of poor foreigners, for the most part Russian and Polish Jews. These Jews are not charged with immorality or with vice of any description, though represented by some witnesses as being uncleanly in their persons and habits. On the contrary, they are represented on all hands as thrifty and industrious, and they seldom or never come on the rates, as the Jews support by voluntary contributions all their indigent members. What is shown is that the Jewish immigrants can live on what would be starvation wages to Englishmen, that they work for a number of hours almost incredible in length, and that until of late they have not easily lent themselves to trade combinations.

Machinery, by increasing the sub-division of labour, and consequently affording great opportunities for the introduction of unskilled labour is also charged with being a cause of sweating. The answer to this charge seems to be, that in some of the largest clothing and other factories in which labour is admitted to be carried on under favourable conditions to the workers, machinery, and sub-division of labour to the greatest possible extent, are found in every department of the factory.

With more truth it may be said that the inefficiency of many of the lower class of workers, early marriages, and the tendency of the residuum of the population in large towns to form a helpless community, together with a low standard of life and the excessive supply of unskilled labour, are the chief factors in producing sweating. Moreover, a large supply of cheap female labour is available in consequence of the fact that married women working at unskilled labour in their homes, in the intervals of attendance on their domestic duties and not wholly supporting themselves, can afford to work at what would be starvation wages to unmarried women. Such being the conditions of the labour market, abundant materials exist to supply an unscrupulous employer with workers helplessly dependent upon him.

The most important question is, whether any remedy can be found for this unhappy state of a portion of the labouring class. With respect to the low wages and excessive hours of labour, we think that good may be effected by the extension of co-operative societies, and by well-considered combination among the workers. We are aware that home-workers form a great obstacle in the way of combination, inasmuch as they cannot readily be brought to combine for the purpose of raising wages. To remove this obstacle we have been urged to recommend the prohibition by legislation of working at home, but we think such a measure would be arbitrary and oppressive, not sanctioned by any precedent in existing law, and impossible to be effectually enforced.

We now proceed to make recommendations in respect of the evils, which appear to us, under existing circumstances, to require immediate parliamentary interference.

Under the factory law work-places for the purposes of sanitation are divided into three classes:—Factories, Workshops, and Domestic workshops. We are of opinion that all work-places included under the above descriptions should be required to be kept in a cleanly state, to be lime-washed or washed throughout at stated intervals, to be kept free from noxious effluvia, and not to be overcrowded; in other words, to be treated for sanitary purposes as factories are treated under the factory law. We are also of opinion that an adequate number of inspectors should be appointed to enforce a due observance of the law. We think that inspectors should have power to enter all work-places within their jurisdiction at reasonable times without warrant.

We consider that the establishment of County Councils provides in every county a body capable of being trusted with the control and super-intendence of sanitary inspection. We think it a disadvantage that different departments of the Government should be concerned with matters relating to the labour question. . . .

Evidence has been brought before us that the use of the 'oliver', or heavy sledge hammer, used for cutting cold iron, is unfit work for women and girls, with the exception of the 'light oliver', adapted for making hobnails; and we recommend that women and girls should be prohibited by law from working the 'oliver' when the hammer exceeds a certain specified weight.

We also recommend that women and girls should be prohibited by law from making chains the links of which are made of iron exceeding a certain specified thickness.

We are glad to find that efforts are being made to put an end to the grave scandal of sweating in the making up of Government contracts for clothing and accoutrements.

We cannot conclude without expressing our earnest hope that the exposure of the evils which have been brought to our notice will induce capitalists to pay closer attention to the conditions under which the labour which supplies them with goods is conducted. When legislation has reached the limit up to which it is effective, the real amelioration of conditions must be due to increased sense of responsibility in the employer and improved habits in the employed. We have reason to think that the present inquiry itself has not been without moral effect. And we believe that public attention and public judgment can effectually check operations in which little regard is shown to the welfare of work-people and to the quality of production, and can also strongly second the zealous and judicious efforts now being made to encourage thrift, promote temperance, improve dwellings, and raise the tone of living.

S.C. on the Sweating System, 5th Report, pp. iii-xlv; P.P. 1890, vol. 17.

CHAPTER 7

'PAGES FROM A WORKGIRL'S DIARY'

[The article, 'Pages from a Workgirl's Diary', was written by Miss Beatrice Potter (Mrs Sidney Webb: 1858-1943) for the *Nineteenth Century* and was published in the October 1888 issue of that influential monthly review. This was a few months after she had given evidence before the Select Committee of the House of Lords on the Sweating System, as mentioned in the previous chapter.

Miss Potter's appearance on that occasion had created something of a sensation. Thoroughly self-possessed, so well spoken and mannered, so obviously cultured and intelligent, so very much the lady—she stood out in strong contrast with the other members of her sex who came to tell their Lordships of their experiences in East End tailoring workshops.

At the time she was just thirty. She was the youngest but one of the nine daughters of Richard Potter, a man of wealth and high esteem in the business world, chairman for some years of the Great Western Railway and for ten years, when Beatrice was a girl, president of the Grand Trunk Railway of Canada. She accompanied him on some of his business trips, and after her mother's death acted as his housekeeper. But as she grew into womanhood she found the conditions of wealthy existence increasingly irksome, and made friends with cousins on her mother's side who had not got on in the world but were wage-earning operatives in cotton mills at Bacup, in Lancashire. This 'Bacup adventure', as she styles it, 'gave a decisive twist' to her mind, and decided her to adopt the career of a 'social investigator'. She became a rent collector in a block of model dwellings in London's dockland, and this led to her engagement by Charles Booth (whose wife was her cousin) to collaborate with him in his 'grand inquest'. She wrote several chapters of *Life and Labour of the People in London*, and had a number of articles accepted by the *Nineteenth Century*.

'Pages from a Workgirl's Diary' was the best received of these: so well received, in fact, that she felt a little ashamed of the fuss that was made about it. 'My one and only literary success' is how she describes it in her autobiography, *My Apprenticeship* (1926); 'a cheap triumph', seeing that it was little more than a transcript of her MS. diary, with 'the facts just enough disguised to avoid recognition and possible actions for libel, and sufficiently expurgated to be "suited to a female pen"!'— this being a reference to her omission of what she had written in her

243

diary about the prevalence of incest among some of her workmates in the tailoring workshops who were living in one-room tenements. But it may be noted that the woman who wrote *My Apprenticeship* was in her middle sixties, and may have found it difficult to recapture the eager insight of forty years earlier.

Six months after her father's death in 1892 Beatrice Potter married Sidney Webb (1859-1947), an unpretentious looking little man who had a clerkship in the Civil Service. But he was a leading Fabian Socialist, and Beatrice had the good sense to recognize his possession of a 'clear, analytic brain' that was the necessary complement of her own. So began 'Our Partnership' that, extending over half a century, was to prove so extraordinarily fruitful in the production of massive works of social research and Socialist ideology.]

It is mid-day. The sun's rays beat fiercely on the crowded alleys of the Jewish settlement: the air is moist from the heavy rains. An unsavoury steam rises from the downtrodden slime of the East End streets and mixes with the stronger odours of the fried fish, the decomposing vegetables, and the second-hand meat, which assert their presence to the eyes and nostrils of the passers-by.

For a brief interval the 'whirr' of the sewing-machines and the muffled sound of the presser's iron have ceased. Machinists and pressers, well-clothed and decorated with heavy match-chains; Jewish girls with flashy hats, full figures, and large bustles; furtive-eyed Polish immigrants with their pallid faces and crouching forms; and here and there poverty-stricken Christian women—all alike hurry to and from the mid-day meal; while the labour-masters, with their wives and daughters, sit or lounge round about the house-door, and exchange notes on the incompetency of 'season hands', the low price of work, the blackmail of shop foremen; or else discuss the more agreeable topic of the last 'deal' in Petticoat Lane and the last venture on race-horses.

Jostled on and off the pavement, I wander on and on, seeking work. Hour after hour I have paced the highways and byways of the London Ghetto. No bills up except for a 'good' tailoress, and at these places I dare not apply, for I feel myself an impostor, and as yet my conscience and my fingers are equally unhardened. Each step I take I am more faint-hearted and more weary in body and limb. At last, in sheer despair, I summon up my courage. In a window the usual bill, but seated on the doorstep a fat cheerful-looking daughter of Israel, who seems to invite application.

'Do you want a plain 'and?' say I, aping ineffectually a workwoman's manner and accent, and attaining only supreme awkwardness.

The Jewess glances quickly, first at my buttonless boots, then at my short but already bedraggled skirt, upwards along the straight line of my ill-fitting coat, to the tumbled black bonnet which sits ill at ease over an unkempt twist of hair.

'No', is the curt reply.

'I can do all except buttonholes', I insist in a more natural tone. She looks at my face and hesitates. 'Where have you worked?' 'In the country', I answer vaguely.

She turns her head slowly towards the passage of the house. 'Rebecca, do you want a hand?' 'Suited an hour ago', shouts back Rebecca.

'There, there, you see', remarks the Jewess in a deprecating and kindly voice as her head sinks into the circles of fat surrounding it. 'You will find plenty of bills in the next street; no fear of a decent young person, as knows her work, staying out o' door this time of year'; and then, turning to the woman by her side; 'It's rare tho' to find one as does. In these last three days, if we've sat down one, we've sat a dozen to the table, and not a woman amongst them as knows how to baste out a coat fit for the machine.'

Encouraged by these last words I turn round and trudge on. I ask at every house with a bill up, but always the same scrutinizing glance at my clothes, and the fatal words, 'We are suited!'

Is it because it is the middle of the week, or because they think I'm not genuine? think I. And at the next shop window I look nervously at my reflection, and am startled at my utterly forlorn appearance— destitute enough to be 'sweated' by any master.

'Sure, there's not much on 'er back to take to the h'old uncle', remarks an Irish servant to her mistress, as I turn away from the last house advertising for a 'good tailoress'.

I feel horribly sick and ill; and I am so painfully conscious of my old clothes that I dare not ask for refreshment at an eating-house or even at a public. Any way, I will have air, so I drag one foot after another into the Hackney thoroughfare. Straight in front of me, in a retail slop-shop of the lowest description, I see a large placard: 'Trouser and Vest Hands Wanted Immediately.' In another moment I am within a large work-room crowded with women and girls as ill-clothed as myself. At the head of a long table, examining finished garments, stands a hard-featured, shrewd-looking Jewess, in a stamped cotton velvet and with a gold-rimmed eyeglass.

'Do you want trouser hands?'

'Yes we do—indoor.'

'I'm a trouser finisher.'

The Jewess examines me from head to foot. My standard of dress suits her. 'Call at eight o'clock to-morrow morning.' And she turns from me to look over a pair of trousers handed up the table.

'What price do you pay?' say I with firmness.

'Why, according to the work done, to be sure. All prices,' she answers laconically.

'Then to-morrow at eight.' And I leave the shop hurriedly to escape that hard gaze of my future mistress. Again in the open street . . . Only one drawback to perfect content: *Can* I 'finish' trousers?

At a few minutes past eight the following morning I am standing in front of 'MOSES AND SON. CHEAP CLOTHING'. In the window two shop-boys are arranging the show garments: coats and vests (sold together), 17s. to 22s.; trousers from 4s. 6d. up to 11s. 6d.

'Coats evidently made out: I wonder where and at what price?' ponders the investigator as the work-girl loiters at the door.

'You'd better come in', says the friendly voice of a fellow-worker as she brushes past me. 'You're a new-comer; the missus will expect you to be there sharp.'

I follow her into the retail shop, and thence through a roughly-made wooden door. The workroom is long and irregularly shaped, somewhat low and dark near the entrance, but expanding into a lofty skylight at the further end. The walls are lined with match-boarding; in a prominent place, framed and under glass, hang the Factory and Workshop Regulations. Close by the door, and well within reach of the gas-stove (used for heating irons), two small but high tables serve the pressers: a long low plank-table, furnished with a wooden rail for the feet, forms on either side of it, chairs top and bottom, runs lengthways for the trouser finishers; a high table for the basters; and, directly under the skylight, two other tables for machinists and vest hands complete the furniture of the room. Through an open door, at the extreme end of the workshop, you can see the private kitchen of the Moses family; and beyond, in a very limited back-yard an outhouse, and, near to it, a tap and sink for the use of all the inmates of the establishment.

Some thirty women and girls are crowding in. The first arrivals hang bonnets and shawls on the scanty supply of nails jotted here and there along the wooden partition separating the front shop from the work-room; the later comers shed their outdoor garments in various corners. There is a general Babel of voices as each 'hand' settles down in front of the bundle of work and the old tobacco or candlebox that holds the cottons, twist, gimp, needles, thimble, and scissors belonging to her. They are all English or Irish women, with the exception of some half-dozen well-dressed 'young ladies' (daughters of the house), one of whom acts as forewoman, while the others are already at work on the vests. The 'missus' is still at breakfast. A few minutes after the half-hour the two pressers (English lads, and the only men employed) saunter lazily into the room, light up the gas-jet, and prepare the irons.

The forewoman calls for a pair of trousers, already machined, and hands them to me. I turn them over and over, puzzled to know where to begin. The work is quite different from that of the *bespoke* shop, at which I was trained—much coarser and not so well arranged. The woman next me explains: 'You'll 'ave to bring trimmings; we h'aint' supplied with them things y'ere; but I'll lend you some, jist to set off with.'

'What ought I to buy?' I ask, feeling rather helpless.

At this moment the 'missus' sweeps into the room. She is a big woman, enormously developed in the hips and thighs; she has strongly marked Jewish features, and, I see now, she is blind of one eye. The sardonic and enigmatical expression of her countenance puzzles me with its far-off associations, until I remember the caricatures, sold in City shops for portraits, of the great Disraeli. Her hair is crisp and oily—once jet-black, now, in places, grey—it twists itself in scanty locks over her forehead. The same stamped cotton velvet, of a large flowery pattern, that she wore yesterday; a heavy watch-chain, plentiful supply of rings, and a spotlessly clean apron.

'Good morning to you', she says graciously to the whole assembly as she walks round our table towards my seat. 'Sarah, have you given this young person some work?'

'Yes', replies Sarah; 'fourpence halfpenny's.'

'I have not got any trimmings. I did not know that I had to supply them. Where I worked before they were given', I ejaculate humbly.

'That's easily managed; the shop's just round the corner—Or, Sarah', she calls across the table, 'you're going out—just get the young person her trimmings. The lady next you will tell you what you want', she adds in a lower tone, bending over between us.

The 'lady' next me is already my friend. She is a neat and respectable married woman with a look of conscious superiority to her surroundings. Like all trouser hands she is paid by the piece; but in spite of this she is prepared to give up time in explaining how I am to set about my work. 'You'll feel a bit strange the first day. 'Ave you been long out o' work?'

'Yes', I answer abruptly.

'Ah! that accounts for you're being a bit awkward-like. One's fingers feel like so many thumbs after a slack time.'

And certainly mine do. I feel nervous, and very much on trial. The growing heat of the room, the form so crowded that one must sit sideways to secure even a limited freedom for one's elbows; the general strangeness of my position—all these circumstances unite to incapacitate a true hater of needlework for even the roughest of sewing. However, happily for me no one pays me much attention. As the morning wears on, the noise increases. The two pressers have worked up their spirits, and a lively exchange of chaff and bad language is thrown from the two lads at the pressing (immediately behind us) to the girls round our table. Offers of kisses, sharp dispatches to the devil and his abode, a constant and meaningless use of the inevitable adjective, form the staple of the conversation between the pressers and the younger hands; while the elder women whisper scandal and news in each other's ears. From the further end of the room catches of music-hall songs break into the monotonous whirr of the sewing-machine. The somewhat crude and unrhythmical chorus—

> Why should not the girls have freedom now and then?
> And if a girl likes a man, why should she not propose?
> Why should the little girls always be led by the nose?

seems the favourite refrain, and, judging from the gusto with which it is repeated, expresses the dominant sentiment of the work-girls. Now and again the mistress shouts out, 'Sing in time, girls; I don't mind you singing, but sing in time'. There is a free giving and taking of each other's trimmings, a kindly and general supervision of each other's work—altogether a hearty geniality of a rough sort. The enigmatical and sardonic-looking Jewess sits at the upper end of our table, scans the finished garment through her gold-rimmed eyeglass, encourages or scolds as befits the case; or, screwing up her blind eye, joins in the chatter and broad-witted talk of the work-women immediately surrounding her. . . .

'The missus 'as sixteen children', remarks my friend Mrs Long confidentially—'h'eight by Mr Moses, and h'eight by the master she buried years ago. All them girls at the bottom table ar' 'er daughters.'

'They are a nice-looking set', say I, in a complimentary tone. 'Yes, it's a pity some of the girls in the shop h'ain't like them', mutters my respectable friend. 'They're an awful bad lot, some of them. Why, bless you, that young person as is laughing and joking with the pressers jist be'ind us'—and there follow horrible details of the domestic vice and unnatural crime which disgrace the so-called 'Christian' life of East London.

'Eh, eh!' joins in the woman next her, with a satisfied sniff at the scandal (a regular woman of the slums, with her nose and skin patched by drink), 'it's h'ill thinking of what you may 'ave to touch in these sort of places. . . .'

*   *   *

'One o'clock', shouts a shrill boy's voice.

'Stop work', orders the mistress.

'I wish I might finish this bit', I say pathetically to my friend, painfully conscious of the shortcoming in the quantity, if not in the quality of my work.

'You mustn't; it's the dinner hour.'

The pressers are already off, the mistress and her daughters retire into the kitchen; the greater number of women and girls turn out into the street, while one or two pull baskets from under the table, spread out before them, on dirty newspapers, cracked mugs, bits of bread and butter, cold sausage or salt fish; and lift, from off the gas-stove, the tin teapot wherein their drink has been stewing since the early morning. Heartily thankful for a breath of fresh air and a change from my cramped posture, I wander up and down the open street, and end my 'dinner hour' by turning into a clean shop for a bun and a fresh cup of tea. Back again at two.

'You must work sharper than this', remarks the mistress, who is inspecting my work. I colour up and tremble perceptibly as I meet the scrutinizing gaze of the hard-featured Jewess. She looks into my eyes with a comically puzzled expression, and adds in a gentler voice: 'You must work a little quicker for you own sake. We've had worse buttonholes than these, but it don't look as if you'd been 'customed to much work'.

But now the drama of the day begins. The two pressers saunter in ten minutes after the hour. This brings down upon them the ire of the Jewess. They, however, seem masters of the situation, for they answer her back in far choicer language than that in which they were addressed —language which I fear (even in a private diary) I could hardly reproduce; they assert their right to come when they choose; they declare that if they want a day off they 'will see her to the devil and take it'; and lastly, as a climax to all insults, they threaten her with the 'factory man', and taunt her with gambling away on racehorses money she 'sweats' out of them.

At these last words the enigmatical and sardonic expression of the Jewess changes into one of outbursting rage. All resemblance of the City caricatures of that great passionless spirit vanishes . . . A perfect volley of oaths fly in quick succession between the principal combatants; while woman after woman joins in the fray, taking the missus's side against the pressers. The woman of the slums actually rises in her seat and prepares to use her fists; while her daughter seizes the opportunity to empty the small bottle of brandy hidden under her mother's trimmings . . . At this critical moment—enter the master.

Mr Moses is a corpulent, well-dressed English Jew. His face is heavy and sensual, his eyes sheepish, his reputation among his wife's 'hands' none of the best. At this moment, his one desire is to keep the Queen's

peace . . . 'Sit down, Mrs Jones', he shouts to the woman of the slums—
'sit down, or you and that——daughter of yours leave the shop this very
instant. Now, lads, just you be quiet; go on with your work and don't
speak to my wife.' And then, turning to his wife, in a lower tone—'Why
won't you leave them alone and not answer them?' and the rest of his
speech we cannot hear; but judging from the tone and the look, it takes
the form of deprecating expostulation. I catch the words 'push of work'
and 'season hands'.

'Why, if you were only a bit of a man', cries the mistress, raising her
voice so that all may hear, 'you'd throw those two b — y rascals out. I'd
throw them out at any price, if I were a woman's husband. The idea of
saying how I spend my money—what's that to him?' 'It isn't their
business what you do with your money', rejoins the master soothingly.
'But just let them alone, and tell those girls to be quiet. It's more than
half the girls' fault—they're always at the fellows', he adds, anxious to
shift the blame into a safe quarter. The storm lulls, and Mr Moses
returns into the front shop . . .

At length tea-time breaks the working day. Pence have already been
collected for the common can of milk; innumerable teapots are lifted
off the gas-stove, small parcels of bread and butter, with a relish or a
sweet, are everywhere unrolled. My neighbours, on either side, offer me
tea, which I resolutely refuse. The mistress sips her cup at the head of
the table. The obnoxious pressers have left for the half-hour. Her
feelings break out—

'Pay them 5s. a day to abuse you! As if I couldn't spend my money on
what I like; and as if Mr Moses would ever ask—I'd like to see him
ask me—how the money'd gone!'

All the women sympathize with her, and vie with each other in
abusing the absent pressers. 'It's h'awful, their language', cries the slum
woman; 'if I were the missus, I'd give the bl — y scoundrels tit for tat.
Whativer's the use of bein' a missus if you've got to 'old in y're tongue?'

'As for the factory man', continues the irate Jewess, turning to the
other sore point, 'just fancy threatening me with him! Why they ar'n't
fit to work in a respectable shop; they're d — spies . . .'

At the word spy, I feel rather hot; but conscious of the innocence of
my object, I remark, 'You have nothing to fear from the factory
inspector; you keep the regulations exactly'.

'I don't deny', she answers quite frankly, 'that if we're pressed for
work I turn the girls upstairs; but it isn't once in three months I do it;
and it all tells for their good.'

Two hours afterwards, and I have finished my second pair. 'This
won't do', she says as she looks over both pairs together. 'Here, take
and undo the band of that one; I'll set this one to rights. Better have

respectable persons, who know little, to work here, than blaguards who know a lot—and a deal too much', she mutters . . .

'Eight o'clock by the Brewery clock', cries the shrill voice.

'Ten minutes to', shouts the missus, looking at her watch. 'However, it ain't worth breaking the law for a few minutes. Stop work.'

This is most welcome to me. The heat since the gas has been lit is terrific, my fingers are horribly sore, and my back aches as if it would break. The women bundle up their work; one or two take it home. Every one leaves her trimmings on the table, with scissors and thimble. Outside, the freshness of the evening air, the sensation of free movement, and rest to the weary eyes and fingers constitute the keenest physical enjoyment I have ever yet experienced. . . .

BEATRICE POTTER (Mrs Sidney Webb); from an article contributed to the *Nineteenth Century*, October 1888; reprinted in *Problems of Modern Industry* (1902).

"MAMMON'S RENTS"!!

House-Jobber. "NOW, THEN, MY MAN; WEEK'S HUP! CAN'T 'AVE A 'OME WITHOUT PAYIN' FOR IT, YER KNOW!"

Punch (1883)

TROPICAL.

Maid (to Irish Milkman). "MISSIS SAYS SHE'S SURE THERE'S BEEN A GREAT DEAL O' WATER IN THE MILK LATELY, AND THAT IF——"

Pat. "AN' CAN YE WANDER AT IT, MY DEAR! SMALL BLAME TO THE COWS THIS THUR-RSTY WEATHER, POOR CRATURS!"

Punch (1885)

CHAPTER 8

DANGEROUS TRADES

(Departmental Committees of the Home Office, 1893-99)
After the 'sweated industries' it was the turn of the 'dangerous trades' to be subjected to official investigation. The Home Office was the responsible department, and the appointment in 1892 of H. H. Asquith as Home Secretary in Gladstone's fourth Liberal Government was the signal for vigorous action. Asquith turned out to be one of the best in the long line of Home Secretaries, although he was in office for only three years; not the least of his admirable innovations was the appointment of the first women Factory Inspectors.

In 1893 departmental committees were set up to inquire into the conditions of labour in Chemical Works and the Lead Industries. The Liberals went out of office in 1895, but the good work was continued by Lord Salisbury's Conservative administration. In 1896 a great new field of industrial activities was laid open, when the Miscellaneous Dangerous Trades Committee was set up under the chairmanship of H. J. Tennant, M.P., who had served as secretary to the departmental committee on Various Lead Industries in 1893. Among the committee members were Miss May Abraham (1869-1946), the first woman inspector to be appointed in England (in 1893), who was now H.M. Superintending Inspector of Factories, and Professor Thomas Oliver, MD, (1853-1942), a Scotsman who practised medicine in Newcastle from 1879 and was a professor at the medical school there for many years. Oliver (who was knighted in 1908) was recognized as one of the greatest experts in the developing field of industrial medicine, and was the author of standard works on *Dangerous Trades* (1902) and *Diseases of Occupations* (1908).

It may be of interest to learn what were the trades which in 1896 were considered to be specially dangerous. As listed in the terms of reference of the Dangerous Trades Committee they were:—India rubber works; paper staining, colouring, and enamelling; dry cleaning; basic slag works, and manufacture of silicate of cotton; electric generating works; sole-stitching by American machinery; glass polishing; file-cutting; flour mills; use of steam locomotives in factories; use of inflammable paints in shipbuilding yards; manufacture and use of grindstones and emery wheels; use of lead in various forms in print and dye works; bottling of aerated water; manufacture of salt, etc.

As will be clear from the extracts given here from the successive 'dangerous trades' reports, some distressing and even dreadful facts were brought to light, and in a number of cases the Home Office took remedial action.

I

Dreadful Effects of Lead Poisoning

It is known that if lead (in any form) even in what may be called infinitesimal quantities, gains entrance into the system for a lengthened period . . . there is developed a series of symptoms, the most frequent of which is colic.

Nearly all the individuals engaged in factories where lead or its compounds are manufactured look pale, and it is this bloodlessness, and the presence of a blue line along the margin of the gums, close to the teeth, that herald the other symptoms of *plumbism.*

A form of paralysis known as wrist-drop, or lead palsy, occasionally affects the hands of the operatives. There is, in addition, a form of acute lead poisoning, most frequently met with in young girls from 18 to 24 years of age, which is suddenly developed, and is extremely fatal. In it, the first complaint is headache, followed, sooner or later, by convulsions and unconsciousness. Death often terminates such a case within three days. In some cases of recovery from convulsions total blindness remains.

There has been considerable doubt as to the channels by which the poison enters the system. The Committee have taken much evidence on this subject, and have arrived at the conclusion—(*a*) that carbonate of lead may be absorbed through the pores of the skin, and that the chance of this is much increased during perspiration and where there is any friction between the skin and the clothing; (*b*) that minute portions of lead are carried by the hands, under and round the nails, etc., on to the food, and so into the stomach; (*c*) but that the most usual manner is by the inhalation of the lead dust. Some of this becomes dissolved in the alkaline secretions of the mouth, and is swallowed with the saliva, thus finding its way into the stomach. Other particles of dust are carried to the lungs, where they are rendered soluble and absorbed by the blood.

Report on the Various Lead Industries, p. 9; P.P. 1893-4, vol. 17.

2

Annie Harrison's Story

Miss Annie Harrison was called in and examined.

Chairman: (Mr Gould). How old are you?—Twenty on the 28th of February last. Where have you been working?—At Bilston, at Messrs Ralph & Jordan's.

Are you working there now?—No, sir . . . I was very ill; obliged to leave. I had lead poison.

What did you feel?—The mornings I went to work—I stayed away one Monday, the morning; and on the Tuesday morning when I went to work I felt very ill, very low, I trembled. I went to one of the girls and I said, 'I cannot stay any longer; I think I will have to go home badly'. She said, 'I would stay till dinner time'. I went to one of the furnace-men, who were firing, and he said, 'You will have to go home now: I see it coming over you'. I said, 'Yes, I feel very ill this morning; I can hardly tell you how I feel'. I was trembling at the same time, and I fell back, and I do not remember anything more.

You fainted?—Well, I must have done. I no remember anything more. When I found myself right again, I was in the dinner house, what they call the dinner house, a little bit of a room.

Have you pain here (*indicating stomach*)?—Very bad pain in the stomach. This morning I felt something frightful drawing me in two. I was on chairs furniture pasting; I had to go and lie down, leaving them. I have been across the country hop-picking to see if that would do me any good, and really I have had to fall across the crib in the morning, I have been so ill. It is a most frightful feeling in the stomach.

When you first went, a year ago, to Messrs Ralph & Jordan's, what was the state of your health?—I was in very good health then.

Then why did you leave the situation that you were in—in domestic service?—I did not have enough wages when I was in service. I did not have but 1s. 9d. a week in my first place.

Then you left because you wanted to better yourself?—Yes, sir; I got very good wages while I stopped at Messrs Ralph & Jordan's some weeks, and some weeks were very bad ones.

What were you doing: brushing?—Yes, sir.

What did you earn there a week?—Some weeks 11s., and some weeks it made it out. You would have to stand about, and you would perhaps not get above 2s. 6d. At the very lowest I have got 2s. 7d.

That was piecework?—Yes, piecework.

Did you always take your breakfast before you went in the morning?—Yes, sir; I always had a breakfast before I started out of the house in the morning.

Could you eat it; had you a pretty good appetite?—Well, not always; I was a very poor eater; it fell off when I had been there a little time.

Now, tell me, do you wear a handkerchief over your mouth?—No, sir.

Never?—When I went there first there were some very old gowns made with glazed linings—some of this cheap stuff. Well, they were very ragged, torn all to pieces. There were no caps then, not when I went.

Were there any overalls?—These were the overalls; what they call pinafores.

Handkerchiefs?—There was not any until there came these fresh bye-laws; then they gave you those flannel things to go over your mouth, respirators.

Did you find that the dust got down your throat much? Yes, sir; and it tastes very sweet, and I fetched it up off my stomach like that.

Black?—Yes, in a large lump. If you have worked in the reds, it will come up red; if you have worked in the blues, it will come up blue; if you have worked in the blacks, it will come up black, and there is not one girl on the ground, if she will speak the truth, but will say it to you, and the yellow too. But it was the yellow that done me the best. I was working on Old Brook's for the last three months; three months of the time Colman's, Old Brook's.

You mean that the sign that you were brushing was Colman's, Old Brook's?—Yes, Old Brook's sauce and Old Brook's mustard and things.

What I want to ask you is this, did you ever find that your clothes became covered with dust underneath?—Yes, sir, it goes straight through.

Through the overalls?—Yes, sir, it goes through the overalls. Through the gown?—Yes, sir.

Through the stays?—Well, I will not say through the stays; it will go straight through the lower part.

The Secretary. Did you have any headache at the time you were ill?—Yes, sir. I had a fearful headache for which I brought buckets of water up; I put my head almost in water, I had such a fearful headache. When you were taken ill, what doctor attended you?—Of course, Messrs Ralph & Jordan had the doctor from Bilston, Dr Smith.

Did Dr Smith come to see you at your home at Sedgley?—Yes, sir. You are not married, are you?—No, sir.

Did you wash your hands carefully when you were at the works?—Yes, sir.

Chain-makers' workshops at Cradley Heath

dbook of Sweated Industries Exhibition (*Daily News, 1906*)

Bromsgrove nail-maker

A woman chain-maker at work

16. Women worker
in a white-lea
factory

R. H. Sherard 'Whi
Slaves of England' (189

Interior of a typic
file-cutting 'sho
in Sheffield

Report of Departmental Committees on Miscellaneous Dangerous Trades (1898): British Museum Ph

Did all the girls wash their hands?—Yes, sir; all that I have ever seen.

Did the foremen see that you washed your hands?—There did not use to be any pails to wash their hands in, until they became so strict on that inspector's order, never; there had not used to be pails.

But now there are?—Yes, there are now.

Mr Cameron: What did Dr Smith say to you when he saw you at home, that time that you fainted, and went home and were ill?—When I was taken first, Mr Stone wanted to know whether I had better have a cab to go home in; so, when I got home, about an hour after, he sent one of the girls to know whether he had better send a doctor. The doctor did not come till about half-past five, and so I was in 'two-double'. I could not ease myself with nothing, nor mother could not. She had tried salt, and all manner of things, too. When Dr Smith's assistant came first, of course, he put me to bed, and he used the instruments on me, and I was much easier after he used the instruments. He said that it loosed it from the bowels; so after then I felt better. On the next day he came, he said it was lead colic. Next day Dr Smith said it was lead colic.

The Secretary. What are you doing now?—I am at home yet.

You are not in any employment?—No, sir; I have not been able to go anywhere just yet.

Chairman. You are not quite well now?—No, sir; but I am going to a situation soon.

You are not going back to enamelling?—Never; no more. I think I shall get turned out of home if I go again.

Departmental Committee on White Lead; C 7239 (1893), pp. 347–8; P.P. 1893/4, vol. 17.

3

'Melting eyes'

The Chairman: Do you think women are more susceptible then men to [lead] poisoning?—No, I do not; I think that they throw if off more than men but there are some women I should not employ if I were the manager of white lead works.

What would be your grounds of objection?—Women with large eyes, and what you would call melting eyes, that is to say, full of tears.

Liquid eyes?—That is to say, as it flows over the eyeball; they are very susceptible to the dust of white lead, and it causes brain disease with them and frequently blindness.

JOHN IVES VAUGHAN, of Norwood, who had 'a good deal of practical experience with respect to the making of white lead', in evidence; Minutes of Evidence to the White Lead Committee, C. 7239 (1893), p. 201; P.P. 1893/4, vol. 17.

4

The Death of Harriet Walters

The Committee are directed to investigate the circumstances under which Harriet Walters met her death, 12th June last, at the age of 17.

Her History as an Enamel Worker

She lived with her grandparents in rather poor circumstances at Sedgley. She entered the enamel works of Messrs Ralph & Jordan at Bilston, at the age of 16, in 1892, working as a brusher, and was there for six months.

From the foregoing Report it will be seen that the brushing department is the one where most danger exists in enamelling works.

The distance between her home and the enamelling works at Bilston is about three miles, which distance the girl had to walk in all weathers; in addition to which she had to stand practically all day, stooping over the plate upon which she was engaged, and brushing off this deleterious powder.

In January 1893 she entered Messrs Orme, Evans and Company's works at Wolverhampton, where she also worked at brushing, the distance she had to walk to and from her work being about the same as in her previous employment. Here she worked up to 5th June, on which day she felt so ill she asked the foreman to be allowed to go home. This she was permitted to do, and she accordingly walked back to Sedgley in company of a fellow worker.

On the 6th she was first seen by Mr Ballenden, who attended her and prescribed for her until her death. This occurred rather suddenly on the 12th June. It seems that, although she never compained, she was actually laid up for three or four days while employed at Bilston, that she had constant headaches, and that her anaemic appearance dated from her first employment. It also appears that, although reluctant to complain to her family, who were all along opposed to her employment in the enamelling trade, she did complain to her fellow workers before being taken ill on 5th June.

The Inquest

At the coroner's inquest, held at Sedgley, the jury returned a verdict of death from chronic lead poisoning, accidentally contracted through her employment.

The Committee's Finding

The Committee agreed that she died of lead poisoning, but, as she was only seriously ill a week, they consider that her death was the result of an acute attack, acting on a constitution already enfeebled by long exposure to the influence of lead, and therefore probably contaminated by it. They further believe that her death was accelerated by a persistence in the practice before mentioned, viz. of walking from Sedgley to Wolverhampton, a distance of three miles, without having tasted food, and of then working till the dinner hour, for, although the employers provided milk at one time, the milk was discontinued when the special rules were issued necessitating the supply of acid drink. By this means the deceased got into a very low state of health, with great anaemia and constant want of appetite. The result was that, when attacked by lead poisoning, she had no reserve of health with which to resist it. Since the death of this girl the firm have recommenced the supply of milk at 11 a.m.

It has been stated she was very poor and half-starved. The Committee find that though the family was distinctly poor they never reached that pitch of poverty where there was an insufficiency of plain but nutritious food. There was always breakfast for her if she could have eaten it.

The Committee regret that on 5th June, when the foreman gave her leave of absence, he did not comply with the special rules and give her an order upon a doctor for professional attendance and medicine. Mr Ballenden was sent for by her friends, although his charges were afterwards defrayed by the firm.

The Committee found that the respirator in use at the time of Harriet Walter's death was in reality a common handkerchief. It is probable that in the extreme heat of last May and June the younger and more inexperienced workers would take many opportunities of slipping these off.

Report from the Departmental Committee on the Various Lead Industries: C 7239 (1893), pp. 20-21; P.P. 1893/4, vol. 17.

5

'British Slaughter-Houses'

The duties of the powder packer consist of filling casks with bleaching powder. To do that he has to enter the chamber, which for several days has been filled with chlorine gas. Though the worst of this gas has been allowed to pass out of the chamber before the packer enters it, the atmosphere is still charged with the deadly fumes. The heat is sometimes tremendous, especially as the poor wretch who has to endure it is swathed about the head in a way that would protect him for arctic cold.

How does the packer protect himself? Ten year ago he simply wound a few folds of flannel round his mouth, which sufficed to filter the air through. The strength of the gas then was nothing like it is now . . . The man now wears a round paper cap; his eyes are covered with a pair of enormous goggles. Then the muzzle, composed of twenty-six folds of flannel, wide enough to cover the space from the upper lip to the neck, is lashed tightly under the chin and round the neck with cords. No space on any account must be left through which the horrible chlorine may find its way into the mouth.

When the muzzle is on, the effort of breathing appears to be most painful even in the open air. The chest heaves like that of a man struggling for breath in the violent stages of lung disease. The appearance of the face of the muzzled man gives you an impression that he is being suffocated; the eyes seem distended as they stare out through the goggles; the veins of the forehead are swollen, and the flesh is puffed up in a scarlet ridge round the top of the muzzle.

I ought to have mentioned an additional precaution which is taken before the muzzle is put on. The men grease themselves thoroughly all over the face and neck and wherever the skin is exposed. Round their legs they tie paper closely, and in these gaiters, with their feet encased in thick wooden clogs, they step into the powder. It is like stepping into the flames, for, although they shovel a clear place to stand in, the feet and legs are exposed to tremendous heat.

Their arms, in spite of the grease, frequently bleed. 'Let me see', I said to one of the packers, who in a quiet matter-of-fact way was giving his version; 'pull up your sleeve.' He hadn't been working for a week, he said, so that his arms were nearly well. They were covered with little half-healed scars, where the corrosive fluid seemed to have burnt in. The packers' arms are in a constant state of inflammation. To use their own expression, 'they are on fire'. At night they cannot keep them under the bedclothes.

'What is it like being gassed?' I asked the man. 'Like having a hot poker shoved down your throat', was the answer. 'You feel done for . . . Whether you lie by a day or longer, it takes you fully a week to get over it. Sometimes your mate will help you with your share, and you stay about and make a show of helping, but it is no good. When the stuff has got down your throat, you can't eat anything. If you manage to swallow a bit, you vomit it up again directly. All you can take is drink—whisky is the best thing.'

'But you old hands don't get gassed, do you?' I queried. But I was mistaken. Every man is liable to a visit of the gas right through the muzzle. Gassing is such a common matter, that the men would describe its symptoms as they would tell you what their Sunday's dinner was like.

'Is it ever fatal?' Yes, sometimes. The length of time which has to be passed in the torture chamber cannot be stated exactly. There is so much work to be done in the time, and each man sticks at it as long as he can hold out. Then whilst he goes to recover himself, his mate takes a turn.

The man who lent me his muzzle was in his working togs, wooden clogs, paper leggings over his trousers. I got him to give me his clothes bill for a fortnight. The items are as follows. They were checked by a number of other men, and are under rather than over the mark:

	s.	d.
5 cotton shirts at 1s. 2d.	5	10
1 pair of clogs in 3 weeks at 3s. 6d.	2	4
1 singlet at 3s.	3	0
1 pair of trousers, with patchings, at 3s.	3	0
Flannel for renewing muzzle	1	0
	15	2

These particulars were somewhat staggering, but the packer asked me to look at his clothes. His shirt was torn, I noticed, and in several parts hung in strips. It was hardened by the acid or powder, and tore freely wherever one laid hold of it. This shirt has seen two days' work, and was now good for nothing. Through the rents the chlorine gas gets at the flannel singlet and attacks that. His trousers were held together by some rough patches. Patching clothes is, however, out of the question as a rule. I tried to get a pin through the shirt, but the stuff was so caked and stiffened with the sweat and powder that it was like pushing it through plaster.

'Besides,' said the man, 'we can't ask our wives to patch our clothes.

The acid gets at the ends of their fingers and burns them. There is nothing for it but to be continually buying fresh things as the old ones give out.'

From an article in a 'trade journal' by a 'special commissioner to St Helens', entitled 'British Slaughter-Houses'; quoted in Report of Chemical Works Committee: C 7235 (1893), page 18; P.P. 1893-4, vol. 17.

6

Whisky 'cuts the gas'

William Dooley, employed as a burner in the vitriol department a t Kurts's works, St Helens: giving evidence.
Mr Richmond.—What is the gas you are subjected to?—Sulphur gas; it catches you in the chest and gives you a heavy feeling . . . You cannot eat anything, and are always dry, and always want some sort of drink to stimulate you and give you wind to last your time out, or else you could not work.

Do you mean that you must have drink, and that it must be alcohol? —Yes, sir, to put a false spirit in you. Whisky puts a false spirit in you, and gives you a bit of wind, whisky does. It cuts the gas . . . the gas which tightens you.

Dr O'Neill. Do all the men in the place drink whisky?—Yes, when they can get it.

Chemical Works Committee, pp. 10-11; P.P. 1893-4, vol. 17.

7

India-rubber Works

Some years ago the attention of the Secretary of State was drawn to numerous cases of illness among persons employed in india-rubber factories. Similar complaints were received by the Factory Department.

An inquiry was instituted at that time, and Dr John T. Arlidge, MD, was requested to undertake the investigation of the matter. That eminent scientist visited the works in London, Manchester and the neighbourhood, and at Retford, and reported on the question in October

1894. The Committee will have occasion to make references as they proceed to Dr Arlidge's report.

India-rubber enters into the composition of a large number of articles, such as tubes, mechanical appliances, waterproof garments, children's balloons and toys of various kinds, patent packing for electric wires or cables, tobacco pouches, golf and lawn tennis balls, carriage-aprons, rugs, etc. The part of the trade in which most people are employed is the manufacture of waterproof garments and shoes . . .

It will be gathered that is is impossible to escape from the fumes of naphtha in a rubber factory. Dr Arlidge asserts 'that the inhalation of pure naphtha vapour would be incompatible with life'; but he considers it 'not injurious to any serious extent' in the 'very diluted' form in which it is encountered in these factories. He admits it to be 'penetrating and somewhat nauseous, and this, doubtless, as in all effluvia, much more to some persons than to others'.

The Committee feel that they must rank themselves in the first class. They have visited rubber factories where the vapour attacked eyes and nose, making them smart and water; to such they confess that the expression 'very diluted' would seem to them to be scarcely applicable. And these were not the minority. A visit to almost any 'spreading' or 'making-up' room on a cold winter's evening, when the windows are closely shut and the gases well ablaze, and any fresh atmosphere there may have been originally has long been exhausted, should convince an impartial observer that the fumes which assail your eyes on such an occasion are not 'very diluted'; the heat and the naphtha together to the new-comer are almost overpowering. . . .

Dr Arlidge goes on, 'It is common to many on first commencing employment to experience slight embarrassment of breathing, lightness of head or giddiness, temporary confusion and nausea. These symptoms usually last only a few hours or days, but in slighter degree will at times recur on recommencing work.'

The Committee might add to Dr Arlidge's list of ailments, faintness, headache, general lassitude, and disinclination for food. It is not an infrequent thing to hear from the workers that they are obliged to leave the factory and go into the open air to seek relief from the overpowering effects of the naphtha fumes. They soon lose this giddiness and lightness of head by breathing fresh air. They often taste the naphtha when they get home in the evening, and also when they wake in the morning, which naturally makes them disinclined for food.

It is a common custom in the trade to let the workers eat their meals in the shop in which they have been working. The reason alleged for this is that the food which has been brought into a room in which it is exposed to the vapour of naphtha becomes so tainted that it cannot be eaten outside. The occupiers are anxious, it would appear, in these cases to avoid the expense of providing a dining-room, so that meals must be eaten in the work room by those living at a distance. The Committee strongly condemn this practice. They have seen factories where the most admirable arrangements are made for supplying the workers with meals at cheap rates in a comfortable dining-room.

Of the effects of working in the carbon bisulphide process, the Committee have seen enough to indicate the very grave risks to health which those employed must daily encounter. All the witnesses the Committee examined were quite conscious that the occupation was a dangerous one, and that they had been ill more or less frequently from the effects of their work. These effects were in many instances enduring.

Cases have been brought to the Committee's notice of persons who were so prone to mania or temporary insanity that the windows of the room in which they worked had to be barred up to prevent them precipitating themselves below. In one case a man escaped by the window, ran into a carpenter's shop, and covered himself with shavings, to hide from his supposed pursuers . . .

Interim Report of the Departmental Committee appointed to Inquire into and Report upon certain Miscellaneous Trades; c.8149 (1896), pp. 14-17; P.P. 1896, vol. 33.

8

Ships' Painters

When ships come into a dock or alongside a wharf or quay for repair the chief anxiety of the owner or master is to get away again. That 'time is money' is true of ships probably more than of any other profit making machine in existence. To meet this demand of speed in the repairing of ships ingenuity has been expended, and many devices invented. Among them the invention of quick-drying paints is one of the most ingenious, if not one of the most injurious.

It appears that the time for a ship to be in a dock under the system of using these quick-drying, or spirit compositions, is about three days. These patent, or inflammable paints, are composed of a composition containing methylated spirit, petroleum spirit, or benzine, instead of oil, to mix with the colouring material. Naturally they are very volatile and highly inflammable. The Committee have heard of many cases of accident through the use of these compositions.

The use of spirit, or patent compositions, involve a twofold danger to those who work with them. There is the risk of fire; and there is the risk of intoxication, followed by unconsciousness and asphyxiation by the inhalation of the fumes. The latter is not uncommonly seen in more modified forms, such as a temporary loss of the faculties, and many of the same effects as are produced by drunkenness. It also, when inhaled in considerable quantities, produces nausea and vomiting, loss of appetite, colic, extreme torpor, feebleness of muscles, bleeding at the nose and ears and temporary dementia.

The men who have used spirit paints describe how common and how constant are fires. The Committee have heard from many witnesses that when men are engaged in painting the outside of a ship with an inflammable paint the ship's side suddenly, for no apparent reason, often becomes momentarily in flames. The flames rise with great rapidity, giving off generally large volumes of smoke and great heat, and as suddenly become extinguished. It usually happens that such a blaze as this is attributable to the presence of a candle or some naked flame. Either this flame has been held too near to the freshly painted ship's side, or the wind has blown the volatile spirit on to the candle flame, and this has communicated fire to that portion of the ship's side, from which any spirit could evaporate.

The holds of many ships are enormous, of more are of considerable size, and of all are large enough of three or four men working together, in itself a safeguard against accident. It is generally possible for the men to work standing upright, and to dispense with the use of artificial light. It is where the men are obliged to go in alone, to paint stooping, lying down, or standing on a ladder to creep through manholes in order to get to and from their work, and finally to use artificial lights, that they are exposed to the gravest risks.

Horrible cases of stupefaction in the first instance, and fire subsequently, followed by months of illness from burning, or ultimate death, have been brought to the notice of the Committee . . .

Dangerous Trades Committee; C. 8149 (1896), pp. 19-20; P.P. 1896, vol. 33.

9

'Acting silly' at the Dry-Cleaner's

The process of 'Dry cleaning', sometimes called 'French' or 'Chemical cleaning', originated in France, where it is known as 'Nettoyage-à-sec'.

As carried on upon a small scale in many works in London and elsewhere, this is an extremely simple process. The gloves or garments are scrubbed with a small brush, soap, and benzine; they are then rinsed in benzine and 'made up'. The Committee was informed that this has been carried on in kitchens and small rooms where cooking was going on at the same time, and in rooms above the ground floor, from which escape in case of fire would be sometimes impossible.

When done on a large scale it becomes an elaborate business, involving the use of much and carefully devised machinery, employing large numbers of workpeople, and necessitating most careful precautions.

In spite of all precautions which can be, and usually are, taken in the larger and more carefully conducted factories, [including] among others, searching the workpeople's pockets, small fires seem to be inevitable. Sometimes they result from carelessness; a match is left in the pocket or lining of a garment, or is dropped on the floor by a worker emptying his own or somebody else's pockets. But they also not unfrequently originate from an electric spark, generated by the friction of rinsing or rubbing a silk fabric on a close thundery day. The spontaneous combustion of benzine may be avoided by the addition of a small quantity of oil soap . . .

Similar effects are noticeable in the trade as have been traced in india-rubber works to the inhalation of naphtha fumes, and in docks to the use of inflammable paints. The workers complain of giddiness, nausea, vomiting, and headaches, sometimes of tasting the spirit, and usually loss of appetite, intoxication with hysterical symptoms, sleepiness, and, in the more severe cases, of loss of consciousness.

These effects are more noticeable and severe among the young workers and in some people than others . . . In one place, visited by the Committee, the girls in the glove-cleaning department told them that they had to come out for fresh air 'pretty often', that the spirit got into their heads and made them 'act silly'.

Dangerous Trades Committee, Interim Report: C. 8149 (1896), pp. 22-4; P.P. 1896, vol. 33.

10

Mineral Water Bottlers

The trade of manufacturing and bottling of aerated waters is carried on very largely in our great towns, London, Dublin, and Belfast being among the more important centres. One firm in London informed the Committee that they sent out, during the year 1895, over nine million bottles of different kinds of aerated water.

Dangers of working are almost entirely confined to the risk of being cut, more or less severely, from the bursting of bottles. That this is no rare occurrence only may be gathered from the fact that in one factory in Newcastle, visited on December 2, when neither the excessive heat nor pressure of work could be made accountable for the occurrence, no fewer than six bottles 'flew' in about ten minutes.

The bottling machines are, in most instances, carefully fenced and guarded, but even when this is done all risk to the worker is not eliminated. The bottles are apt to 'fly' after they have been filled and corked, or when they are being labelled or moved about. The percentage of breakages at these stages is, however, much smaller than during the filling operation.

In many cases the workers in mineral water factories wear face-guards and gauntlets. Sometimes they only wear a gauntlet on one arm, or they have only wire gauze spectacles; or the face-guards or spectacles are limited to the bottlers, and not supplied to the wirers or labellers. The style of gauntlet varies; some, like a mitten, come down to the finger-joints, while others reach up as far as the wrist.

Dangerous Trades Committee, C. 8149 (1896), pp. 25-7; P.P. 1896, vol. 33.

II

Sheffield File-cutters

The industry of cutting files is performed both by hand and by machinery, and is carried on in many parts of the country, but chiefly in Sheffield.

In hand cutting the worker is seated at what is known in the trade as a 'stock'. This consists of a stone block into the centre of which a smaller steel block, called a 'stiddy', is inserted, the surface of which is raised slightly above that of the 'stock'. Upon the 'stiddy' the file to be cut is placed. Each individual tooth is formed by a stroke of a heavy hammer or a chisel. In order to support the file while it is being thus heavily struck by the hammer and chisel a substance between the file and the 'stiddy' is necessary which, while it will give a certain amount of resistance to the blow, is not so hard as to cause a recoil. For this purpose what is known as a 'lead bed' is used, which consists of a piece of lead varying in size with the size of the file . . . If the work is at all heavy, the lead flattens out where the file presses upon it; a groove is thus formed in the lead into which the file fits. When one face has been cut charcoal is rubbed upon it before the file is turned, and when both faces are finished the file is briskly brushed.

Where the file is large, and the teeth to be cut consequently deep, the work is extremely heavy. The hammers weigh $7\frac{1}{2}$ to 8 lbs., even as much as 9 lbs., and it has been calculated that in a day's work a man may lift 100 tons. A 12-inch file requires 3,500 teeth to be cut in it, counting both sides; this, with an 8-lb. hammer, would entail the lifting of 13 tons per file.

The Committee do not propose to deal with the process of file cutting by machinery, as it is generally carried on in modern 'shops' with good ventilation and air space; as the 'bed' is of spelter, containing only a small proportion of lead; and as the operative rarely leans over the file while it is being cut.

The dangers of file cutting are to be traced to several causes, the most important of which is the 'lead bed'. But there are many accessories to this, which make file cutting one of the most serious subjects into which the Committee has been directed to inquire. The conditions under which the occupation is carried on in numerous instances tend unnecessarily to aggravate the risks of lead poisoning.

Bad ventilation, overcrowding, dirtiness, want of light in the workshops, their close proximity to privy middens, general disinclination to take precautions, the cramped position in which the work is carried on, the practice of licking the fingers to hold the chisel and of brushing the dust off the cut file, the juxtaposition of the 'stocks', dilapidation of the floors and neglect of lime-washing are governing conditions which produce in this industry a vitality as low and a mortality as high as can be found in any industry considered by the Committee.

With so little space between the workers it is inevitable under existing conditions that they should inhale the dust created by the constant hammering and brushing of files. This dust contains a large proportion of lead as well as of chalk, charcoal, steel, and granite, and is found on the floor and on the 'stocks'. Even in the dust removed from the rafters careful analysis reveals the presence of lead. Workers in so sedentary an occupation naturally object to the draught caused by the opening of windows immediately in front of or beside them. In the absence of other means of admitting fresh air there is practically no ventilation.

Speaking generally, Dr Henry Harvey Littlejohn, who for six years filled the post of Medical Officer of Health for Sheffield, says that file makers as a class show evidence of impaired nutrition and health, and, in his experience, it is rare to find a robust file cutter. He adds, 'I do not mean that they all complain of any special form of ill health, but they are for the most part sallow, poorly nourished, and deficient in muscular development'.

Of the file-cutting 'shops' to which attention should be specially drawn, the Committee would again quote from the valuable statement Dr Littlejohn was good enough to hand in.

'Most of these shops are of such a rude and primitive description that they appear not to have been built for the purpose, and to have been simply out-houses in the yards belonging to dwelling-houses, which in the absence of control and restrictions have been transformed into workshops. They are frequently built against a blank wall, with a shed and sloping roof so that through ventilation is impossible, and all light and air is admitted by the windows that are situated low down and immediately in front of the bench at which the work is carried on. Under these circumstances, when the windows are opened, the cold air blows directly on the workpeople ... The floors often consist only of bricks or earth loosely laid, and are frequently foul from the accumulation of dust and other refuse ... I have been frequently told by workpeople that the only way to make the temperature at all bearable is to block up every opening to the outer air and to have as many workpeople in them as possible.'

Dangerous Trades Committee, 3rd Interim Report; C. 9073 (1898), pp. 6-8; P.P. 1899, vol. 12.

12

'Stamp-lickers' tongue'

The attention of the Chief Inspector of Factories was drawn by Miss Anderson, Her Majesty's Principal Lady Inspector, to the practice of licking labels in thread mills in 1895. Miss Anderson found a very large number of little girls employed in the licking process, and that several of them had suffered from swollen glands. This practice is not confined to the thread industry, but may be seen also in the silk and in the aerated water industries, and probably in other trades where small packages are made up, such as the tobacco trade, and the wholesale chemists' or drapery trades.

Dr Oliver has been good enough to draw up a minute from the medical point of view, which follows:—Although the Committee have not been brought into direct contact with any person who had suffered seriously from licking labels, they venture to express the opinion that since the work is usually done by young persons and children at an age when growth is active and the system requires all its digestive secretions, the daily loss of saliva to the system cannot but be prejudicial to health. Analysis of the labels show that they sometimes contain copper and lead, the presence of which constitutes a danger. A kindred practice, that of licking postage stamps, has given rise to what is known as 'stamp licker's tongue', and the application of stamp paper to an open wound has been credited with causing blood poisoning.

In the labels which have been submitted to the Committee for analysis, nothing but gum was found in the adhesive part of the label, but since it is believed that substances of an animal nature are occasionally substituted for gum, serious risk to health might be incurred by licking materials thus prepared. The mouth might become the seat of irritable ulcers. From the surface of these sores infective material might be carried to the glands underneath the jaw, and thus a serious constitutional illness follow. There is no reason why the saliva of young people should be put to such a use as the moistening of labels for bobbins. It is, to say the least, a nasty practice and one which can be just as effectively done by mechanical methods.

That Dr Oliver is correct in his closing statement may be gathered from the fact that at one of the large thread mills in Lancashire the tickets for the bobbins were, at the first visit of the Committee, almost entirely moistened by application to the mouth. There were employed at that time some twelve full-timers, who each licked from 40 to 50 gross of labels per day, and 35 half-timers, who accomplished from 20 to 25 gross per day. To give an indication of the amount of licking possible to be done, one woman informed the Committee that when busy she could complete 45 gross of bobbins in a day, or allowing for a ticket for each end of the bobbin, 90 gross of labels a day! This firm have now entirely abandoned licking, and the whole of the work is done by means of a damper which they obtain from Messrs Coats of Paisley. At their last visit the Committee were informed by the authorities at this important Lancashire mill that the work was done more expeditiously and better by artificial means than by the mouth . . .

Dangerous Trades Committee, 5th and Final Report; C. 9509 (1899), pp. 31-2; P.P. 1899, vol. 12.

CHAPTER 9

THE STRIKE OF THE MATCHGIRLS

(*Mrs Annie Besant's articles in 'The Link'*)

In the long history of labour disputes the Strike of the Matchgirls in 1888 fills a most interesting page. No strike can ever have been more popular. The sex of the strikers, their youth and inexperience, the deplorable conditions under which they had been working, their peculiar helplessness as against their employers—all these things combined to arouse public sympathy to an exceptional degree. And there was still something more. 'Matchgirls—*striking*—what a lark!'

Every history of the period gives the strike a few lines of mention, but the best place to read about it—from the strikers' angle—is in the pages of *The Link*, the little Socialist weekly (four pages for a halfpenny) that was edited by Mrs Annie Besant.

But for her there might well have been no strike at all. In 1888 she was just turned forty, strikingly handsome, full-charged with personal magnetism, and a powerful platform speaker. Twenty years earlier she had married a Lincolnshire clergyman, but she had 'lost her faith'— quite a serious matter in Victorian times—obtained a legal separation from her husband, and had joined that doughty Radical, Charles Bradlaugh, in his freethinking and birth-control propaganda. But fairly recently she had taken up the new gospel of Socialism which had led to a break with Bradlaugh, and she was one of the first to join the Fabian Society on its formation in 1884. It was at a Fabian meeting that she first heard of the plight of the matchgirls, and as a result decided to investigate the matter for herself. She wrote up what she had learnt in her next article in *The Link*. Entitled 'White Slavery in London', this appeared in the issue of June 23, 1888, and is here reprinted in full (No. 1).

Not surprisingly, in the light of the article's high-pitched virulence, she was at once threatened with an action for libel by Messrs Bryant & May. But this did not worry her in the slightest: she must have expected it, and would have been disappointed if it had not been forthcoming. She kept at the charge, and when, to her amazement, the matchgirls struck work in a body, she took charge of the strike and led it to a triumphant conclusion. The course of events may be followed in the extracts from her successive articles in *The Link*.

When the strike was over and the girls had gone back to work with most of their demands satisfied, Mrs Besant acted as secretary of the trade union that had been organized. But not for long. The very next year she put Socialism behind her, and under the influence of Madame Blavatsky embraced the new religion of Theosophy. In due course she removed to India, where for more than forty years she was prominent in nationalist politics in addition to maintaining her pre-eminence in the worldwide Theosophical movement. She died in India in 1933.

I

'White slavery in London'

At a meeting of the Fabian Society held on June 15th, the following resolution was moved by H. H. Champion, seconded by Herbert Burrows, and carried *nem. con.* after a brief discussion: 'That this meeting, being aware that the shareholders of Bryant and May are receiving a dividend of over 20 per cent., and at the same time are paying their workers only 2¼d. per gross for making match-boxes, pledges itself not to use or purchase any matches made by the firm.'

In consequence of some statements made in course of the discussion, I resolved to personally investigate their accuracy, and accordingly betook myself to Bromley [Poplar] to interview some of Bryant and May's employees, and thus obtain information at first hand. The following is the outcome of my enquiries:

Bryant and May, now a limited liability company, paid last year a dividend of 23 per cent. to its shareholders; two years ago it paid a dividend of 25 per cent., and the original £5 shares were then quoted for sale at £8 7s. 6d. The highest dividend paid has been 38 per cent.

Let us see how the money is made with which these monstrous dividends are paid. (The figures quoted were all taken down by myself, in the presence of three witnesses, from persons who had themselves been in the prison-house whose secrets they disclosed.)

The hour for commencing work is 6.30 in summer and 8 in winter; work concludes at 6 p.m. Half-an-hour is allowed for breakfast and an hour for dinner. This long day of work is performed by young girls, who have to stand the whole of the time. A typical case is that of a girl of 16, a piece-worker; she earns 4s. a week, and lives with a sister, employed by the same firm, who 'earns good money, as much as 8s. or 9s. per week'. Out of the earnings 2s. is paid for the rent of one room; the child lives on only bread-and-butter and tea, alike for breakfast and dinner, but related with dancing eyes that once a month she went to a meal where 'you get coffee, and bread and butter, and jam, and marmalade, and lots of it'; now and then she goes to the Paragon [music-hall], someone 'stands treat, you know'; and that appeared to be the solitary bit of color in her life.

The splendid salary of 4s. is subject to deductions in the shape of fines; if the feet are dirty, or the ground under the bench is left untidy, a fine of 3d. is inflicted; for putting 'burnts'—matches that have caught fire during the work—on the bench 1s. has been forfeited, and one unhappy girl was once fined 2s. 6d. for some unknown crime. If a girl leaves four or five matches on her bench when she goes for a fresh 'frame' she is fined 3d., and in some departments a fine of 3d. is inflicted for talking. If a girl is late she is shut out for 'half the day', that is, for the morning six hours, and 5d. is deducted out of her day's 8d.

One girl was fined 1s. for letting the web twist round a machine in the endeavor to save her fingers from being cut, and was sharply told to take care of the machine, 'never mind your fingers'. Another, who carried out the instructions and lost a finger thereby, was left unsupported while she was helpless. The wage covers the duty of submitting to an occasional blow from a foreman; one, who appears to be a gentleman of variable temper, 'clouts' them 'when he is mad'.

One department of the work consists in taking matches out of a frame and putting them into boxes; about three frames can be done in an hour, and ½d. is paid for each frame emptied; only one frame is given out at a time, and the girls have to run downstairs and upstairs each time to fetch the frame, thus much increasing their fatigue. One of the delights of the frame work is the accidental firing of the matches; when this happens the worker loses the work, and if the frame is injured she is fined or 'sacked'. 5s. a week had been earned at this by one girl I talked to.

The 'fillers' get ¾d. a gross for filling boxes; at 'boxing', *i.e.* wrapping papers round the boxes, they can earn from 4s. 6d. to 5s. a week. A very rapid 'filler' has been known to earn 'as much as 9s.' in a week, and 6s. a week 'sometimes'. The making of boxes is not done in the factory; for these 2¼d. a gross is paid to people who work in their own homes, and 'find your own paste'. Daywork is a little better paid than piecework, and is done chiefly by married women, who earn as much sometimes as 10s. a week, the piecework falling to the girls. Four women day workers, spoken of with reverent awe, earn—13s. a week.

A very bitter memory survives in the factory. Mr Theodore Bryant, to show his admiration of Mr Gladstone and the greatness of his own public spirit, bethought him to erect a statue to that eminent statesman. In order that his workgirls might have the privilege of contributing, he stopped 1s. each out of their wages, and further deprived them of half a day's work by closing the factory, 'giving them a holiday'. ('We don't want no holidays', said one of the girls pathetically, for—needless to say —the poorer employees of such a firm lose their wages when a holiday is 'given'.) So furious were the girls at this cruel plundering, that many went to the unveiling of the statue with stones and bricks in their pockets, and I was conscious of a wish that some of those bricks had made an impression on Mr Bryant's—conscience. Later on they surrounded the statue—'we paid for it' they cried savagely—shouting and yelling, and a gruesome story is told that some cut their arms and let their blood trickle on the marble paid for, in very truth, by their blood. There seems to be a curious feeling that the nominal wages are 1s. higher than the money paid, but that 1s. a week is still kept back to pay for the statue and for a fountain erected by the same Mr Bryant. This, however, appears to me to be only of the nature of a pious opinion.

Such is a bald account of one form of white slavery as it exists in London. With chattel slaves Mr Bryant could not have made his huge fortune, for he could not have fed, clothed, and housed them for 4s. a week each, and they would have had a definite money value which would have served as a protection. But who cares for the fate of these white wage slaves? Born in slums, driven to work while still children, under-sized because underfed, oppressed because helpless, flung aside as soon as worked out, who cares if they die or go on the streets, provided only that the Bryant and May shareholders get their 23 per cent., and Mr Theodore Bryant can erect statues and buy parks? Oh if we had but a people's Dante, to make a special circle in the Inferno for those who live on this misery, and suck wealth out of the starvation of helpless girls.

Failing a poet to hold up their conduct to the execration of posterity, enshrined in deathless verse, let us strive to touch their consciences, *i.e.* their pockets, and let us at least avoid being 'partakers of their sins', by abstaining from using their commodities.

ANNIE BESANT, *The Link*, July 7, 1888.

2

'How Messrs Bryant and May Fight'

No sign of the 'legal attention' announced in such hot haste by Mr Theodore Bryant last week has yet reached me, but Messrs Bryant and

May have not been idle. They apparently shirk the straightforward course of prosecuting me for libel, knowing full well that my statements are true and can be proved up to the hilt, and they fear the publicity that such a suit would give to their shameful treatment of the helpless girls they employ.

Determined, however, to revenge themselves for the exposure of their iniquities, they have fallen on the girls themselves, selecting as victims three. In order to make the punishment of these as heavy as possible they did not dismiss them at once, but kept them on for a week making their work very slack, and finally discharged one of them with 2s. 8d. for her week's wages, promising a second 3s. 6d., and a third 1s. 8d. These wages are to pay for food and rent for the week. It is hard to understand what kind of non-human beings they can be who can put into a woman-child's hand 1s. 8d. as the price of her week's labor, and then bid her go forth workless into the cruel streets. How can a man do this thing, and go home to his comfortable house, and perhaps to wife and child?

* * *

On Wednesday the three girls went crying to a friend in Bromley who is good enough to act for me, saying that they had 'got the sack'. He brought them to Mile End to see me, and I promised them they should not be left unsupported, but urged them to go back and try and get the wages due to them. During the week they had been kept short of work, and on the Saturday one of them was given 2s. 8d. for the week's labor, and with a sneering quotation from my article was bidden not to show her face in the factory again. The other two were ordered to call for their wages on Monday, one having hers fixed at 3s. 6d. and the other at 1s. 8d. for the week.

My friend made up on Saturday to them the wages usually earned, as they owed for rent and food, and were penniless. One of these girls was taken back to work on the Monday, the other was put off—still without her wages—till the Wednesday, and at the time of writing I do not know whether or not she has been reinstated. It is probable that the commotion raised has made Messrs Bryant and May feel that they had better try to undo some of the wrong inflicted.

Their last device is to force the girls to sign a paper that they are satisfied with their position. The public will estimate the value of such a production, extorted from the helpless.

ANNIE BESANT, *The Link*, July 7, 1888.

3

'*The Revolt of the Matchmakers*'

Last week the following touching letter was received by Annie Besant, who, however, little guessed that it was the signal of the coming storm. 'My Dear Lady.—We thank you very much for the kind interest you have taken in us poor girls, and hope that you will succeed in your undertaking. Dear Lady, you need not trouble yourself about the letter I read in the *Link* that Mr Bryant sent you, because you have spoke the truth, and we are very pleased to read it. Dear lady, they are trying to get the poor girls to say it is all lies that has been printed, and trying to make them sign papers to say it is lies; dear lady, no one knows what we have to put up with, and we will not sign them. We all thank you very much for the kindness you have shown us. My dear lady, we hope you will not get into any trouble in our behalf, as what you have spoke is quite true; dear lady, we hope that if there will be any meeting we hope you will let us know it in the book. Dear lady, do not mention the date this letter was written or I might have put my or our names, but we are frightened, do keep that as a secret. We know you will do that, dear lady.'

On Friday, a little before three o'clock, the meaning of the letter became clear; between one and 2 hundred girls flocked down Fleet Street, cheered vigorously as they saw Annie Besant's photograph in the window, and turning into Bouverie Street filled that narrow thoroughfare. The irruption caused considerable excitement, and numerous heads appeared at all available windows. After a little puzzled delay, a message was sent down explaining that it was not possible for any address to be delivered in a thoroughfare where the block caused serious inconvenience, that the office of the *Link* was too small to accommodate the crowd, but that Annie Besant would gladly see a deputation.

Three sturdy respectable women soon appeared in the *Link* office, and told their story which was briefly as follows. The foreman had brought round on Wednesday a paper certifying that the girls were well treated and contented and repudiated the statements made on their condition, and this paper was laid to receive signatures during the dinner hour. When the foreman of one department returned, expecting to find it filled, it offered to his angry eyes a white unsullied surface. In vain he threatened and scolded; the girls would not sign; as one of them said to Annie Besant in recounting the story, 'you had spoke up for us and we weren't going back on you'. A girl pitched on apparently as ringleader was threatened with dismissal, but she stood firm. On the following morning she was suddenly discharged for a pretended act of insubordination, and the women, promptly seeing the reason of her punishment, put down their work with one accord and marched out. The news spread, and the rest of the wood-match girls followed their example, some 1,400 women suddenly united in a common cause. An offer was made to take back the girls, but the spirit of revolt against cruel oppression had been aroused, and they declared they would not go in 'without their pennies'.

Puzzling Pennies
These 'pennies' have been a pain and a grief to us. We long strove to hunt them down, but they eluded our grasp. Some of the young girls said they were a continuing tax for the Gladstone statue, which has remained in their minds as an ogre responsible for all non-understood reductions, but this was manifestly a myth. Still, we heard on all sides: 'I earned 6s. and took 5s. 6d.' 'I earned 4s. 4d. and took 3s. 11d.'; and so on. That a penny in the shilling vanished was clear. At length we obtained the following explanation: at one time young girls were employed to carry to and fro the work for the box-filling women, who could thus get through more work, and did not therefore complain of the ½d. out of each 3d. deducted for the wages of their young attendants. After a while these girls were put to other work, but the farthings remained as a permanent reduction, making the penny off each shilling.

The girls will go back to work if Bryant and May will either restore them their pennies, letting them have a shilling when they have earned it, or give them back the help for which the deduction was originally made. The demand is surely modest enough, but a firm mean enough to 'scoop up' farthings in this way will probably be callous to any sense of justice. . . .

ANNIE BESANT, *The Link*, July 14, 1888.

4

At the House of Commons

Fifty-six of the matchworkers came down to the *Link* office on Tuesday, to go thence to the House of Commons to lay some of their grievances before Messrs Cunninghame Graham and Conybeare. As the girls tramped along the embankment in orderly array, 3 or 4 deep, they made a striking object-lesson for the careless well-to-do folk who gazed at them with supercilious puzzlement as they passed. Some very young, pale, thin, undersized, ragged, their very appearance eloquent of hard labor unfit for childish frames. Others older, who were still growing physically when wages were better, looked stronger in health, more vigorous and more resistant.

At the House of Commons permission to enter was only granted to twelve, and these filed in, with Annie Besant and H. Burrows as introducers, and found themselves in the famous lobby of the House, the observed of all observers. They were ushered into a committee room, and there told their own story and answered a number of questions put to them by the hon. members, with a quick intelligence, directness, and frankness, which shewed how much might be made of them under fair and wholesome life-conditions.

But may be some thought, as certainly did one in that strange procession, that the appearance among the sleek, comfortable, well-to-do West End folk, who crowded the lobby, of the gaunt, ragged group, representing the suffering of the East, was a portent not lightly to be disregarded by those who will one day have to answer in their own or their children's persons for the ruined lives of these. . . .

ANNIE BESANT, The Link, July 14, 1888.

5

'Complete victory'

The sudden and complete victory which has crowned the brave Revolt of the Match Girls has made the strike a matter of history.

The deputation of match girls who waited on the London Trades' Council had no cause to regret their visit. They were accompanied by Annie Besant, Herbert Burrows, and Miss Clementina Black, and after their case had been briefly laid before the Council by Annie Besant they were carefully and closely examined by the members. Extreme pains were taken by the representatives of the Trades to get exact information, and the intelligent women and girls who represented the matchmakers answered with a precision and careful accuracy which evidently created a good impression.

After a long interview the deputation retired to a substantial supper provided for them by the kindness of the Council, and after a while they were joined by their hosts, and Mr Shipton announced that they had come to the following resolution: 'That this Council, representing the interests of over 25,000 artisans and mechanics, having heard an account of the dispute pending between Messrs Bryant and May and their employees, offer, as practical workmen, to mediate in any way, with a view of honorably determining the contest, and that in the meantime, the Council will use every effort to support the girls till a satisfactory conclusion is come to.'

On Monday a number of members of the Council saw the Directors [of Bryant and May], and after long discussions it was agreed that these gentlemen should bring a deputation of the matchgirls to meet the directors the following day, when it was hoped that a settlement would be arrived at.

Accordingly on Tuesday the Strike Committee accompanied members of the London Trades' Council into the presence of the directors, and put their own case. It was finally agreed that: (1) all fines should be abolished; (2) all deductions for paint, brushes, stamps, etc., should be put an end to; (3) the 3d. should be restored to the packers; (4) the 'pennies' should be restored, or an equivalent advantage given in the system of payment of the boys who do the racking; (5) all grievances should be laid directly before the firm, ere any hostile action be taken; (6) all the girls to be taken back. The firm hoped the girls would form a union; they promised to see about providing a room for meals away from the work; and they also promised to provide barrows for carrying the boxes, which have been hitherto carried by young girls on their heads, to the great detriment of their hair and their spines.

It is small wonder that these terms were enthusiastically endorsed by the girls as a whole, when they were submitted to them at a meeting held at 6 p.m. the same day. Mr Shipton received warm applause as he explained the details of the settlement, and the acceptance was carried amid wild cheering, the girls feeling that they had won a victory which would materially better their conditions.

Seldom has a strike had a more successful ending, and this happy result is due, first to the hearty and ungrudging support and help rendered to the girls by the London Trades' Council; and secondly, to the courage, steadfastness, and thorough loyalty to each other of the girls. . . .

ANNIE BESANT, *The Link*, July 21, 1888.

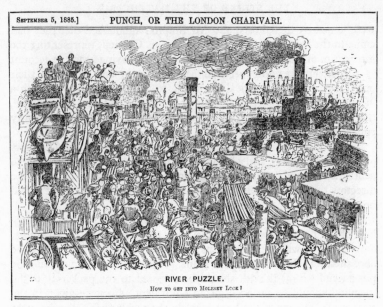

RIVER PUZZLE.

How to get into Molesey Lock?

DEA EX MACHINÁ!

(A Reminiscence.)

Punch, (1891)

CHAPTER 10

THE MAIDEN TRIBUTE

'Sensational' is surely the right word to apply to the series of articles that W. T. Stead wrote in July, 1885, for the *Pall Mall Gazette* under the general title of 'The Maiden Tribute of Modern Babylon'.

To understand their 'why and wherefore' we must go back a few years. For a long time there had been growing public concern at the spread of juvenile prostitution and the existence of a 'white slave traffic' between England and the Continent. The matter was raised by Lord Dalhousie and Lord Shaftesbury in the House of Lords, and in 1881 a Select Committee was appointed to 'investigate the law relating to the protection of young girls'. Dalhousie was elected chairman, and the Committee issued its first report in July 1882; the chief paragraphs are given in (*a*).

Speaking in support of his Committee's report, Dalhousie told the Lords that the continental traffic in girls 'surpassed in villainy any other trade in human beings in any part of the world, in ancient or modern times', and certainly the revelations made shocking reading. Harcourt, Home Secretary in the Gladstone administration, proceeded to introduce a bill that would raise the 'age of consent' from the existing thirteen to sixteen years, as the Committee had recommended, but this was strongly opposed in the House of Commons and the bill had to be dropped. Bill after bill on similar lines was introduced in subsequent sessions, and all met the same fate. The latest in the series had been introduced in the spring of 1885, and already there was talk of its being sacrificed on the ground of pressure of other business. Could it be saved? Some of its supporters thought that it might, if public opinion were brought to bear. What was wanted was Publicity, and (they decided) the right man for *that* was Mr Stead.

Born in 1849, the son of a Congregationalist minister, William Thomas Stead had been appointed editor of the *Northern Echo* at Darlington when only twenty-two. Before long his reputation as a hard-hitting campaigner reached London, and in 1880 he became chief assistant to John Morley, the rising Liberal politician who had just been made editor of the *Pall Mall Gazette* following a take-over. Three years later he succeeded Morley in the editorial chair, and under his direction the newspaper displayed a vigorously crusading tone. When, therefore, he was urged to champion the Criminal Law Amendment Bill, he was not long in making up his mind.

Acting in close co-operation with his friend Bramwell Booth, son of General Booth of the Salvation Army, in which he was Chief of Staff, Stead spent some six weeks in a personal exploration of London's underworld. Then having gathered his material he wrote the articles for the *Pall Mall* from which our Nos. (*b*) 1 to 7 have been drawn.

The effect on the public was tremendous. The newspaper was banned from W. H. Smith's bookstalls, but newsboys did good business in selling it in the streets for a shilling. Indignant readers bombarded Stead with protests, jealous rivals accused him of muck-raking, and in the Houee of Commons the question was asked, why he was not being prosecuted for obscenity. On the other hands, he received a great volume of support from Church leaders and women's organizations. Very shortly he had the satisfaction of seeing the Criminal Law Amendment Bill rushed through all its stages and become law. Henceforth a girl had to be sixteen before she could give her consent to sexual relations with a man.

But now Stead and his associates ran into serious trouble. To prove how easy it was to get hold of a girl for immoral purposes and ship her abroad he had employed Mrs Rebecca Jarrett (the reformed brothel-keeper of No. 4) to 'purchase' Eliza Armstrong, a girl of thirteen, from her mother, after which she had been taken to a house in Soho, where she was visited by Stead just as though he had been a man intent on her seduction, and then placed in charge of some women officers of the Salvation Army, who took her across the Channel to their place in Paris.

So far everything had gone according to plan, but when the story of 'Lily', as Stead had named the girl in his article, was published, the hunt began for her original. Mrs Armstrong got talking to the newspapers—according to her she had believed that her Eliza was being taken away to enter domestic service, the neighbours turned nasty, the police got on the scent, with the result that in September, Stead, Bramwell Booth, Mrs Jarrett, and several others who had been engaged in the affair were charged at Bow Street police court with having removed a girl under 16 years of age from her parents' custody without their consent. At the consequent trial at the Old Bailey all save Boooth were found guilty and sentenced to terms of imprisonment—in Stead's case, three months.

In after years Stead looked back on the affair as constituting his chief claim to fame. 'I achieved my end', he wrote. 'The C.L.A. Act was swept in triumph through both Houses of Parliament by members who had assured me positively that it was a physical impossibility to do such a thing. The act of Parliament still stands as the Charter of the girlhood of the country.' Stead left the *Pall Mall* in 1889, and in the next year started the *Review of Reviews*. He was drowned in the Titanic disaster in 1912.

(a) PROTECTION OF YOUNG GIRLS REPORT

The Committee appointed in 1881, and re-appointed in the present Session, have met and further considered the subject-matter referred to them . . .

I. *As to Young Girls alleged to have been induced by Artifices to go to Belgium, or elsewhere Abroad, for immoral purposes.*

1. The Committee are satisfied on the evidence produced before them that in recent years, chiefly between 1871 and 1879, a certain number of girls have been induced by agents in London to go over to Belgium, and have been placed in licensed houses ('*maisons de débauche*') there.

2. The agents, or *placeurs*, have been in the habit of receiving money, from £8 to £12 and upwards, for each girl, from the keepers of these houses.

3. The girls whose cases were brought in evidence before the Committee would appear (with possibly a few exceptions) to have already led immoral lives in this country, and to have known that they were going abroad for immoral purposes, but not to have known that they would be confined and kept under restraint in these houses to the extent to which they were.

4. Although, as a general rule, not otherwise ill-treated, they were practically prisoners, being, in most cases, in debt to the keepers for whose benefit they were employed, and their own clothes being taken from them; and although the houses were periodically inspected by the police, and notices put up to the effect that girls could not be detained against their will, still from fear, ignorance, and unacquaintance with the language, as well as from being poor and friendless, they had no power to escape, until found by those who made it their business to inquire into their cases.

5. In many instances these girls were under 21, and the Belgian law on this point was evaded by the production of false certificates of birth

283

procured by the *placeurs* from Somerset House, that is to say, certificates that were really those of other women whose names these girls were made to assume.

6. The Belgian authorities rendered assistant in rescuing these cases, and prosecuted and severely punished the *placeurs* and others, is so far as they had violated the Belgian law, and at the time when this Committee made their first Report in 1881 it was stated to them, by those most likely to know the facts, that there were no longer any cases of English girls being kept in any of the Belgian brothels. . . .

II. *As to the amount of Protection at present given by the Law to Young Girls in England.*

8. In other countries female chastity is more or less protected by law up to the age of 21. No such protection is given in England to girls above the age of 13.

9. The evidence before the Committee proves beyond doubt that juvenile prostitution, from an almost incredibly early age, is increasing to an appalling extent in England, and especially in London.

10. Various causes are assigned for this: a vicious demand for young girls; overcrowding in dwellings, and immorality arising therefrom; want of parental control, and in many cases, parental example, profligacy, and immoral treatment; residence, in some cases, in brothels; the example and encouragement of other girls slightly older, and the sight of the dress and money, which their immoral habits have enabled them to obtain; the state of the streets in which little girls are allowed to run about, and become accustomed to the sight of open profligacy; and sometimes the contamination with vicious girls in schools. . . .

Report of the Select Committee of the House of Lords on the Law relating to the Protection of Young Girls (188, Session 1882, pp. iii-lv; P.P. 1881, vol. 9.

(*b*) W. T. STEAD'S ARTICLES IN THE '*Pall Mall Gazette*'

I

'*The Maiden Tribute of Modern Babylon*'

In ancient times, if we may believe the myths of Hellas, Athens, after a disastrous campaign, was compelled by her conqueror to send once every nine years a tribute to Crete of seven youths and seven maidens. The doomed fourteen, who were selected by lot amid the lamentations of the citizens, returned no more. The vessel that bore them to Crete unfurled black sails as the symbol of despair, and on arrival her passengers were flung into the famous Labyrinth of Daedalus, there to wander about blindly until such time as they were devoured by the Minotaur, a frightful monster, half man, half bull, the foul product of an unnatural lust. . . .

The fact that the Athenians should have taken so bitterly to heart the paltry maiden tribute that once in nine years they had to pay to the Minotaur seems incredible, almost inconceivable. This very night in London, and every night, year in and year out, not seven maidens only, but many times seven, will be offered up as the Maiden Tribute of Modern Babylon. Maidens they were when this morning dawned, but to-night their ruin will be accomplished, and to-morrow they will find themselves within the portals of the maze of London brotheldom.

Within that Labyrinth wander, like lost souls, the vast host of London prostitutes, whose numbers no man can compute, but who are probably not much below 50,000 strong. Many, no doubt, who venture but a little way within the maze make their escape. But multitudes are swept irresistibly on and on to be destroyed in due season, to give place to others, who also will share their doom. The maw of the London Minotaur is insatiable. After some years' dolorous wandering in this palace of despair, most of those ensnared tonight will perish, some of them in horrible torture. Yet, so far from this great city being convulsed with woe, London cares for none of these things. . . .

Although I am no vain dreamer of Utopias peopled solely by Sir Galahads and vestal virgins, I am not without hope that there may be some check placed upon this vast tribute of maidens, unwitting or unwilling, which is nightly levied in London by the vices of the rich upon the necessities of the poor.

London's lust annually uses up many thousands of women, who are literally killed and made away with—living sacrifices slain in the service of vice. That may be inevitable, and with that I have nothing to do. But I do ask that those doomed to the house of evil fame shall not be trapped into it unwillingly, and that none shall be beguiled into the chamber of death before they are of an age to read the inscription above the portal— 'All hope abandon ye who enter here'. If the daughters of the people must be served up as dainty morsels to minister to the passions of the rich, let them at least attain an age when they can understand the nature of the sacrifice which they are asked to make. And if we must cast maidens nightly into the jaws of vice, let us at least see to it that they assent to their own immolation, and are not unwilling sacrifices procured by force and fraud. That is surely not too much to ask from the dissolute rich.

w. t. stead, *Pall Mall Gazette*, July 6, 1885.

2

'It doesn't even raise the neighbours'

Before beginning this inquiry I had a confidential interview with one of the most experienced officers who for many years was in a position to possess an intimate acquaintance with all phases of London crime [Sir Charles Howard Vincent, former director of the Criminal Investigation Department at New Scotland Yard]. I asked him, 'Is it or is it not a fact, that, at this moment, if I were to go to the proper houses, well introduced, the keeper would, in return for money down, supply me in due time with a maid—a genuine article, I mean, not a mere prostitute tricked out as a virgin, but a girl who had never been seduced?'

'Certainly', he replied, without a moment's hesitation. 'At what price?' I continued. 'That is a difficult question', he said. 'I remember one case which came under my official cognizance in Scotland-yard in which the price agreed was stated to be £20. Some parties in Lambeth undertook to deliver a maid for that sum to a house of ill fame, and I have no doubt it is frequently done all over London.'

'But', I continued, 'are these maids willing or unwilling parties to the transaction—that is, are they really maiden, not merely in being each a *virgo intacta* in the physical sense, but as being chaste girls who are not consenting parties to their seduction?' He looked surprised at my question, and then replied emphatically: 'Of course they are rarely willing, and as a rule they do not know what they are coming for.'

'But', I said in amazement, 'then do you mean to tell me that in very truth actual rapes, in the legal sense of the word, are constantly being perpetrated in London on unwilling virgins, purveyed and procured to rich men at so much a head by keepers of brothels?'

'Certainly,' he said, 'there is not a doubt of it.' 'Why', I exclaimed, 'the very thought is enough to raise hell.'

'It is true', he said, 'and although it ought to raise hell, it does not even raise the neighbours.'

'But do the girls cry out?' 'Of course they do. But what avails screaming in a quiet bedroom? Suppose a girl is being outraged in a room next to your house? You hear her screaming, just as you are dozing to sleep. Do you get up, dress, rush downstairs, and insist on admittance? Hardly. But suppose the screams continue and you get uneasy, you begin to think whether you should not do something? Before you have made up your mind and got dressed the screams cease, and you think you are a fool for your pains.'

'But the policemen on the beat?' 'He has no right to interfere, even if he heard anything. Suppose that a constable had a right to force his way into any house where a woman screamed fearfully, policemen would be almost as regular attendants at childbed as doctors. Once a girl gets into such a house she is helpless, and may be ravished with comparative safety.'

'But surely rape is a felony punishable with penal servitude. Can she not prosecute?'

'Whom is she to prosecute? She does not know her assailant's name. She might not even be able to recognize him if she met him outside. Even if she did, who would believe her? A woman who has lost her chastity is always a discredited witness. The fact of her being in a house of ill fame would possibly be held to be evidence of her consent. The keeper of the house and all the servants would swear she was a consenting party; they would swear that she had never screamed, and the woman would be condemned as an adventuress who wished to levy blackmail.'

'And this is going on to-day?'

'Certainly it is, and it will go on, and you cannot help it, as long as men have money, procuresses are skilful, and women are weak and inexperienced.'

W. T. STEAD, Pall Mall Gazette, July 6, 1885.

3

Confessions of a Brothel-keeper

Here is a statement made to me by a brothel-keeper who formerly kept a house in the Mile-end Road, but who is now endeavouring to start life afresh as an honest man. I saw both him and his wife, herself a notorious prostitute whom he had married off the streets, where she had earned her living since she was fourteen.

'Maids, as you call them—fresh girls as we know them in the trade—are constantly in request, and a keeper who knows his business has his eye open in all directions. His stock of girls is constantly getting used up, and needs replenishing, and he has to be on the alert for likely 'marks' to keep up the reputation of his house.

'The getting of fresh girls takes time, but it is simple and easy enough when once you are in it. I have gone and courted girls in the country under all kinds of disguises, occasionally assuming the dress of a parson, and make them believe that I intended to marry them, and so got them in my power to please a good customer. How is it done? Why, after courting my girl for a time, I propose to bring her to London to see the sights. I bring her up, take her here and there, giving her plenty to eat and drink—especially drink. I take her to the theatre, and then I contrive it so that she loses her last train. By this time she is very tired, a little dazed with the drink and excitement, and very frightened at being left in town with no friends. I offer her nice lodgings for the night; she goes to bed in my house, and then the affair is managed. My client gets his maid, I get my £10 or £20 commission, and in the morning the girl, who has lost her character, and dare not go home, in all probability will do as the others do, and become one of my "marks"—that is, she will make her living in the streets, to the advantage of my house.'

'Another very simple mode of supplying maids is by breeding them. Many women who are on the streets have female children. They are worth keeping. When they get to be twelve or thirteen they become merchantable. For a very lively "mark" of this kind you may get as much as £20 or £40. I sent my own daughter out on the streets from my own brothel. I know a couple of very fine little girls now who will be sold before very long. They are bred and trained for the life. They must take the first step some time, and it is bad business not to make as much out of that as possible. Drunken parents often sell their children to brothel keepers. In the East-end you can always pick up as many fresh girls as you want.'

W. T. STEAD, Pall Mall Gazette, July 6, 1885.

4

'How girls are bought and ruined'

Making inquiries at the other end of the town, by good fortune I was brought into intimate and confidential communication with an ex-brothel-keeper [Rebecca Jarrett].

When a mere girl she had been seduced by Colonel S—, when a maid-servant at Petersfield, and had been thrown upon the streets by that officer at Manchester. She had subsequently kept a house of ill-fame at a seaport town, and from thence had gravitated to the congenial neighbourhood of Regent's Park. There she had kept a brothel for several years. About a year ago, however, she was picked up, when in a drunken fit, by some earnest workers [of the Salvation Army], and after a hard struggle was brought back to a decent and moral life.

She was a woman who bore traces of the rigorous mill through which she had passed. Her health was impaired; she looked ten years older than her actual age, and it was with the greatest reluctance she could be prevailed upon to speak of the incidents of her previous life, the horror of which seemed to cling to her like a nightmare. By dint of patient questioning, however, and the assurance that I would not criminate either herself or her old companions, she became more communicative. Her narrative was straightforward, and I am fully convinced that it was entirely genuine. Her story was somewhat as follows:—

'As a regular thing, the landlady of a bad house lets her rooms to gay women and lives on their rent and the profits of the drink which they compel their customers to buy for the good of the house. She may go out herself, or she may not. If business is very heavy she will have to do her own share, but as a rule she contents herself with keeping her girls up to the mark . . . Girls often shrink from going out, and need almost to be driven into the streets. If it was not for gin and the landlady they could never carry it on. Some girls I used to have would come and sit and cry in my kitchen and declare that they could not go out, they could not stand the life. I had to give them a dram and take them out myself, and set them agoing again, for if they did not seek gentlemen where was I to get my rent?

'Did they begin willingly? Some; others had no choice. How had they no choice? Because they never knew anything about it till the gentleman was in their bedroom, and then it was too late. I or my girls would entice fresh girls in, and persuade them to stay out too late till they were locked out, and then a pinch of snuff in their beer would keep them snug until the gentleman had his way.

'Has that happened often? Lots of times. It is one of the ways by which you keep your house up. Every woman who has an eye to business is constantly on the look out for likely girls. Pretty girls who are poor, and have either no parents or are away from home, are easiest picked up. How is it done? You or your decoy find a likely girl and then you track her down. I remember I once went a hundred miles and more to pick up a girl. I took a lodging close to the board school, where I could see the girls go backwards and forwards every day. I soon saw one that suited my fancy. She was a girl of about thirteen, tall and forward for her age, pretty, and likely to bring business. I found out she lived with her mother. I engaged her to be my little maid at the lodgings where I was staying. The very next day I took her off with me to London and her mother never saw her again. What became of her? A gentleman paid me £13 for the first of her, soon after she came to town. She was asleep when he did it—sound asleep. To tell the truth, she was drugged. It is often done. I gave her a drowse. It is a mixture of laudanum and something else. Sometimes chloroform is used, but I always used either snuff or laudanum. We call it drowse, or black draught, and they lie almost as if dead, and the girl never knows what has happened till morning. 'And then? Oh! then she cries a great deal from pain, but she is 'mazed and hardly knows what has happened except that she can hardly move from pain. Of course, we tell her it is all right; all girls have to go through it some time, that she is through it now without knowing it, and that it is no use crying. It will never be undone for all the crying in the world. She must now do as the others do. She can live like a lady, do as she pleases, have the best of all that is going, and enjoy herself all day. If she objects, I scold her and tell her she has lost her character, no one will take her in; I will have to turn her out on the streets as a bad and ungrateful girl. The result is that in nine cases out of ten, or ninety-nine out of a hundred, the child, who is usually under fifteen, frightened and friendless, her head aching with the effect of the drowse and full of pain and horror, gives up all hope, and in a week she is one of the attractions of the house.'

W. T. STEAD, Pall Mall Gazette, July 6, 1885.

5

'A dreadful profession'

When I was prosecuting these inquiries at the East-end, I was startled by a discovery made by a confidential agent at the other end of the town. This was nothing less than the unearthing of a house, kept apparently by a highly respectable midwife, where children were taken by procurers to be certified as virgins before violation, and where, after violation, they were taken to be 'patched up', and where, if necessary, abortion could be procured.

The existence of the house was no secret. It was well known in the trade, and my agent was directed thither without much ado by a gay woman with whom he had made a casual acquaintance.

No doubt the respectable old lady has other business of a less doubtful character, but in the trade her repute is unrivalled, first as a certificator of virginity, and secondly for the adroitness and skill with which she can repair the laceration caused by the subsequent outrage.

w. t. stead, *Pall Mall Gazette*, July 6, 1885.

6

A Firm of Procuresses

The recruiting for the brothel is by no means left to occasional and irregular agents. It is a systematized business. Mesdames X. and Z., procuresses, London, is a firm whose address is not to be found in the 'Post Office Directory'. It exists, however, and its operations are in full swing at this moment. Its members have made the procuration of virgins their speciality. They do nothing else. They keep no house of ill fame.

One of the members of this remarkable firm lives in all the odour of propriety if not of sanctity with her parents; the other, who has her own lodgings, nominally holds a position of trust and of influence in the establishment of a well-known firm in Oxford-street. The office of the firm is at the lodgings of the junior partner, where letters and telegrams are sent and orders received, and the necessary correspondence conducted.

Both partners are young. The business was started by Miss X., a young woman of energy and ability and great natural shrewdness, almost immediately after her seduction in 1881. She was at that time in her sixteenth year. A girl who had already fallen introduced her to a 'gentleman', and pocketed half the price of her virtue as commission. The ease with which her procuress earned a couple of pounds came like a revelation to Miss X., and she began to look about to find maids for customers and customers for maids. After two years, business had increased to such an extent that she was obliged to take into partnership Miss Z., an older girl, about twenty, of slenderer figure and fairer complexion.

I heard accidentally of the operation of this famous firm in conversation with a bright-looking young girl about sixteen who was telling me the way in which she was first brought out. An interview was arranged without much difficulty . . . with Mesdames X. and Z. . . . and in the course of the evening they gave me a good idea of the whole art and mystery of procuration, as practised by its most skilful professors.

'I was told the other day', said I, by way of opening the conversation, 'that the demand for maidenheads has rather fallen away of late, owing to the frauds of the procurers. The market has been glutted with vamped-up virgins, of which the supply is always in excess of the demand, and there are fewer inquiries for the genuine article.'

'That is not our experience', said the senior partner, a remarkable woman, attractive by the force of her character in spite of the ghastliness of her calling, compared to which that of the common hangman is more honourable. 'We do not know anything about vamped virgins. Nor, with so many genuine maids to be had for the taking, do I think it worth while to manufacture virgins. I should say the market was looking up. Prices may have fallen, but that is because our customers give larger orders. For instance, Dr—, one of my friends, who used to take a maid a week at £10, now takes three a fortnight at from £5 to £7 each.'

'What!' I exclaimed; 'do you actually supply one gentleman with seventy fresh maids every year?'

'Certainly', said she; 'and he would take a hundred if we could get them. But he is so very particular. He will not take a shop-girl, and he always must have a maid over sixteen.'

'Why over sixteen?' said I. 'Because of the law', she replied; 'no one is allowed to take away from her home, or from her proper guardians, a girl who is under sixteen. She can assent to be seduced after she is thirteen, but even if she assented to go, both the keeper of the house where we took her, and my partner and I, would be liable to punishment if she was not over sixteen. That diminishes the age from which maids can be drawn. The easiest age to pick them up is fourteen or fifteen. At thirteen they are just out of school, and still more or less babies under the influence of their mothers. But at fourteen and fifteen they begin to get more liberty without getting much more sense; they begin to want clothes and things which money can buy, and they do not understand the value of what they are parting with in order to get it. After a girl gets past sixteen she gets wiser, and is more difficult to secure.'

'You seem to know the law', said I, 'better than I know it myself.' 'Have to', she said promptly. 'It is my business. It would never do for me not to know what was safe and what was not. We might get both ourselves and our friends into no end of trouble if we did not know the law.'

The Speciality of their Business

'Then do you do anything in the foreign trade?' I asked. 'Oh no', she said. 'Our business is in maidenheads, not in maids. My friends take the girls to be seduced and take them back to their situations after they have been seduced, and that is an end of it so far as we are concerned.

We do only the first seductions, a girl passes only once through our hands, and she is done with. Our gentlemen want maids, not damaged articles, and as a rule they see them only once.'

'What comes of the damaged articles?' 'They all go back to their situations or their places. But,' said the procuress reflectively, 'they all go to the streets after a time. When once a girl has been bad she goes again and again, and finally she ends like the rest. There are scarcely any exceptions.'

'Do they ever have children?' 'Not very often the first time. Of course, we tell them that it never happens. Girls are so silly, they will believe anything . . . But of course sometimes they get in the family way the first time.'

'And then', said I, 'I supposed they affiliate the child?' 'On whom, pray?' said the senior partner, laughing. 'We make it a special feature of our business that the maid never knows who is her seducer, and in most cases they never know our address. How can she get to know? I have to take a cook, for instance, next Sunday at church time to Mr —, who has a place in Bedford-square. I take the girl in a cab. We drive through street after street. Then we stop opposite a door and go in. The cook will see a gentleman who may be with her a few minutes, or he may be with her half an hour. During that time she is naturally somewhat excited and suffers more or less pain. As soon as she is dressed I take her away in a cab and she never sees that gentleman again. Even if she noticed the house, which is doubtful, she does not know the name of its owner, and in many cases the house is merely a brothel. What can she do?'

The Forcing of Unwilling Maids

'Do the maids ever repent and object to be seduced when the time comes?' 'Oh yes', said Miss X., 'sometimes we have no end of trouble with the little fools. You see they often have no idea in the world as to what being seduced is. We do not take the trouble to explain, and it is enough for us if the girl willingly consents to see or to meet or to have a game with a rich gentleman. What meaning she attaches to seeing a gentleman it is not our business to inquire. All that we have to do is to bring her there and see that she does not make a fool of the gentleman when she gets there.'

'You always manage it though?' I inquired. 'Certainly', she said. 'If a girl makes too much trouble, she loses her maidenhead for nothing instead of losing if for money. The right way to deal with these silly girls is to convince them that now they have come they have got to be seduced, willing or unwilling, and that if they are unwilling, they will be first seduced and then turned into the streets without a penny. Even then they sometimes kick and scream and make no end of a row. You remember Janie?' she said, appealing to Miss Z. 'Don't I just', said that amiable lady. 'We had fearful trouble with that girl. She wrapped herself up in the bed-curtains and screamed and fought and made such a rumpus, that I and my friend had to hold her down by main force while she was being seduced.'

'Tell me', said I, 'when these maids scream so fearfully does no one ever interfere?' 'No; we take them to a quiet place, and the people of the house know us, and would not interfere, no matter what noise went on. Often we take them to private houses, and there of course all is safe. The time for screaming is not long. As soon as it is over the girl sees it is no use howling. She gets her money and goes away. . . .'

Where Maids are Picked Up

'Who supplies most of your maids?' 'Nurse-girls and shop-girls, although occasionally we get a governess, and sometimes cooks and other servants. We get to know the servants through the nurses. Young girls from the country, fresh and rosy, are soon picked up in the shops or as they run errands. But nurse-girls are the great field.'

'But how do you manage to pick up so many?' The senior partner replied with conscious pride, 'It takes time, patience, and experience. Many girls need months before they can be brought in. You need to proceed very cautiously at first. Every morning at this time of the year my friend and I are up at seven, and after breakfast we put a shawl round our shoulders and off we go to scour the park. Hyde Park and the Green Park are the best in the morning; Regent's Park in the afternoon. As we go coasting along, we keep a sharp look out for any likely girl, and having spotted one we make up to her; and week after week we see her as often as possible, until we are sufficiently in her confidence to suggest how easy it is to earn a few pounds by meeting a man. In the afternoon off goes the shawl and on goes the jacket, and we are off on the same quest. Thus we have always a crop of maids ripening, and at any time we can undertake to deliver a maid if we get due notice.'

w. t. stead, *Pall Mall Gazette*, July 7, 1885.

7

Night Prowler

As to the extent of the evil of importunate solicitation I can bear personal testimony as to the gross exaggeration of the popular notion. I have been a night prowler for weeks. I have gone in different guises to most of the favourite rendezvous of harlots. I have strolled along Ratcliff-highway, and sauntered round and round the Quadrant at midnight. I have haunted St James's Park, and twice enjoyed the strange sweetness of summer night by the sides of the Serpentine. I have been at all hours in Leicester-square and the Strand, and have spent the midnight in Mile-end-road and the vicinity of the Tower.

Sometimes I was alone; sometimes accompanied by a friend; and the deep and strong impression which I have brought back is one of respect and admiration for the extraordinary good behaviour of the English girls who pursue this dreadful calling. In the whole of my wanderings I have not been accosted half-a-dozen times, and then I was more to blame than the woman. I was turned out of Hyde Park at midnight in company with a drunken prostitute, but she did not begin the conversation. I have been much more offensively accosted in Parisian boulevards than I have ever been in an English park or English street, and on the whole I have brought back from the infernal labyrinth a very deep conviction that if there is one truth in the Bible that is truer than another it is this, that the publicans and harlots are nearer the kingdom of heaven than the scribes and pharisees who are always striving to qualify for a passport to bliss hereafter by driving their unfortunate sisters here to the very real hell of a police despotism.

W. T. STEAD, *Pall Mall Gazette*, July 10, 1885.

A QUIET SUNDAY IN LONDON; OR, THE DAY OF REST.

Punch (1886)

CHAPTER II

THE SUBMERGED TENTH

(*General Booth's 'In Darkest England, and the Way Out'*)

Very shortly after Charles Booth had disturbed Victorian complacency with the estimate that a third of the population were living in the condition of 'poverty sinking into want', his namesake (but no relation) William Booth, 'General' of the Salavation Army, more than disturbed it with the calculation that there were about three millions of men, women, and children, who were living in such conditions of misery and destitution, vice and crime, as put them outside the limits of civilized society. For this festering mass of blighted humanity he coined the phrase, the 'Submerged Tenth'.

This was in his book, *In Darkest England, and the Way Out*, that was published in 1890. The book created a profound impression, not only on social workers (who might be expected to know most of its facts already) but on the general public, who were attracted by its clever title and the 'popular' style in which it was written. (Sometimes it has been said that it was largely written by W. T. Stead, but Stead himself asserted that he had merely acted as a 'hack' to get Booth's huge and ever growing mass of material into shape.)

Even those who detested 'the General's' ferocious theology and even more, perhaps, the drum-banging and trumpet-blasting of the Salvation Army's bands, could not but admit that he knew what he was talking about. For nearly forty years he had been a revivalist preacher, a dozen years had passed since he had converted his Christian Mission in Whitechapel into the Salvation Army, and all those years he had spent among the lowest of the low. His claim that he and his Salvationists could reach lower social strata than any other organization, religious or social, had even attempted to reach, was generally conceded. When this man, then, who looked like an Old Testament prophet and often spoke and acted like one, not only pointed out the horrible evils of modern society but made bold to say that he knew how to cure them, and could and would do so if he only had the money . . . the money started to roll in. A hundred thousand pounds was what he asked for, and before the year was out most of it had been subscribed.

In his book he listed and explained the methods he proposed to adopt in order to get rid of pauperism, vice and crime. The most important of these were: farm colonies for the unemployed, large-scale emigration, travelling hospitals, household salvage brigade, rescue homes for fallen women and homes for unfallen girls in moral danger, prison-gate brigade to assist discharged prisoners, refuges for the children of the streets, industrial schools, mission of rescue to drunkards, enquiry office for missing persons, a poor man's bank and poor man's lawyer, and 'Whitechapel-by-the-Sea', a bright and breezy name for schemes to enable slum-dwellers to have a day at the seaside for a few shillings.

Of course, there were plenty to scoff and criticize and condemn. Booth was accused of being a 'Socialist', of aiming at a personal dictatorship backed by his army of men and women pledged to absolute obedience. He had misread the statistics, he was setting himself against the 'laws' of economics, he would damage irreparably the springs of charity. The most serious charge was of mismanagement of the funds subscribed, and a public inquiry was instituted—which at length reported that Booth had not derived any personal financial benefit and that the accounts were being properly kept. In the event, nothing like all that 'the General' had proposed was carried out, but in many directions there was considerable progress. When Booth died in 1912 his funeral was the occasion for a vast demonstration of public sympathy and support.

I

Darkest England

This summer the attention of the civilized world has been arrested by the story which Mr Stanley has told of 'Darkest Africa' and his journeyings through the heart of the Lost Continent . . . It is a terrible picture. But while brooding over the awful presentation of life as it exists in the vast African forest, it seemed to me only too vivid a picture of many parts of our own land. As there is a darkest Africa is there not also a darkest England?

The Equatorial Forest travelled by Stanley resembles that Darkest England of which I have to speak, alike in its vast extent, its monstrous darkness, its malaria and its gloom, its dwarfish de-humanized inhabitants, the slavery to which they are subjected, their privations and their misery.

Hard it is, no doubt, to read in Stanley's pages of the slave-traders coldly arranging for the surprise of a village, the capture of the inhabitants, the massacre of those who resist, and the violation of all the women; but the stony streets of London, if they could but speak, would tell of tragedies as awful, of ruin as complete, of ravishments as horrible, as if we were in Central Africa; only the ghastly devastation is covered, corpse-like, with the artificialities and hypocrisies of modern civilization.

The lot of a Negress in the Equatorial Forest is not, perhaps, a very happy one, but is it so very much worse than that of many a pretty orphan girl in our Christian capital? A young penniless girl, if she be pretty, is often hunted from pillar to post by her employers, confronted always by the alternative—Starve or Sin. And when once the poor girl has consented to buy the right to earn her own living by the sacrifice of her virtue, then she is treated as a slave and an outcast by the very men who have ruined her. Her word becomes unbelievable, her life an ignominy, and she is swept dowward, ever downward, into the bottomless perdition of prostitution.

The blood boils with impotent rage at the sight of these enormities, callously inflicted, and silently borne by these miserable victims. Nor is it only women who are the victims, although their fate is the most tragic.

Those firms which reduce sweating to a fine art, who systematically and deliberately defraud the workman of his pay, who grind the faces of the poor, and who rob the widow and the orphan, and who for a pretence make great professions of public-spirit and philanthropy, these men nowadays are sent to Parliament to make laws for the people. The old prophets sent them to Hell—but we have changed all that. They send their victims to Hell, and are rewarded by all that wealth can do to make their lives comfortable. Read the House of Lords' Report on the Sweating System, and ask if any African slave system, making due allowance for the superior civilization, and therefore sensitiveness, of the victims, reveals more misery.

Darkest England, like Darkest Africa, reeks with malaria. The foul and fetid breath of our slums is almost as poisonous as that of the African swamp. Fever is almost as chronic there as on the Equator. Every year thousands of children are killed off by what is called defects of our sanitary system. They are in reality starved and poisoned, and all that can be said is that, in many cases, it is better for them that they were taken away from the trouble to come.

Just as in Darkest Africa it is only a part of the evil and misery that comes from the superior race who invade the forest to enslave and massacre its miserable inhabitants, so with us, much of the misery of those whose lot we are considering arises from their own habits. Drunkenness and all manner of uncleanness, moral and physical, abound. Have you ever watched by the bedside of a man in delirium tremens? Multiply the sufferings of that one drunkard by the hundred thousand, and you have some idea of what scenes are being witnessed in all our great cities at this moment. As in Africa streams intersect the forest in every direction, so the gin-shop stands at every corner with its River of the Water of Death flowing seventeen hours out of the twenty-four for the destruction of the people. A population sodden with drink, steeped in vice, eaten up with every social and physical malady, these are the denizens of Darkest England amidst whom my life has been spent, and to whose rescue I would now summon all that is best in the manhood and womanhood of our land.

The Cab Horse's Charter

What, then, is Darkest England? For whom do we claim that 'urgency' which gives their case priority over that of all other sections of their countrymen and countrywomen?

I claim it for the Lost, for the Outcast, for the Disinherited of the World.

But I will be more precise. The denizens of Darkest England, for whom I appeal, are (1) those who, having no capital or income of their own, would in a month be dead of sheer starvation were they exclusively dependent upon the money earned by their own work; and (2) those who by their utmost exertions are unable to attain the regulation allowance of food which the law prescribes as indispensable even for the worst criminals in our goals.

I sorrowfully admit that it would be Utopian in our present social arrangement to dream of attaining for every honest Englishman a gaol standard of all the necessaries of life. Some time, perhaps, we may venture to hope that every honest worker on English soil will always be as warmly clad, as healthily housed, and as regularly fed as our criminal convicts—but that is not yet. Neither is it possible to hope for many years to come that human beings generally will be as well cared for as horses.

What, then, is the standard towards which we may venture to aim with some prospect of realization of our time? It is a very humble one, but if realized it would solve the worst problems of modern Society. It is the standard of the London Cab Horse.

When in the streets of London a Cab Horse, weary or careless or stupid, trips and falls and lies stretched out in the midst of the traffic, there is no question of debating how he came to stumble before we try to get him on his legs again. The Cab Horse is a very real illustration of poor broken-down humanity; he usually falls down because of overwork and underfeeding. If you put him on his feet without altering his conditions, it would only be to give him another dose of agony; but first of all you'll have to pick him up again. It may have been through overwork or underfeeding, or it may have been all his own fault that he has broken his knees and smashed the shafts, but that does not matter. If not for his own sake, then merely in order to prevent an obstruction of the traffic, all attention is concentrated upon the question of how we are to get him on his legs again. The load is taken off, the harness is unbuckled, or, if need be, cut, and everything is done to help him up. Then he is put in the shafts again and once more restored to his regular round of work. That is the first point. The second is that every Cab Horse in London has three things; a shelter for the night, food for its stomach, and work allotted to it by which it can earn its corn.

These are the two points of the Cab Horse's Charter. When he is down he is helped up, and while he lives he has food, shelter and work. That, although a humble standard, is at present absolutely unattainable by millions—literally by millions—of our fellow-men and women in this country.

The Submerged Tenth

The first question, then which confronts us is, what are the dimensions of the Evil? How many of our fellow-men dwell in this Darkest England? How can we take the census of those who have fallen below the Cab Horse standard to which it is our aim to elevate the most wretched of our countrymen?

The moment you attempt to answer this question, you are confronted by the fact that the Social Problem has scarcely been studied at all scientifically. One book there is, and so far as I know at present, only one, which even attempts to enumerate the destitute. In his 'Life and Labour in the East of London' Mr Charles Booth attempts to form some kind of an idea as to the numbers of those with whom we have to deal.

How do his statistics work out? . . . Let us suppose that the East London rate is double the average for the rest of the country. That would bring out the following figures:—

	East London	United Kingdom
Houseless		
Loafers, Casuals, and some Criminals	11,000	165,500
Starving		
Casual earnings or chronic want	100,000	1,550,000
Total Houseless and Starving	111,000	1,715,500
In Workhouses, Asylums, etc.	17,000	190,000
	128,000	1,905,500

To these must be added the inmates of our prisons . . . indoor paupers and lunatics—and we have an army of nearly two millions belonging to the submerged classes. To this must be added, at the very least, another million, representing those dependent upon the criminal, lunatic and other classes, not enumerated here, and the more or less helpless of the class immediately above the houseless and starving. This brings my total to three millions, or, to put it roughly, to one-tenth of the population.

Darkest England, then, may be said to have a population about equal to that of Scotland. Three million men, women, and children, a vast, despairing multitude in a condition nominally free, but really enslaved. Is anything to be done with them? Can anything be done for them? Or is this million-headed mass to be regarded as offering a problem as insoluble as that of the London sewage, which, feculent and festering, swings heavily up and down the basin of the Thames with the ebb and flow of the tide?

This Submerged Tenth—is it, then, beyond the reach of the nine-tenths in the midst of whom they live, and around whose homes they rot and die?

In Darkest England, chs. 1 and 2.

2

'Born slaves of the bottle'

The bastard of a harlot, born in a brothel, suckled on gin, and familiar from earliest infancy with all the bestialities of debauch, violated before she is twelve, and driven out into the streets by her mother a year or two later, what chance is there for such a girl in this world—I say nothing of the next? Yet such a case is not exceptional. And with boys it is almost as bad.

There are thousands who were begotten when both parents were besotted with drink, whose mothers saturated themselves with alcohol every day of their pregnancy, who may be said to have sucked in a taste for strong drink with their mothers' milk, and who were surrounded from childhood with opportunities and incitements to drink. How can we marvel that the constitution thus disposed to intemperance finds the stimulus of drink indispensable? Even if they make a stand against it, the increasing pressure of exhaustion and scanty food drives them back to the cup. Ot these poor wretches, born slaves of the bottle, predestined to drunkenness from their mother's womb, there are—who can say how many? Yet they are all men. . . .

In Darkest England, page 47.

3

The Girls of the 'Dusthole'

There is scarcely a lower class of girls to be found than the girls of Woolwich 'Dusthole'. The women living and following their dreadful business in this neighbourhood are so degraded that even abandoned men will refuse to accompany them home. Soldiers are forbidden to enter the place, or to go down the street, on pain of twenty-five days' imprisonment; pickets are stationed at either end to prevent this.

One public-house is shut up three or four times a day sometimes for fear of losing the licence through the terrible brawls which take place within. A policeman never goes down this street alone at night—one having died not long ago from injuries received there—but our two [Salvation Army] lasses go unharmed and loved at all hours, spending every other night always upon the streets.

The girls sink to the 'Dusthole' after coming down several grades. There is but one on record who came there with beautiful clothes, and this poor girl, when last seen by the officers, was a pauper in the work-house infirmary in a wretched condition.

The lowest class of all is the girls who stand at the pier-head—these sell themselves literally for a bare crust of bread and sleep in the streets.

In Darkest England, p. 55.

4

Life in a Casual Ward

Now, what is the existing machinery by which Society, whether through the organization of the State or by individual endeavour, attempts to deal with the submerged residuum?

The first place must naturally be given to the administration of the

Poor Law. Legally the State accepts the responsibility of providing food and shelter for every man, woman or child who is utterly destitute. This responsibility it, however, practically shirks by the imposition of conditions on the claimants of relief that are hateful and repulsive, if not impossible.

No Englishman can come upon the rates so long as he has anything whatever left to call his own. When long-continued destitution has been carried on to the bitter end, when piece by piece every article of domestic furniture has been sold or pawned, when all efforts to procure employment have failed, and when you have nothing left except the clothes in which you stand, then you can present yourself before the relieving officer and secure your lodging in the workhouse, the administration of which varies infinitely according to the disposition of the Board of Guardians under whose control it happens to be.

If, however, you have not sunk to such despair as to be willing to barter your liberty for the sake of food, clothing, and shelter in the Workhouse, but are only temporarily out of employment, seeking work, then you go to the Casual Ward. There you are taken in, and provided for on the principle of making it as disagreeable as possible for yourself, in order to deter you from again accepting the hospitality of the rates— and of course in defence of this a good deal can be said by the Political Economist.

But what seems utterly indefensible is the careful precautions which are taken to render it impossible for the unemployed Casual to resume promptly after his night's rest the search for work. Under the existing regulations, if you are compelled to seek refuge on Monday night in the Casual Ward, you are bound to remain there at least till Wednesday morning.

The theory of the system is this, that individuals casually poor and out of work, being destitute and without shelter, may upon application receive shelter for the night, supper and a breakfast, and in return for this, shall perform a task of work, not necessarily in repayment for the relief received, but simply as a test of their willingness to work for their living. The work given is the same as that given to felons in gaol, oakum-picking and stone-breaking.

The work, too, is excessive in proportion to what is received. Four pounds of oakum is a great task to an expert and an old hand. To a novice it can only be accomplished with the greatest difficulty, if indeed it can be done at all. It is even in excess of the amount demanded from a criminal in gaol.

The stone-breaking test is monstrous. Half a tone of stone from any man in return for partially supplying the cravings of hunger is an outrage which, if we read of as having occurred in Russia or Siberia, would find Exeter Hall crowded with an indignant audience, and Hyde Park filled with strong oratory.

But because this system exists at our very doors, very little notice is taken of it. These tasks are expected from all comers, starved, ill-clad, half-fed creatures from the streets, foot-sore and worn out; and yet unless it is done, the victim is liable to be dragged before a magistrate and committed to gaol as a rogue and vagabond, while in the Casual Ward their treatment is practically that of a criminal.

They sleep in a cell with an apartment at the back, in which the work is done, receiving at night half a pound of gruel and eight ounces of bread, and next morning the same for breakfast, with half a pound of oakum and stones to occupy himself for a day.

The beds are mostly of the plank type, the coverings scant, the comfort *nil*. Be it remembered that this is the treatment meted out to those who are supposed to be Casual poor, in temporary difficulty, walking from place to place seeking some employment.

The treatment of the women is as follows: Each Casual has to stay in the Casual Wards two nights and one day, during which time they have to pick 2 lb. of oakum or go to the wash-tub and work out their time there. While at the wash-tub they are allowed to wash their own clothes, but not otherwise. The inspector, who is a male person, visits the wards at all unexpected hours, even visiting while the females are in bed. The beds are in some wards composed of straw and two rugs; in others cocoanut fibre and two rugs.

The Casuals rise at 5.45 a.m. and go to bed at 7 p.m. If they do not finish picking their oakum before 7 p.m. they stay up till they do. If a Casual does not come to the ward before 12.30, midnight, they keep them one day extra.

The result of the deliberate policy of making the night refuge for the unemployed labourer as disagreeable as possible, and of placing as many obstacles as possible in the way of his finding work the following day, is, no doubt, to minimize the number of Casuals, and without question succeeds. In the whole of London the number of Casuals in the wards at night is only 1,136. That is to say, the conditions which are imposed are so severe, that the majority of the Out-of-Works prefer to sleep in the open air, taking their chance of the inclemency and mutability of our English weather, rather than go through the experience of the Casual Ward.

The second method in which society endeavours to do its duty to the lapsed masses is by the miscellaneous and heterogeneous efforts which are clubbed together under the generic name of Charity . . . The third method by which society professes to attempt the reclamation of the lost is by the rough, rude surgery of the Gaol. . . .

In Darkest England, pp. 67-73.

5

Night on the Embankment

There are still a large number of Londoners and a considerable percentage of wanderers from the country in search of work, who find themselves at nightfall destitute. These now betake themselves to the seats under the plane trees on the Embankment. Formerly they endeavoured to occupy all the seats, but the lynx-eyed Metropolitan Police declined to allow any such proceedings, and the dossers, knowing the invariable kindness of the City Police, made tracks for that portion of the Embankment which, lying east of the Temple, comes under the control of the Civic Fathers. Here, between the Temple and Blackfriars, I found the poor wretches by the score; almost every seat contained its full complement of six—some men, some women—all reclining in various postures and nearly all fast asleep.

Just as Big Ben strikes two, the moon, flashing across the Thames and lighting up the stone work of the Embankment, brings into relief a pitiable spectacle. Here on the stone abutments, which afford a slight protection from the biting wind, are scores of men lying side by side, huddled together for warmth, and, of course, without any other covering than their ordinary clothing, which is scanty enough at the best. Some have laid down a few pieces of waste paper, by way of taking the chill off the stones, but the majority are too tired even for that, and the nightly toilet of most consists of first removing the hat, swathing the head in whatever old rag may be doing duty as a handkerchief, and then replacing the hat.

The intelligent-looking elderly man, who was just fixing himself up on a seat, informed me that he frequently made that his night's abode. 'You see', quoth he, 'there's nowhere else so comfortable. I was here last night, and Monday and Tuesday as well, that's four nights this week. I had no money for lodgings, couldn't earn any, try as I might. I've had one bit of bread today, nothing else whatever, and I've earned nothing today or yesterday; I had threepence the day before. Gets my living by carrying parcels, or minding horses, or odd jobs of that sort. You see, I haven't got my health, that's where it is. I used to work on the London General Omnibus Company and after that on the Road Car Company, but I had to go to the infirmary with bronchitis and couldn't get work after that. What's the good of a man what's got bronchitis and just left the infirmary? Who'll engage him, I'd like to know? Besides, it makes me short of breath at times, and I can't do much. I'm a widower; wife died long ago. I have one boy, abroad, a sailor, but he's only lately started, and can't help me. Yes! it's very fair out here of nights, seat's rather hard, but a bit of waste paper makes it a bit softer. We have women sleep here often, and children, too. They're very well conducted, and there's seldom many rows here, you see, because everybody's tired out. We're too sleepy to make a row.'

A Salvation Army Officer; *In Darkest England*, pp. 25-6.

THE PASSING OF THE FORSYTES

The Forsyte Saga opens on the afternoon of June 15, 1886, when 'the highest efflorescence of the Forsytes' might have been seen in the drawing-room of old Jolyon Forsyte's house in Stanhope Gate, the occasion being the celebration of the engagement of his granddaughter Miss June with Philip Bosinney. Some time in the late November of the following year there occurs what may be taken as the climax of the story, in the violated privacy of Irene Forsyte's bedroom.

In this same year of 1887 was celebrated the Jubilee of Queen Victoria, and we may be sure that 'the Forsytes' were not behindhand in their demonstrations of loyal fervour and thankfulness. We can hardly be wrong in taking this as the height of the 'Age of the Forsytes'. Soames Forsyte must have thought so. Thirty-five years later we over-hear him saying, 'In my belief the world reached its highest point in the 'eighties, and will never reach it again'.

The Diamond Jubilee ten years later was an even more magnificent affair, but whereas the first had been primarily and essentially royal the second was a splendid advertisement of Imperial might and grandeur. The Forsyte soul must have sensed the difference, and been troubled. As the century drew to its close, the signs of change multiplied apace and gathered ever-increasing speed.

Motor-cars, for instance: as Jolyon looked out through the window of his hansom when on the way to Irene's flat in Chelsea he had noted that whereas only a year before they seemed to number about one in thirty of the vehicles on the streets now they were one in twenty. ('They've come to stay. Just so much more rattling round of wheels and general stink.') Very soon flying-machines would be stuttering across the sky. 'Kinemas' and 'Bioscopes' were opening in back streets. The telephone had already become something more than a gurgling gadget. Cheap railway fares were emptying the masses on to the seaside beaches. Everybody could afford a daily newspaper now that they were only a halfpenny. Tinned foods in the larder, carpet-sweepers in the home, typewriters in the office, light by pressing a switch. Free schooling for every child, and a secondary education for the brightest and most promising of even the poorest class. Women were wearing fewer clothes, and claiming larger liberties; some of them were even demanding the right to the vote in parliamentary elections. Every year more and more private businesses were being converted into limited liability companies. In local government the old 'vestries' had been supplanted by 'councils' of various types and sizes, and not only Socialists were advocating a large extension of 'municipal trading'.

Yes, times were changing, and the people with them. Soames Forsyte's experiences on 'Mafeking Night' (May 18, 1900) must have been a real eye-opener. Never had he encountered such a crowd as engulfed him when he wandered into Regent Street. Shrieking and whistling, dancing and playing the fool with false noses and mouth-organs and long feathers. A youth knocked his top-hat off. Crackers exploded about his feet. Rude girls called out after him to 'keep his hair on'. The crowd was cheerful, but some day their mood might change. 'They were hysterical—it wasn't English! This, then, was the populace, the innumerable living negation of gentility and Forsyteism'.

When did the 'Age of the Forsytes' come to an end? One date that may be suggested is when 1905 turned into 1906 and the masses of the lower middle and working classes demonstrated their voting strength for the first time, giving to Campbell-Bannerman and his Liberals the greatest electoral triumph in our parliamentary history. Another might be 1909-10 when Lloyd George's budget showed how the rich might be 'soaked' to provide benefits for the poor. And yet another might be that 4th of August in 1914, when (in Grey's memorable phrase) the lamps went out all over Europe, after which things were never the same again. But a somewhat earlier date than any of these may be suggested, and on the whole with better reason. That date is the 22nd of January, 1901, when Queen Victoria died at Osborne House in the Isle of Wight. For once the death of the Sovereign did indeed represent a definite break in the march of history, and the fact that it occurred within a few weeks of the birth of a new century seemed to add to its significance.

'The Queen was dead, and the air of the greatest city upon earth grey with unshed tears.' With these finely chosen, appropriately solemn words John Galsworthy introduces his account, in one of the concluding chapters of *In Chancery*, of the old Queen's funeral procession through the streets of the capital on the way to the burial at Windsor.

Crushed in the crowd against the railings in Hyde Park on that morning in early February was Soames Forsyte, fur-coated and top-hatted, with his young, newly married wife beside him, snuggling against the cold in her dark furs. On the other side of Park Lane his father, old James Forsyte, stood looking out through his bedroom window, his nose flattened by the chilling glass.

Half-masted flags, tolling bells, muffled music of the military bands, and the slow tramp, tramp, tramping of soldiers' feet. And then behind the white draped coffin on the gun-carriage came the captains and the kings of much more than half the world.

'There it was—the bier of the Queen, coffin of the Age slowly passing! And as it went by there came a murmuring groan from all the long line of those who watched, a sound such as Soames had never heard, so unconscious, primitive, deep and wild . . . Tribute of an Age to its own death. . . .'

INDEX